Mutiny!

Mutiny!

Naval insurrections in Australia and New Zealand

Tom Frame and Kevin Baker

ALLEN & UNWIN

First published in 2000

Copyright © Tom Frame and Kevin Baker, 2000

All rights reserved. No part of this book may be reproduced or transmitted in any form or by any means, electronic or mechanical, including photocopying, recording or by any information storage and retrieval system, without prior permission in writing from the publisher. *The Australian Copyright Act* 1968 (the Act) allows a maximum of one chapter or 10% of this book, whichever is the greater, to be photocopied by any educational institution for its educational purposes provided that the educational institution (or body that administers it) has given a remuneration notice to Copyright Agency Limited (CAL) under the Act.

Allen & Unwin
9 Atchison Street
St Leonards NSW 2065
Australia
Phone: (61 2) 8425 0100
Fax: (61 2) 9906 2218
Email: frontdesk@allen-unwin.com.au
Web: http://www.allenandunwin.com

National Library of Australia
Cataloguing-in-Publication entry:

Frame, Tom.
  Mutiny!: naval insurrections in Australia and New Zealand.

  Includes index.
  ISBN 1 86508 351 8.

  1. Mutiny – Australia – History. 2. Mutiny – New Zealand – History. 3. Australia – History, Naval. 4. New Zealand – History, Naval. I. Baker, Kevin. II. Title

Set in 10/12 pt Trump Mediaeval by DOCUPRO, Sydney
Printed by South Wind Productions, Singapore

10 9 8 7 6 5 4 3 2 1

Contents

Acknowledgments	vi
Acronyms and abbreviations	vii
Introduction	ix
1 The evolution of mutiny	1
2 Mutiny and the Royal Navy	11
3 The New South Wales Corps: were they really mutineers?	30
4 Mutiny in the Australian colonial forces	45
5 A democratic navy	58
6 World War I	75
7 Mutiny in whose flagship?	97
8 The turbulent twenties	111
9 Depression disputes	121
10 The tumultuous thirties	138
11 World War II	151
12 Vanity and mutiny	164
13 Mutiny in New Zealand	185
14 Postwar disappointment	207
15 Mutiny in the Australian Army and Air Force	219
16 Volunteers and mutiny	234
17 Conscience and mutiny	249
18 Looking back and moving on	260
Endnotes	266
Index	279

Acknowledgments

The authors acknowledge the assistance and support of the staff of the Australian War Memorial and the National Library of Australia in researching this work. Thanks also to Vic Cassells; Robert Gillam of the HMAS *Pirie* Association; David Stevens of the Maritime Studies Program of the Department of Defence; John Seymour of the Department of Legal Studies at the Australian National University; Frank Walker from the RAN Corvettes Association (New South Wales) and many others who have been generous in sharing advice and offering suggestions. Particular acknowledgment is made of the work of Kathryn Spurling of the University College, Australian Defence Force Academy, whose pioneering work on lower deck life in RAN ships in the period 1911–52 challenged the authors to think more broadly about the social and economic contexts of mutinous attitudes and actions. Dr Frame is grateful for the assistance of Commodore Ian Burnside, OBE RAN Rtd, and Lieutenant Commander John Nash, RAN Rtd. Dr Baker expresses his thanks to his wife Jane and their children, without whose help nothing would be possible.

Acronyms and abbreviations

AB	Able Seaman
ACNB	Australian Commonwealth Naval Board
ADF	Australian Defence Force
AIF	Australian Imperial Force
ANMEF	Australian Naval & Military Expeditionary Force
AWM	Australian War Memorial
CPD	*Commonwealth Parliamentary Debates*
CPO	Chief Petty Officer
DFDA	*Defence Force Discipline Act*
DSC	Distinguished Service Cross
HMAS	His (Her) Majesty's Australian Ship
HMS	His (Her) Majesty's Ship
HMCS	His (Her) Majesty's Canadian Ship
HMNZS	His (Her) Majesty's New Zealand Ship
HREOC	Human Rights and Equal Opportunity Commission
KR & AI	*King's Regulations and Admiralty Instructions*
LAC	Leading Aircraftman
LS	Leading Seaman
NDA	*Naval Discipline Act*
OBE	Officer, Order of the British Empire
PO	Petty Officer
QR & AI	*Queen's Regulations and Admiralty Instructions*
SBA	Sick Berth Attendant
SGT	Sergeant
S/SGT	Staff Sergeant
RAAF	Royal Australian Air Force
RAN	Royal Australian Navy
RANB	Royal Australian Naval Brigade
RANR	Royal Australian Naval Reserve
RANVR	Royal Australian Naval Volunteer Reserve

RCN	Royal Canadian Navy
RN	Royal Navy
Rtd	Retired
RTN	Royal Thai Navy
RNZN	Royal New Zealand Navy
USN	United States Navy
USS	United States Ship

Introduction

There are few words in the English language more evocative of intrigue and drama than 'mutiny'. Mutinies have occurred wherever and whenever ships have gone to sea. From Homer's *Odyssey*, which depicts a mutinous act by a crew who unleash an ox-skin of winds while in sight of home, to the casting adrift of Lieutenant William Bligh from HMS *Bounty* by Fletcher Christian off Tahiti in 1789, the tensions of shipboard life have often erupted into violent protest and open insurrection. These stresses and the conflicts they ultimately produce have attracted poets, novelists and historians eager to exploit the drama and danger of the mutiny and the presumed daring and courage of the mutineer. Indeed, the word 'mutiny' has come to be associated with powerful images of desperation and violence, of romance and adventure.

Despite their enduring fascination with Bligh, Christian and the *Bounty*, few Australians or New Zealanders are aware of the large number of mutinies within their national histories. They occur in the very first pages of the history of European contact with the Southern Hemisphere. The earliest 'mutiny' followed the wreck of the Dutch ship *Batavia* off the West Australian coast in June 1629. The first mutinous action after the colonisation of Australia was the so-called 'Rum Rebellion', an uprising of corrupt and venal military officials against Captain William Bligh, then Governor of New South Wales. Another form of mutiny was seen in 1854 in the action of the goldminers who revolted against the arbitrary acts of the Victorian colonial government. Their declaration of an Australian republic at the Eureka Stockade stands within the technical definitions of a mutiny. This book, however, is mainly concerned with those that have taken place in and around the coastlines of Australia and New Zealand, and within the naval forces of those two countries. The official naval histories are curiously but perhaps predicably silent on their occurrence.

Mutiny! is an attempt to insert the missing pages into the published chronicles of both the Royal Australian Navy (RAN) and the Royal New Zealand Navy (RNZN). It describes and analyses a succession of naval mutinies within a chronological framework. The RNZN has suffered a mutiny only once, although that was one of the most widespread of mutinies in recent naval history. By way of contrast, mutinies have not been uncommon in Australian ships. There have been at least eleven and possibly as many as nineteen mutinies in the RAN during both peacetime and war. The uncertainty of the number arises from two sources. The first is a conscious desire among naval administrators and commanders to avoid the controversy which invariably attaches itself to the charge of mutiny. Consequently, sailors whose actions appear *prima facie* to be mutinous have been charged with a range of offences other than mutiny. Second, the definition of mutiny in most disciplinary codes is open to wide interpretation. Demonstrating before a tribunal that an action or attitude was mutinous has often proved to be a complicated undertaking. But for these requirements, and the many incidents which went unreported by officers concerned about their professional reputations, there might have been many more mutinies in the RAN's history.

In examining a succession of incidents in an attempt to explain when and why mutinies occur, our central thesis is this: most navies lack a mechanism whereby sailors can complain about some aspect of their naval service in the knowledge that the grievance will be treated seriously and with complete confidence that reprisals will not follow. In the absence of such a mechanism, and given that sailors are otherwise powerless, there have been occasions in which men have resorted to the only means available to them in an effort to be heard—mutiny. The charge of mutiny is frequently misunderstood and misapplied, however, so that instances in which men have resorted to collective action or 'combination' have been labelled mutiny when the intention of the participants was never mutinous. Indeed, in some cases mutiny provisions in naval disciplinary codes have been used to exploit sailors and to deprive them of their basic rights—including the prerogative to complain when mistreated. Where sailors are respected as human beings and processes do exist whereby grievances are acknowledged and sincerely considered, mutinies do not seem to occur.

Creating the conditions in which the appeal of mutiny becomes remote involves the whole social and cultural ethos of a navy. It requires a commitment to the individual, a concern for their well-being and esteem of human dignity. Such a commitment has not always been universally embraced or upheld in the navies of either Australia or New Zealand. Mutinies have been the consequence.

All navies take pride in the maintenance of good order and discipline. For the greatest part, and in contrast to military officers and soldiers, naval officers and sailors have generally not been party to civil insurrections or political intrigues. In fact, most navies have been extraordinarily docile in a political sense. Sailors' love for the sea, and their physical remoteness from the causes and expression of political unrest, have enabled most naval high commands to preserve stability while ensuring loyalty to properly constituted authority, however tenuous its hold on legal or political legitimacy. Naturally, there is a sense of shame in nations and navies when internal insurrections occur. The commanding officer of any ship in which a mutiny takes hold regards the event as a criticism of his command and of the collective capability of his officers and senior sailors. That a mutiny occurred, notwithstanding whatever mitigation might be offered in defence of either the captain or the ship's company, is enough to signal serious organisational ill health. It is for this reason that most sympathetic histories recoil from tackling the complex cultural problems implicit in a navy which has suffered from insurrection. While great victories in battle proclaim how much a navy can achieve, a mutiny reveals how brittle are the foundations on which these same institutions sometimes exist.

Mutinies are the 'midnight of the soul' in every sea-going service. They prompt, or at least ought to prompt, self-questioning, and raise an element of doubt that all is well. It is for this reason that they deserve far more attention than they have received to date. *Mutiny!* is an attempt to show that sailors are earthly creatures and that human frailty is great. Mutinies are worthy of more understanding while those who perpetrate them are entitled to a little more sympathy. This book tries to give both.

THE LAWS OF THE NAVY

*Dedicated to his friends in the Service
by the author Ronald A. Hopwood*

Now these are the Laws of the Navy,
Unwritten and varied they may be;
And he that is wise will observe them,
Going down to his ship in the sea . . .

. . . Canst follow the track of the dolphin
Or tell where the sea swallows roam?
Where Leviathan taketh his pastime?
What ocean he calleth his home?
Even so with the words of thy Rulers,
And the orders those words shall convey.
Every law is as naught beside this one—
'Thou shalt not criticise, but obey!'
Saith the wise, 'How may I know their purpose?'
Then acts without wherefore or why:
Stays the fool but one moment to question,
And the chance of his life passeth by . . .

Now these are the laws of the Navy,
Unwritten and varied they be;
And he that is wise will observe them,
Going down to his ship in the sea.
As the wave rises clear to the hawse pipe,
Washes aft, and is lost in the wake,
So shall ye drop astern all unheeded,
Such time as the law ye forsake.

1

The evolution of mutiny

Whenever and wherever men have gone down to the sea in ships, there has been disobedience, insubordination and mutiny. The first European legal proceedings in Australia resulted from what was said to be a 'mutiny' following the grounding of the *Batavia*, the newest and finest ship operated by the Dutch East India Company (also known as the VOC, the *Verenigde Oostindische Compagnie*), on the Abrolhos Islands off Western Australia en route to Java in June 1629. The mutiny and its brutal consequences involved the dramatic clash of three vastly different personalities: the master, Ariaen Jacobsz, the under-merchant, Jeronimus Cornelisz, and *Batavia*'s *Commandeur*, Francisco Pelsaert. While all VOC ships carried a *Commandeur*, a landsman-merchant vested with administrative oversight during a voyage, the master was responsible for the safe navigation of the ship and exercised command over the crew. From the outset, Jacobsz and Pelsaert disliked and resented each other. Their mutual disdain was exploited by the cruel and ruthlessly self-serving under-merchant Cornelisz. With this tension underscoring command of the voyage, *Batavia* was doomed when it set out from Amsterdam bound for the East Indies in October 1628.

Jacobsz, a gifted seafarer but a corrupt employee, had been planning a mutiny early into the voyage. At this time and in this context, mutiny was understood to be the supplanting of lawfully constituted authority by an unlawful authority. Pelsaert's authority would be replaced by that of Jacobsz and those acting in concert with him for the sole purpose of the mutineers' self-interest. This plan was mutinous in two elements: first, the supplanting of authority, and second, its perpetration by a group of men acting together. To effect the mutiny, Jacobsz planned to separate *Batavia* from the other ships in the fleet, including the accompanying warship *Buren*, and create an atmosphere which would incite the entire crew to turn against Pelsaert and join Jacobsz. Jacobsz and his initial co-conspirator Cornelisz would then seize the ship, kill the passengers and take possession of the ship's cargo for themselves. It was a risky plan with grave consequences, as Hugh Edwards notes:

> The punishments for mutiny were terrible. If a whisper escaped, the very kindest fate they could expect was to be publicly hanged in chains on the gibbet outside the Castle of Batavia and left to dangle as a warning to others until they became sun-blackened husks. It was more likely that the judges, scowling under their tall black hats, would order something like breaking while spread-eagled on a wheel—bones large and small, from the toes and fingers inward to the trunk, pulp-broken with a metal rod while the crowd watched and savoured until death came in the end as sweet relief. That was more the measure of mutineers.[1]

Batavia's grounding was unintended. The ship was well to the south of her intended track when she struck. Pelsaert was critical of Jacobsz for his error in navigation. While such a miscalculation was understandable, Pelsaert was unforgiving. It seemed at first that the plans of Jacobsz and Cornelisz would be thwarted by the disaster—instead, however, the mutineers were unwittingly assisted when Pelsaert decided to leave the ship and the survivors and head for help at the port of Batavia, sailing in the ship's boat with Jacobsz. Over the next few weeks, with the mutineers now numbering around twenty under the leadership of Cornelisz, all of the soldiers embarked in *Batavia* and most of the other male survivors were systematically and brutally murdered. The women were spared to satisfy the carnal lusts of the mutineers. Pelsaert reached the port of Batavia on 7 July. He was given charge of the yacht *Sardam* and told to return to the Abrolhos Islands, rescue the survivors and salvage as much of the company's property as possible. He sailed from Batavia with Jacobsz on 15 July.

The *Commandeur* was horrified to find the carnage which had followed his departure. Supposedly disciplined men who had served, he thought, loyally and with restraint under his charge, had rapidly become unrestrained and vicious murderers.

All of the mutineers were captured with the aid of *Sardam*'s crew. After a brief trial conducted by Pelsaert, the seven leading mutineers were hanged on 2 October 1629 at Seal's Island, one of the Albrolhos group. Cornelisz had both hands cut off before he faced the gallows. Those who were not executed on Seal's

Island met their deaths outside Batavia Castle on 31 January 1630. Ariaen Jacobsz, accused of mutiny and incitement, was imprisoned in Batavia. There is no record of his ultimate fate.

Pelsaert was later criticised for his decision to leave the survivors, the Company contending that he should not have abandoned the survivors to sail to Batavia as his authority would have prevented the mutiny and subsequent slaughter. Certainly Pelsaert was desperately unfortunate to have had Jacobsz and Cornelisz, both scheming and evil men, on board *Batavia*. This disaster confirmed that the dangers of the sea often meant that seamen were drawn from the roughest and least civil of men, whose loyalties could not be taken for granted. This was especially so in merchant ships, which attempted to secure obedience through a financial contract rather than the commitment to a common cause which tended to draw men to a nation's fighting fleet. Sadly, the *Batavia* mutiny did not reveal anything about human behaviour that was not already known.

Defiance of authority by individuals and groups of people has marked human civilisation from ancient times. Regardless of whether the authority is legitimate or otherwise, people often feel exploited by those wielding power flowing from authority and respond by either excusing themselves from the effective operation of the authority by indifference or disobedience, or by rebelling against its source and expression. Defying, resisting or rebelling against authority can be prompted by adherence to a principle involving higher values or virtues or it can be utterly self-serving. Whatever its motivation, collective opposition to authority has at various times in history been described as 'mutiny'. But what distinguishes a mutiny from an uprising, a rebellion, a revolution or a *coup d'état*?

The *Oxford English Dictionary* defines mutiny as 'an open revolt against constituted authority'—this implies that mutiny can be an individual action, while failing to distinguish a rebellion from a mutiny. The *Encyclopaedia Britannica* asserts that mutiny is an 'overt act of defiance upon military, including naval, authority by two or more persons subject to such authority'. It adds that mutiny has 'always been regarded as a most serious offence'. This seems to be closer to the VOC's understanding in

1629. However, it lacks some comment on mutiny's motivation or purpose. The American *Black's Law Dictionary* defines mutiny as '[rising] against lawful or constituted authority in the naval or military service', but this too is inadequate in not allowing for passive acts of resistance to authority. Another American authority, *Naval Terms Dictionary* depicts it as 'rebellion against constituted authority aboard ship; a crime that, when committed at sea in a civilian ship, comes under the jurisdiction of the Coast Guard'.[2]

These descriptions clearly avoid value statements or moral judgments. Does this mean that not all mutinies are bad or unjustified and that not every perpetrator is evil or deserving of condemnation? Are there times when human rights are unnecessarily violated in the name of naval command and occasions when arbitrary authority is used to suppress resistance to ignorance or callousness? Is it possible that mutinies might be symptoms of institutional decline and catalysts for overdue reform? Could mutineers ever be portrayed as defenders of freedom and agitators for progress?

These are far from straightforward questions which those exercising naval authority should not be left to answer alone. They involve complicated philosophical and ethical questions which require intellectual maturity and moral reflection within the entire body politic. Why? Because it is always easy and comfortable to take the institutional position and claim that mutinies are never justified, that lawful authority must always be upheld to prevent society falling into anarchy and chaos. And it is easy to argue that mutineers are an undisciplined minority who fail to understand and respect official channels for the expression of grievance and complaint. The more difficult task is to place these issues in their proper, wider context. The incidence of insurrection has, therefore, to do with the social composition of the navy and the demands being placed upon its leadership as well as the values of the society in whose name the navy acts. In one sense, mutinies can reveal a great deal about the evolving relationship between a navy and a nation, and between authority and freedom. However, the semantic uncertainty and ethical ambiguity of mutiny is reflected in historico-legal descriptions of mutiny and in the changing scale of punishments prescribed for those found guilty of the offence.

The first record of any formal instructions for discipline within a British fleet is King Richard's *Ordinance for the Great Crusade*. The King appointed a number of superior officers to be justiciaries over the combined fleets of England, Normandy, Brittany and Poitou which had assembled to convey crusading troops to the Holy Land. Although an offence equivalent to mutiny was not identified by name, any sailor found guilty of 'defiance of, vilifying or swearing at his fellows' was fined 'one ounce of silver' for every occasion the offence was committed. By way of comparison, those found guilty of murder were [to be] 'tied to the corpse of [their] victim and hove into the sea, or, if on land, to be buried alive' while any sailor who drew a knife to threaten another man would lose a hand as punishment. Ships' companies were sworn to obey these instructions which were copied onto parchment and nailed to the foremast of each vessel. As most of the men were illiterate, however, it was customary for the *Ordinance* to be read publicly at the monthly formal mustering of the sailors.

When the offence of mutiny was finally proscribed in British naval law, it was usual for the most senior officer in the fleet or flotilla to deal with the matter. Other serious naval offences included murder, manslaughter, wounding and fighting. However, all ships' captains were given authority to deal summarily with offences occurring in their ship, and their power to impose punishment was wide. Such was the importance of authority that challenges to its existence and exercise were met with severe penalties.

Both Britain and France had difficulties in controlling their navies during the time of the various revolutions of the seventeenth and eighteenth centuries. In August 1793, royalist mutineers against the Directoire handed the French fleet base at Toulon to the British. Whether or not this was treason rather than mutiny is another philosophical point worth debating.

In England, on Christmas Day 1749, the Lords of the Admiralty promulgated 36 statements intended to define and regulate conduct on board warships. These statements were termed the *Articles of War* and were, continuing the tradition of reading the *Ordinance*, to be read each Sunday on His Majesty's warships so that even illiterate sailors could not claim ignorance of them. The relevant disciplinary regulations were also posted in a prominent position within the ship. If any sailors were found guilty after court martial of 'mutinous assembly', they were to be sentenced to death. There were three other related articles. For 'uttering words of sedition or mutiny' the penalty was to be death or 'such other punishment' as was determined by court martial. Anyone who heard mutinous talk and failed to make a report was to be punished after a court martial. To 'stir up a disturbance' was also deemed a punishable offence. It was also a serious matter to strike, or even to threaten to strike, a senior officer in the course of duty. These offences could be committed on land, not just in a ship or at sea. When ashore, the *Articles* determined these offences be considered as if 'the same had been committed at sea, on board any of His Majesty's ships or vessels of war'.

The definition of mutiny under the *Articles* was plainly broad. But there was no attempt to balance a statement of the sailor's obligations with a positive prescription of the Navy's obligations to the sailor. Too much authority and power resided in the hands of administrators and commanders. By way of contrast, the sailor was both helpless and powerless.

The *Naval Discipline Act* (NDA) of 1866 resulted from the great mid nineteenth century civil legal reforms in Britain and brought the naval justice system into line with the procedures of English criminal law. Summary trials were retained although the maximum punishment to be awarded by commanding officers of Her Majesty's Ships was 90 days imprisonment. The imposition of more severe punishments was made contingent upon gaining formal approval from the Admiralty. The NDA would be amended many times over the next century to reflect changing social mores, clarify ambiguities and remove perceived injustices. By way of example, flogging was suspended as a peacetime naval punishment in 1870. Nine years later it was suspended as a wartime punishment, although it was not formally removed from the list of punishments until 1948. In 1909 the punishment of detention was introduced but was not awarded until 1911, when suitable quarters were first built for detainees. In 1915 the charge of striking an officer was removed from the inventory of capital offences.

Dealing with mutiny was a key aspect of the new Act. Section 8 of the NDA defined mutiny in terms of resisting or seeking to overthrow lawful authority, and disobeying authority in a subversive manner. As a definition, this appeared to be even broader than the descriptions of mutiny contained in the extant *Articles of War* which were in force concurrently because the terms were so wide as to include almost any form of active or passive disobedience. In one respect, however, the definition was more closely defined. Mutiny could not be committed by an individual who did not endeavour to influence other people. The Act required 'a combination between two or more persons' to resist authority.[3] That resistance could be either active or passive. Even if there was no violence associated with the resistance to authority, severe punishments usually applied. Section 11 of the Act stated that 'the ringleader or ringleaders of a mutiny *not accompanied by violence* could suffer death, or such other punishment as is hereafter mentioned' [emphasis added]. This point is worth noting. Some mutinies have been downplayed by senior naval commanders and administrators as 'strikes' or 'protests', and labelled a form of 'mild mutiny'. However, no such distinction existed in the NDA, which did not differentiate between the supplanting of legitimate authority and mere 'protest'.

The development of naval law followed a similar course in the American navy. The United States Congress passed an Act in 1800 to regulate naval matters along similar lines to the British *Articles of War*. Article 13 of that Act demanded that anyone who tried to make 'a mutinous assembly' should be tried by a court martial. If found guilty, the accused could be sentenced to death. It was also an offence for a person to witness a mutiny which they might have prevented. If a sailor treated a superior with contempt that behaviour could also be deemed mutinous. Under American law, the act of mutiny was not required to constitute the crime—it was sufficient for there to be a conspiracy to act.

The definition of mutiny under the American articles was far too inclusive. The crime of mutiny could consist not just of a mutinous assembly but also of hearing of a mutiny, even discussion of a mutiny, and taking no action. Whether an individual was active or passive in the face of a mutiny, that individual could still be found guilty and face serious punishment. Even complaints, if not directed through proper channels, could be construed as mutiny if disturbances accompanied the complaining. There were no mitigating circumstances. Under both the British and American articles, to strike a superior was a serious offence. Even to show contempt or disrespect could incur a charge of mutiny. When the United States Department of Defense was formed to coordinate the American armed forces in the mid nineteenth century, a *Uniform Code of Military Justice* was instituted to supersede both the army and navy articles. Article 94 of the *Uniform Code*, which concerns mutiny, was more carefully and specifically worded than the articles of 1800.

The current definition of mutiny in the US Navy is found in the regulations for the conduct of Naval Courts and Boards. Section 46 defines mutiny as 'unlawful opposition or resistance to or defiance of superior military authority, with a deliberate purpose to usurp, subvert, or override such authority'.[4] Under this definition, still a wide one that could encompass virtually any refusal to disobey orders, there is no longer any question about whether one or more persons are required to commit a mutiny. A single individual can seek to 'usurp, subvert or override . . . authority'.

The most recent official American consideration of mutiny was prompted by disturbances in the aircraft carriers *Kitty Hawk* and *Constellation*. The Senate Armed Services Committee looked at the question of what made a mutiny. They took advice from a number of sources, including the Library of Congress, before concluding that a refusal by a group of servicemen, acting together, to carry out orders with regard to the ship's operation were the essential elements that constituted mutiny.[5]

In addition to regulations and legislation that apply to servicemen and women, Acts have been passed in both Britain and the United States that make unlawful any attempts by civilians to assist or encourage mutiny in the armed services. The first was the 1797 British *Incitement to Mutiny Act* which provided for the death penalty (later amended to transportation for life) for anyone who sought to subvert the loyalty of serving members of the armed forces. In 1934, when legislators were uneasy about supposed Communist infiltration of warships, the provisions of this act were reviewed and extended by the *Incitement to Disaffection Act*. In the United States a similar bill was proposed in 1934 and again during 1938, but did not receive sufficient support to pass Congress.

The difficulty of defining mutiny with any precision is that acts of indiscipline or refusal to obey orders may involve active or passive resistance which may not clearly disclose a mutinous intent. This could encompass individuals acting alone or groups acting with or without prior organisation. An individual who refuses to obey orders is guilty of disobedience at the very least. Even such a celebrated act as Nelson's refusal to 'see' the withdrawal order off Copenhagen was an act of wilful disobedience. If his action had not produced a comprehensive victory, Nelson's career might have ended controversially and ingloriously in a charge of disobedience to orders or even mutiny. Where the disobedience is 'passive', in the sense that aggressive action against authority does not follow, such action cannot easily be called mutiny. By way of example, if a sailor refused to board a ship during time of war his actions would be considered wilful disobedience. A legal argument might then follow as to whether the sailor's action amounted to a technical desertion, cowardice or conduct prejudicial to good naval discipline and order. The question of mutiny does not arise. If the individual's disobedience is active, however, in the sense that he then proceeds to act against authority by seeking to take command of a ship or seeks to induce others to do so, the incident might fall within the meaning of the term 'mutiny' even though only one person was involved. In Bligh's time, a single act of insubordination could, and did, create and constitute mutiny.

Similarly, a group may be involved in passive or active disobedience to orders. A strike is an example of a passive act. A concerted effort to take command of a vessel is clearly active. Whether the actions are passive or active, where they involve servicemen acting together the legal question arises as to whether or not such actions constitute mutiny. Clearly, if two or more sailors were involved in discussing disobedience to orders, under both the British and American Articles they could have been indicted for mutiny. But what if only one person took action or uttered words of complaint or disrespect? If violence was involved, the provisions relating to resisting a superior came into force and the person could be charged. If there was no violence involved, could a sailor still be guilty of mutiny? Under the British *Articles of War*, the answer would have been yes, as the accused could have been 'uttering words of sedition or mutiny'. Under Article 13 of the American code, the position was less clear. The guilty party might have attempted to make a 'mutinous assembly' and not be joined by anyone. Whether this constituted mutiny was not precisely defined. However, the American article on one occasion was interpreted as if just one man could make a mutiny. The first sailor condemned to death for mutiny in the American navy was hanged in 1812 for abusing and resisting a junior officer who broke up a fight.

Under British law, an individual acting alone who disobeys orders has not committed a mutiny unless he seeks to subvert authority in the process. Several historical examples drawn from the punishment log of the light cruiser HMAS *Melbourne* serve to illustrate this point. On 5 May 1915, Armourer Henry Barnacle refused to obey an order. The Chief Armourer ordered him to lubricate the gunsights of the forecastle six-inch gun. Armourer Barnacle refused, citing 'things to settle' with the Chief Armourer, and saying that he did not intend to do anything until their differences were resolved. Barnacle was charged with 'refusing to obey an order' and disrated (reduced in rank). His was an individual act clearly not intended to challenge the authority of the captain or the ship's officers.[6] An example of 'committing an act to the prejudice of good order and naval discipline' was the action of Stoker Reid who, on 11 May 1915, 'did strike Daniel Francis, Stoker First Class, in the execution of his duty'.[7] Stoker Reid drew fourteen days in the cells for his action. The violence of his offence incurred the charge but there was no element of mutiny in his act. Only if the individual's disobedience is active, in the sense that he then proceeds to act against authority by conspiring with others to resist legitimate orders and directions or seeks to induce others to do so, does his behaviour usually fall within the meaning of the term 'mutiny'.

The question of whether one person can commit mutiny is clarified by describing two types of insurrection. If a mutiny involves some violent act, then a single person can be guilty of such an act. If a mutiny involves more than one person, and those persons are acting together to disobey orders or refuse duty, then all those involved are guilty of mutiny. The second type of mutiny brings in a consideration of intent. Those involved in a mutiny must share a common intent whether they are engaged in a concerted action to usurp authority or to disobey orders. One question that remains to be considered is whether servicemen have a moral responsibility to refuse to carry out what they judge to be an unlawful act. This question concerns much larger issues that did not even begin to be covered adequately until the Nuremburg War Crimes Tribunal began in 1946. The question of acting on conscience and the possibility of mutiny will be considered in Chapter 17, but is mentioned here as another complicating factor in defining mutiny.

The following chapter outlines the way in which the charge of mutiny came to be understood in the Royal Navy during the seventeenth and eighteenth centuries, and explains why the offence was prosecuted with such vigour and those found guilty punished so severely.

2

Mutiny and the Royal Navy

For most of the nineteenth century, and the first half of the twentieth, Britain was the world's leading naval power. This supremacy was achieved after years of experience in building a strong fleet and exploiting a maritime spirit among the British people. There were, however, a number of occasions in which the efficiency and effectiveness of the fighting fleets of Britain were threatened by individual discontent and widespread dissatisfaction in the mess decks of individual warships. That the Royal Navy learned slowly but surely from these incidents meant the spirit of the service remained sufficiently strong to overcome internal upheavals while remaining more than equal to the challenge of defending the Empire from every aggressor. But the lessons were many, varied and usually very costly. They began in the seventeenth century when, for the first time, a standing fleet of purpose-built warships served British national interest throughout Europe and to the ends of the known world.

After the imposition by King Charles I in 1634 of 'Ship Money', a tax levied on the maritime counties and seaport towns to provide for a new fleet of battleships which took to the seas from 1635, service conditions in the Navy gradually deteriorated. Britain might have gained naval supremacy in terms of shipping, but the price paid was the loss of loyalty of many of the serving sailors. When the English Civil War broke out in 1642, discontent was so strong that the Fleet virtually defected to the cause of the Parliamentarians.

> This may seem strange to those who remember how completely it was a creation of the King. But the reason is not far to seek. Charles had religiously devoted Ship Money to the purpose for which it was raised, and had found little or nothing to spare for

improving the conditions of service. After half a century of neglect there were ample grounds for complaint, and the seamen, infected by the prevalent discontents, looked to the people's assembly to right their wrongs.[1]

Many sailors had not received their pay for some years, while some ships' captains were gradually dismantling their vessels to maintain the livelihood of their ships' companies. There is no evidence of strong political or religious support for the Parliamentarians within the Navy, although the seaman became 'anti-King' for understandable personal reasons. The gains won from Parliament in the 1650s had been eroded by rising prices after the Restoration of the English monarchy in 1660 and the formal proclamation of Charles II's fighting fleets as the 'Royal Navy' and the designation of individual vessels 'His Majesty's Ship'. The post-Restoration sailor was, 'contrary to the impression apparently prevailing among feminine novelists, usually an extremely matter-of-fact individual, with the greater portion of his attention fixed on the subject of his food and his pay'.[2]

But rates of pay were not the only grievance. Michael Lewis argues that:

> there were other pay anomalies too which, in modern eyes, would furnish quite justifiable grounds for grievance ... It had long been an established custom not to pay wages until they were six months overdue, and for ships long in commission they were often much more overdue than that—even years behind ... Further, even when at length the seaman left his ship, he received only a 'ticket', not the wages in cash. These could usually be obtained only by a personal visit to the Pay Office on Tower Hill [in London], and not always there. And Tower Hill was a far step in those days from even Chatham and Portsmouth, let alone Plymouth. The result was an extensive traffic in pay tickets, often at scandalous rates of discount, between the seamen and the more or less professional 'ticket-buyers'.[3]

To counter discontent and disobedience, disciplinary standards in an eighteenth century British warship were severe and uncompromising. Navy discipline was harsh, exacting and brutal. But was it really necessary? Some would say it was. In those days, very few men actually volunteered to join the Navy. Indeed, Dr Samuel Johnson's acerbic comment, 'No man will be a sailor who has contrivance enough to get himself into gaol', was not too far from the truth. If the British public would not produce the ships' companies needed by the Navy to defend the realm, they would be forcibly obtained. Press-gangs were raised. They were comprised essentially of thugs, and were active throughout Britain, employing violence to subdue reticent recruits. Once on board a warship, the pressed man came under the Navy's regime of discipline notwithstanding his unwillingness to enter the King's service. Most quickly found that it proved pointless to resist. A man would be broken against rather than be allowed to break naval discipline.

While Britain was at war and the Navy was the first and last line of defence, men could be forced to serve their country despite their own wishes or conscientious principles. In spite of the Navy's recruiting methods and the reluctance of its sailors, Britain still managed in 1700 to emerge ascendant from more than two decades of naval warfare with the Dutch and the French. However, the spread of corruption and the effects of mismanagement were obvious by 1745, when a spate of mutinies revealed that all was not well in the King's service. One unhappy ship was HMS *Sutherland*: 'The company of the *Sutherland* having mutinied and refused to go to sea with Captain [John] Brett, resolved that Captain Crookshanks be ordered to repair down to Plymouth and take command of the ship in the room of Captain Brett'.[4]

The matter was referred to the Admiralty which noted on 11 March 1745 that:

> The Lords thinking proper that the captain and company of the *Sutherland* should be parted, in regard to the present dissension between them and the mutiny of the men, they have sent down Captain Crookshanks to command her until Captain Fox (for whom she is designed) who is now at sea in the *Captain* returns to Plymouth; resolved that Lieutenant Kirley be directed to get the men on board, and the ship ready for the sea, and he is to be acquainted that if any disturbance happens and the men do not come to their duty, it will be imputed to him as the cause of it.[5]

The mutiny was caused by inadequate pay and officers who were indifferent to the laments of their men.

There was another outbreak of dissent in HMS *Captain*. Admiral James Steuart, the Port Admiral in Portsmouth, reported to the Admiralty Secretary, Thomas Corbett, from Spithead on 6 February 1746 as the mutiny ended. The severity of the punishments awarded showed the determination of senior officers to crush mutinous tendencies within the fleets.

> The five men belonging to the *Captain* who were lately sentenced by a court-martial to receive five hundred lashes each for mutiny

14   MUTINY!

have yet had but one-fourth of their punishment inflicted on them. As I thought they could not undergo the whole at one time, I ordered the sentence to be put in execution at four different times . . . I have ordered the same to be postponed for a time. They pray that when they are recovered of their illness they may receive the 375 lashes at one time. All which I mention for their Lordships' information.[6]

Steuart had also been directed to visit HMS *Prince Frederick* after a tense confrontation between several of the officers and the men. Steuart agreed to meet the men and hear their complaints. The grievance was against an officer and the boatswain who they alleged treated them harshly and, most specifically, had denied them food and drink while they worked long hours preparing the ship for recommissioning. On one occasion, they went all day without provisions and made a complaint to a Lieutenant Rose and the master, a Mr Spragge. Steuart reported to the Admiralty:

The lieutenant and master own such a complaint was made to them, but it was done in so tumultuous a manner and with such appearance of mutiny that the master called out for his pistols (for near about 150 to 200 of the men in a body left off work without leave [and] came down to them in the wardroom) and told them they deserve to be shot. And the lieutenant told them that he would have no regard to any complaint they should make in so mutinous a manner, but if one or two of them would come to him in a regular way, he would hear what they had to say, which advice was followed.[7]

It being 9pm, the men were then dismissed from work. When asked by Steuart why they had not referred the matter to their captain, 'one or two of them answered that they feared if they made any complaint they should be punished for it'.[8]

A mutiny broke out in HMS *Royal Oak* over the non-payment of Shore Allowance money. The entire ship's company walked off the ship although Captain Hodsoll had pledged to pay them what was owing as soon as the ship was prepared for sailing. After attempts to persuade the men to return, Hodsoll sent his First Lieutenant (as reported by Admiral Byng):

into the fields to them with orders to read the fifteenth Article of War, which he accordingly did, but notwithstanding, they never returned to the ship till two days after in the afternoon. And two or three days after that they mutinied again upon the same account, spirited up by one Jeremiah Donnavan, and near half the ship's company run away from the ship up into the fields.[9]

After noting a similarly hostile spirit in HMS *Dunkirk*, which was part of the same squadron, Admiral Byng told the Admiralty on October 1747:

> If some vigorous step is not taken to put a stop to such licentious liberties these people take of absenting themselves from the King's duty and throwing off all discipline and respect to their captains and officers, and if some public example is not made of these seamen, there must be an end of all command and authority; for surely no captain will be accountable for the conduct of his Majesty's ship he has the honour to be entrusted with, if such capital crimes as these pass with impunity.[10]

By 1780, the causes of mutiny were conforming to a sadly familiar pattern. Mutineers usually complained of being overworked, underpaid and poorly fed. But this did not exhaust all of the possible causes, as the most controversial mutiny in naval history was to reveal in 1789.

A group of sugar planters in the West Indies in early 1787 proposed importing breadfruit trees from Tahiti as a cheap and nutritious staple diet for their slaves. They approached the noted botanist Sir Joseph Banks, who managed to persuade the Admiralty to make a ship available to transport a cargo of young breadfruit trees from Tahiti to Jamaica and St Vincent. *Bethia*, an armed transport of 215 tons with four guns and a ship's company of 46 men, was acquired by the Admiralty and renamed HMS *Bounty*. With persuasion from Banks, Lieutenant William Bligh RN was appointed in command. Bligh had earlier sailed to Tahiti as the Master of HMS *Resolution* under Captain James Cook. Bligh was anxious to make his mark after he had missed out on the general promotions that followed the return of HMS *Discovery*, the consort to Cook's *Resolution*, following the ill-fated search for a navigable passage around the north of America to link the Atlantic and Pacific Oceans in 1779. After a belated promotion to Lieutenant, Bligh was fortunate to be given command of *Bounty*, even though he had established a reputation as a most capable officer and brilliant navigator.

In many respects, *Bounty* was poorly suited to the expedition, while the Admiralty made inadequate provision for the voyage. *Bounty* was too small and limited for the task that lay ahead. By the time the Admiralty issued final instructions to Bligh in December 1787, the European winter had begun. Furthermore, Bligh was not given a single commissioned officer to maintain discipline. A detachment of Marines would not have been an extravagance in such circumstances. The master was John Fryar and the Senior Master's Mate was Bligh's protégé and friend, Fletcher Christian. There were also four midshipmen. Although aged just 33 when appointed to command, Bligh was older than most of the ship's company, including 22-year-old Fletcher Christian.

After heavy weather prevented *Bounty* from rounding Cape Horn, Bligh decided on 22 April to take the longer route around the Cape of Good Hope and Van Diemen's Land. Following a voyage of over 40 000 kilometres in tempestuous seas, *Bounty* finally arrived off Tahiti on 26 October 1788. The men were exhausted after ten months in trying conditions with poor food. In contradiction of an unearned reputation for harsh and uncompromising discipline, Bligh had ordered only two men flogged since the ship left England. One man received 24 lashes for mutinous behaviour, the other six lashes for neglect of duty. Because of *Bounty*'s late sailing from England and the slow passage to Tahiti, it was another five months before the almost 1000 young breadfruit trees were ready for transportation. By this time, most of the ship's company had taken Tahitian mistresses and were thoroughly enjoying life in the Pacific. Indeed, many were reluctant to leave the idyllic conditions.

It is apparent that Bligh was unaware of the discontent which accompanied *Bounty*'s departure from Tahiti on 4 April 1789. The first few weeks at sea passed without incident but tensions rose rapidly when Bligh accused Christian publicly of losing an adze during an expedition ashore to gather wood and water. The adze was actually stolen by some natives but Bligh would hear no excuse for its loss. Two days later there was another dispute between Bligh and Christian, over the ownership of some coconuts. While Bligh saw both matters as trivial incidents he was happy to forgive and forget quickly, Christian was evidently deeply insulted. On the evening following the second argument, Bligh invited Christian to dine with him. Christian declined, saying he was unwell. On the evening of 27–28 April 1789, Christian and a small number of men took control of *Bounty*. At daybreak (4.30am), Bligh was confronted by Christian and several armed men wielding bayonets. They abused Bligh and threatened to kill him if he did not cooperate. The Captain's hands were tied behind his back before he was led to the upper deck clad only in his shirt. When he observed other members of the ship's company under arrest, Bligh realised a mutiny had begun and asked those responsible for an explanation of their actions. He was ordered to be silent or face death.

Bligh and eighteen other men, including the master Fryar, the gunner, the boatswain and the sailmaker, were set adrift in the ship's launch—a small boat just 7 metres long and 2 metres wide—and given enough provisions for a few weeks. Bligh decided their best prospect was to head for Timor, more than 5000 kilometres to the west. They reached the Great Barrier Reef on 24 May 1789 and, after a few days recovering their strength, rounded Cape York en route to Timor. *Bounty*'s launch reached Koepang in Timor on 14 June. The men were exhausted but their arrival was clearly a stunning achievement and testimony to Bligh's leadership and navigational expertise. By skill and sheer determination, he had managed to keep the men working together for 41 days as he guided the small launch, with minimal navigational equipment, to their chosen destination. Bligh made a triumphant return to England in March 1790. News of his unparalleled feat went before him.

At the court martial convened to inquire into the loss of the *Bounty*, Bligh was given an honourable acquittal. The Admiralty then despatched the 24-gun frigate HMS *Pandora*, under Captain Edward Edwards, to hunt down the mutineers. Shortly after *Pandora*'s arrival at Tahiti on 24 March 1791, Midshipmen George Stewart and Peter Heywood from the *Bounty* went on board the frigate and surrendered. Over the next few days, the remaining twelve men on the island were either apprehended or gave up. Edwards lacked sympathy for any of the mutineers, including those who claimed mitigation for their actions. He manacled the men together and confined them in a small cage as *Pandora* sailed throughout the South Pacific in search of the other mutineers. At the entrance to Torres Strait, *Pandora* grounded on a coral reef. In addition to the 30 members of *Pandora*'s ship's company that were drowned, four of the mutineers also perished. Those who survived the shipwreck reached England during June 1792.

Bligh was then at sea commanding HMS *Providence*, which was engaged in a second attempt at transporting breadfruit trees from Tahiti to the West Indies, and the ten surviving mutineers stood trial without the chief witness being present at the court martial over which Lord Hood presided. Four were acquitted. Six were found guilty of mutiny and sentenced to death by hanging. Of the condemned men, Midshipman Heywood and Boatswain James Morrison were granted clemency and pardoned. A third man was pardoned on the eve of his execution. The three remaining mutineers, Thomas Ellison, Thomas Burkitt and John Millward, were hanged from the yardarm of HMS *Brunswick* as a warning to others who defied duly constituted naval authority. The second breadfruit expedition was successful, with more than 1200 plants being delivered to the West Indies. Bligh was rewarded handsomely for his efforts while the hanging of the leading mutineers further restored his reputation. But was this fair to all concerned?

There are six different interpretations of the circumstances and causes of the *Bounty* mutiny. The first is Bligh's own explanation, which was published in *A Narrative of the Mutiny on board HMS* Bounty in 1790. His view was that the men simply could not resist the temptations of the Tahiti Islands. Bligh wrote:

> It will very naturally be asked, what could be the reason for such a revolt? In answer to which, I can only conjecture that the mutineers had assured themselves of a more happy life amongst the Otaheiteans, than they could possibly have in England; which, joined to some female connections, have most probably been the principal cause of the whole transaction.[11]

In effect, an easy life in a warm tropical climate and casual sex were to blame.

Second, there is the view of Fletcher Christian's elder brother, Edward, in *A Short Reply to Captain Bligh's Answers*,[12] that prolonged suffering prompted an erratic outburst from Fletcher Christian. This is the line taken by Rolf Du Reitz in a number of articles published since 1962.[13] He cites the experience of Lieutenant Francis Bond, who served with Bligh on board *Providence* in the same position Fletcher occupied in *Bounty*. Bond was highly critical of Bligh's manner, including his vanity and explosive temper. In sum, Bligh's defective character and flawed personality were to blame.

Third, Gavin Kennedy in *Captain Bligh: the Man and his Mutinies* argues that 'the mutiny had more to do with the state of Christian's mind than with the customary treatment he received from Bligh'.[14] Kennedy contends that Christian was suffering deep emotional anxiety and was on the verge of a personal breakdown which was evidenced by his talk of suicide. Kennedy felt that Christian was too sensitive for Bligh's intimidation and mockery, and could not cope with the stresses that had built up over the preceding months. Clearly, Christian's weak temperament was to blame.

Fourth, there is the view offered by Sir John Barrow in the 1831 volume *The Eventful History of the Mutiny and the Piratical Seizure of HMS* Bounty*: Its Causes and Consequences*. He asserts that Bligh's domineering behaviour and ruthless command methods were intolerable and that action was needed to avert an even worse crisis developing on the lower deck. This is the version that has most appealed to Hollywood feature film makers. The need to preserve the ship from anarchy and save Bligh's life was to blame.

A fifth interpretation is offered by Richard Hough in *Captain Bligh and Mr Christian: The Men and the Mutiny*, who contends that Bligh and Christian were homosexual lovers.[15] Hough asserts that when Christian engaged in a heterosexual relationship with Isabella, his Tahitian lover, Bligh was enraged. When the ship returned to sea, according to this interpretation, Bligh sought to rekindle his relationship with Christian who was now unwilling to continue the covert and highly dangerous liaison. It is claimed that Christian's refusal drove Bligh to tyranny and Christian to mutiny. A curious variation is Madge Darby's somewhat Freudian contention in *Who Caused the Mutiny on the Bounty* that Christian became demented on realising that he loved Bligh rather than Isabella.[16] According to this line of argument, blame ought to be attributed to uncertain social expectations.

Sixth, the most recent addition to the possible interpretations, is presented by Greg Denning in *Mr Bligh's Bad Language*.[17] Denning claims that Bligh's language was so foul and abusive that he violated standards of decency and prompted rebellion. How does he dispose of the most strongly supported charge against Bligh—that he was a cruel disciplinarian? By showing that in comparison with James Cook, Bligh resorted to the 'cat' only half as often as Cook. It would appear that Bligh's attitude to the safe delivery of the 1000 breadfruit plants became a source of ever-increasing personal stress which he sought to alleviate by tirades against his senior personnel, whom he was in the habit of calling 'scoundrels, damned rascals, hounds, hell-hounds, beasts and infamous wretches'. Denning's point is that Bligh's language was 'bad' because it 'was ambiguous, because men could not read it in a right relationship to his authority'. When his language was coupled with a parsimonious attitude towards the ship's stores, a miserly personal disposition and a commitment to depriving his senior personnel of any indication of their standing in the ship, Bligh eroded the pillars on which respect for command at sea is built. Denning's thesis is strengthened by evidence that the main core of mutineers were from among the best seamen who had spent considerable periods ashore in Tahiti, and who had developed a sympathy for Tahitian customs. Plainly, one of the less laudable sides of the Navy's culture was to blame.

Whatever interpretation one favours—and each has some compelling feature—it is clear that William Bligh emerged from the affair at the time with his professional reputation untarnished. Indeed, his reputation in the Royal Navy was enhanced by his achievement in reaching Timor in the launch. But there were a number of political and philosophical questions to be asked of the Navy's ethos, given that the *Bounty* mutiny occurred in the same year as the French Revolution. What influence did Jean Jacques Rousseau, Thomas Paine and the *Rights of Man* have on the attitudes and dispositions of *Bounty*'s men? What place did liberty or democracy have in a disciplined armed service? What recourse was open to sailors when they suffered, or claimed to be suffering, the burden of tyrannical authority? To whom could a sailor defer when his chief grievance was against his captain? What recourse for relief ought to exist when one officer finds the conduct of another officer inhumane, and when should some form of intervention begin?

The *Bounty* mutiny was spontaneous, poorly planned and chaotic. There were shifting loyalties and uncertain actions. Only Christian seems to have recognised the enormity of the step he was taking in seizing Bligh. However, we know least about the motivations and the mental state of Fletcher Christian. We do not know what triggered his dramatic reaction to Bligh's exercise of command. It seems clear that he was gradually becoming disillusioned with naval life; it was not as genteel or congenial as he imagined. But did this justify launching a mutiny? So much remains unclear.

Shortly after the tragedy of the *Bounty*, the Navy suffered another mutiny. But in contrast to *Bounty*, it was bloodthirsty, cruel and without any of the romantic elements that have made the *Bounty* mutiny the stuff of literature and film. The frigate HMS *Hermione* was burdened with a strict and uncaring disciplinarian. Captain Hugh Pigot frequently flogged his men for trivial offences and showed no interest in their health or well-being. Months of cruel and unusual punishments came to a head one afternoon when three sailors, hurrying to the main deck under threat of the lash, fell from the masts to their death. They were thrown overboard and another dozen men were flogged. That night, around 30 men seized weapons and butchered Pigot and thirteen officers in cold blood. *Hermione* was then sailed to Venezuela where the ship was handed over to the Spanish authorities. The mutineers dispersed. Over subsequent years, around half of the mutineers were caught. Fifteen were hanged. The extreme violence of the *Hermione* mutiny deprived the participants of any sympathy in official circles. The British public and decent seafarers alike were disgusted by the violence of the men's actions.

By 1790, there was still unrest and discontent in His Majesty's Ships. The three main grievances continued to be recruitment, food and pay. Navy pay had remained unchanged from 1686 to 1797. The rate was set at 24 shillings for able seamen per lunar month, and 19 shillings for ordinary seamen—although the cost of living in that same period had increased by 30 per cent and wages ashore, including those granted to the Army, had risen proportionately over time. Whereas a minor mutiny in the Fleet had occurred in 1667 because there was no money in the Treasury to cover cheques written to pay wages, by 1790 the sailor was faced with delays and a range of impediments before any money reached his pocket.

Similarly, in the matter of food, there had been little improvement. Although the difficulty of carrying fresh fruit and vegetables was widely acknowledged, the failure of the Navy to provide lime juice and other anti-scorbutics was a source of frustration. Sailors also resented having to eat sea-going rations when their ships were in harbour and fresh food was available. These sentiments were increased by the perennial issuing of food sufficient for six men to messes containing eight men for reasons of economy.

Sea-going service was arduous. Sailors needed a good diet and were reasonably entitled to decent food. In this aspect of their service, sailors were obliged to rely on their superiors to ensure that those ashore made adequate provision for their needs. After all, administrators were not familiar with sea-going service or the requirements of a ship's company. Sailors also expected to be protected from the corrupt practice of allowances for food being siphoned into private pockets. When sailors felt their officers were not concerned for their plight and indifferent to their lot, or when the government took for granted the security provided by the Navy, evidenced by miserly economies, it was not surprising that food joined pay as a leading source of discontent on the lower deck.

The problem of Fleet manning reflected an historic ambivalence towards the Navy by a succession of English kings and their failure to provide a full-time and fully trained body of men to guarantee the naval defence of the country. It was common practice for mediaeval kings to impose upon the merchant fleet for the men and ships required for the defence of the realm. While this custom ended with the reforms initiated by Robert Blake in the 1640s, the Commonwealth was not of sufficient duration to solve the Navy's manning problem. Genuine reforms were on the horizon, however. In theory, those who served in merchant ships were required to make themselves available to man the state-owned and maintained warships when the threat of conflict emerged. In reality, the Parliament was insufficiently concerned with the needs of the Navy and sanctioned the press-gangs. It must be understood that the press-gangs were authorised to search for returning merchant seamen who were under legal obligation to serve in the King's fleet. The press-gangs were needed because most merchant seamen received three to four times in private employ what they were paid in the King's service. When the press-gangs were unable to secure a sufficient number of sailors from the merchant service, Parliament introduced the 'quota' system whereby all local authorities were required to provide a specified number of men for naval service. The easiest way to meet the quota was to arrange for gaoled men and prisoners on remand to be summarily transferred to the Navy. This meant the Navy was burdened with more than its fair share of difficult and dangerous individuals. While naval discipline was uncompromising and quite indifferent to whether or not a man was either willing or suitable for naval service, the task of creating and sustaining an efficient ship's company was the foremost challenge facing naval captains.

Those shunted off to the Navy included men referred to as 'agitators', individuals who had heard of Rousseau's insistence on the inalienable rights of man and the absolute dignity of the citizen. Whereas such men might have been ignored or overlooked by the population ashore, they had a ready audience of disappointed and disaffected men on board His Majesty's Ships, who were increasingly aware of the long-standing grievances suffered by the lower deck. When the French Revolution later unleashed a wave of violence against established authority as it spread a gospel of hope and liberty for the ordinary man, the Navy was not beyond the reach of its underlying socio-political philosophy.

After the Restoration of the Monarchy in 1660 those who had sided with the Parliament still wanted a humane culture to pervade the Navy's ships. They wanted nothing as radical as democracy. But their cry was not heeded. When more than a century later the quality of naval food was still poor, payment still inadequate and irregular, and men compelled against their will to serve in overcrowded ships, the ingredients required for a mutiny existed in abundance. However, it was at this very same time that Britain's reliance on its Navy was greatest. A generous spirit and a compassionate heart was needed, yet one of Britain's finest sailors seemed completely indifferent to the existence of a just cause among his men. Writing to his wife from St Fiorenzo on 12 November 1794, Admiral Horatio Nelson remarked:

> I came in here two days ago and found a most unpleasant circumstance a mutiny on board the *Windsor Castle*, Admiral Linzee's ship. The crew wishing to change their captain [William Shield] and First Lieutenant, the officers have been tried at their own requests and most honourably acquitted but the Admiral [William Hotham] notwithstanding has removed them and forgiven the ship's company who richly deserve a halter. I am of opinion 'tis mistaken leniency and will be the cause of present innocent people being hanged.[18]

Nelson's wife Frances told him on 17 December 1794 that: 'Captain Troubridge has had a terrible mutiny on board *Culloden*, ten will be hanged. Obliged to order a line-of-battle ship to sink her before they would hear reason'.[19]

But it was not only senior officers who abhorred mutiny. Able Seaman James Scott wrote to his brother from HMS *Sovereign* at Spithead on 16 December 1794.

> Seven of our ships have mutinied, particularly the *Culloden* of 74 guns—the principal part of the ship's company took possession of the ship in the most daring manner, set the officers at defiance—broke open the grand magazine and storerooms—got possession of all the arms and fir'd on some of the officers by which one was severely hurt. They continued in this state for six to seven days. [The ringleaders were persuaded to end the mutiny after negotiation with the captains of three other ships] . . . The principal part of the prisoners I believe will be executed—as it is necessary to show some smart example or the mutiny will become general—and render us in a very bad state to face an enemy as we have to repulse.[20]

There was no doubt a crisis was developing. During 1796, England lost 23 warships. One was captured, thirteen wrecked, six foundered and three were burnt. 1797 was a tumultuous year. Eighteen enemy vessels were captured and all but one pressed into British service. These were included in the 696 vessels on the Navy's order of battle. To man this fleet, the Government authorised the payment of 120 000 sailors and marines commanded by 24 admirals, 36 vice-admirals, 44 rear-admirals, 518 post-captains, 338 commanders, 2030 lieutenants and 492 masters. However, in amassing such a mighty fleet, the Admiralty did not make sufficient provision for the average sailor—the one element upon which the success of the fleet would ultimately depend.

In early 1797, a number of ship's companies in the Channel Fleet at Spithead, near Portsmouth, had become unsettled over a combination of poor pay and conditions, long wartime service and an infusion of revolutionary ideas about the 'rights of man'. The greatest insult to the sailors however (still receiving only 19 shillings per month) was the crucial 'shilling a day' which was being paid to soldiers. A petition to the Admiralty to increase sailors' pay was circulated secretly before being forwarded to the Admiralty in March 1797. An answer was slow in coming, even when further petitions were sent. By 16 April there had still been no formal reply. When the Fleet commander gave the order to set the sails, the men in sixteen line-of-battle ships responded only with jeers.

Dismissing their officers, the sailors convened a 'General Assembly' with each ship invited to send delegates to discuss their grievances and to determine a strategy for achieving their demands. Observing a style of parliamentary procedure and honouring the need for discipline, the men devised a charter of liberties and hoisted a red flag to signify their determination to fight for their rights, resolving to remain on strike until their demands were met. There was no overt violence towards officers and the Admiralty held back from precipitate reaction, such as firing on the ships from shore batteries. The 'Breeze at Spithead' was being felt in the corridors of power.

While the sailors' complaints were not unreasonable, Parliament was in no mood to negotiate with mutineers. The Admiralty, however took a more conciliatory view, sending Admiral Lord Howe to meet with the General Assembly and come to an agreement. After this meeting, most of the men believed that their grievances would be remedied and that a new era had begun. Parliament, however, agreed only to debate the subject of pay rises for the sailors and to support one other of the men's demands—a general pardon for their unprecedented actions. The crisis dragged on into May, then seemed to worsen, with unpopular officers being expelled from some ships. A rumour that the Dutch Fleet was sallying to attack the British began to circulate at the same time as the mutineers feared that the Admiralty was planning to attack them.

On 10 May 1797, as the crisis was about to reach boiling point, it was resolved by Parliament voting to increase the men's pay to a shilling a day for an able seaman and 23 shillings and sixpence per month for an ordinary seaman. The King issued a pardon for the mutinous actions of his sailors. No legal actions followed the Spithead mutiny and all parties appeared relieved that the situation was resolved.

The reforms and concessions won at Spithead applied to every ship and sailor in the fleet. Some sailors were unhappy with the outcome, however, while others were encouraged by Lord Howe's response to the General Assembly at Spithead to take their own action later on, in the mistaken belief that discussion rather than suppression was the Navy's new approach to mutiny.

Although termed a mutiny and certainly falling within the legal definition of the time, the events at Spithead had more of the nature of a social movement. The very large number of men involved, the fact that their grievances were recognised, and the relative absence of violence were all factors that made the Spithead mutiny unique. Notwithstanding the undisputed fact that sailors were engaged in a mutinous act, the application of moderation and the exercise of restraint meant a crisis was avoided and the situation resolved constructively. Michael Lewis comments:

> Mutiny can never be condoned in any Service, but it is impossible not to feel, having regard both to the men's moderation and the enormity of their grievances, that this mutiny was more excusable than any before or since.[21]

Events at The Nore several weeks later were a complete contrast. The crews of ships stationed at the naval base on the mouth of the Thames, known as The Nore, started a mutiny on 12 May. The uprising began in HMS *Sandwich*, the flagship of Admiral Buckner, and would last five weeks. Admiral Duncan's ship, the 74-gun *Veteran*, was the only ship's company to remain loyal in this fleet. The ships based at The Nore consisted of a few line-of-battle ships and many smaller ships. Although they were generally overcrowded, other grounds for mutiny did not appear to be present. As at Spithead, some officers were expelled from their ships, but others were held hostage. The mutineers' demands included improvements in conditions over and above those agreed to at Spithead, a greater share of prize money and amnesty for deserters. The Admiralty, having just resolved one problem, was not inclined to make further concessions, and refused to negotiate.

The Spithead mutiny concerned pay and conditions while The Nore mutiny was thought to be mainly about 'politics'. While this was certainly true, the extent to which political motivations were behind the unrest and sustained the mutiny is difficult to determine. While there was the inevitable suspicion of Jacobinism of the French variety, there were no obvious connections either in affiliation or method between the British sailors and the Jacobites. But a revolutionary spirit which owed a debt to Thomas Paine's *Rights of Man* was apparent in the attitudes of the mutiny's leaders.

In contrast to the 'Breeze' at Spithead, events at The Nore assumed a methodical shape. Each ship had a committee of twelve men who governed the vessel and went to a conference each day at Sheerness. The chief organiser of the mutiny was Richard Parker, a former school teacher from Scotland who had been imprisoned for unpaid debt. Parker had taken the parish bounty of £30 and joined the Navy. By the time of the mutiny, which he did not personally start, he had served in the Navy two years and been appointed a petty officer. He was elected president of the mutineers and hoisted his own red flag in *Sandwich* on assuming leadership. Although every officer was deprived of command, the strictest order was maintained in every ship of the Fleet. Concessions made initially to the mutineers were refused, the mutineers resolving to hold out for the terms of settlement they had presented to the Board of Admiralty. The mutineers were formally declared 'rebels' by the Government on 2 June 1797. This had the effect of prompting several ship's companies to abandon the mutiny and reinstate their officers.

On 6 June, when negotiations collapsed, the Government issued a proclamation forbidding any communication with the mutineers on pain of death. Differences then arose among the mutineers, who varied in their degree of zeal for the Revolutionary cause. The sailors in *Ajax*, *Standard* and *Nassau* resolved to return to duty, hauling down the flag of revolt and hoisting the Union Jack. When Admiral Keith arrived with a squadron on 14 June with orders to engage the mutinous vessels, the ship's company of *Sandwich* also hauled down the red flag and indicated their intention to reinstate and accept lawful authority. They were told to surrender unconditionally, which they did. The delegates, led by Parker, were ordered to Keith's flagship, HMS *Standard*, where they were arrested and placed in irons. 'Admiral' Parker was conveyed to Maidstone Gaol in Kent. The other ships' companies then abandoned the mutiny.

Admiral Nelson was unequivocal about the manner in which he thought the Government should handle the mutiny. He told his wife on 30 June 1797:

> Our fleet as yet is most perfectly quiet and orderly and will remain so if government act with proper spirit at The Nore and execute some of the principals. It would be great humanity, for some unfortunate fellows will mutiny too late and will suffer from mistaken humanity. If government gives in, what can we expect of this fleet? I shall believe we shall all be at Spithead. Mankind are all alike and if these people find their brethren in England get their ignorant wishes complied with by being troublesome, it is human nature for others to take the same methods.[22]

At his trial, Parker stated in his defence that:

> he was forced into it, very much against his will, but, when in power, he was determined to use that power, so as to save the ships to his country, and the lives of the deluded men, as far as he was able. For he said it was the determination of most of the mutineers to surrender the Fleet to the Dutch, or the French, and he had much to do to prevent such a horrid transaction. He also was induced to keep them under sobriety, and a mild but firm discipline.[23]

Parker was found guilty of being the ringleader of a mutiny and sentenced to death. At the other courts martial, some of the defendants offered the defence that they had been acting from motives of improving unendurable conditions on the ships. That defence was not accepted. Given the Admiralty's desire to show its intolerance of mutiny after royal pardons had been extended to some of the Spithead mutineers, it was inevitable that those responsible for the uprising at The Nore would face the ultimate punishment under the law. To achieve the greatest effect, the executions would take place in the ships most noted for their mutinous fervour. On 28 June 1797, the first two of the condemned mutineers were hanged.

Two days later, Parker was taken to his former ship, HMS *Sandwich*, which was then anchored off Sheerness, to be hanged from the foreyard. He faced death accepting his punishment but asserting strongly that mutiny was the only means by which the grievances of sailors would be acknowledged. The punishment was carried out with solemn ceremony. A gun was fired from the Flagship HMS *Espion* before Parker's charge and sentence were read publicly in every ship. At 11am, a gun was fired from the *Sandwich* and the sentence carried out. Four men from HMS *St George* were tried by court martial for mutiny on 7 July. They were hanged the following day, although it was Sunday. Marine Private George Thompson wrote from HMS *London* to his wife:

There have been two men hung on board the *Royal Sovereign* since we came into Torbay for mutiny and attempting to hang a Boatswain's Mate, whom they knew to be inimical to their proceedings, and there is an account brought aboard by some Marines who came from Plymouth a few days ago that there are twelve condemned on board the *Powerful* at Spithead. It was Monday September 3 the two suffered in our Fleet. At 10 o'clock the yellow flag was hoisted and a gun fired which is always a signal for executions, and at 11 two guns were fired and the two unfortunate men were run up one at each yard arm in the smoke, where they hung for three quarters of an hour, they were then lowered into the boat, and put into coffins with two two-and-thirty pound shots at their feet to sink them and taken out to sea and buried.[24]

Nelson was content with the outcome, confiding to his wife on 11 July 1797: 'Our mutinies are I hope stopped here, the Admiral having made some severe examples, but they were absolutely necessary'.[25] On 9 October, a general mutiny broke out in the Fleet at the Cape of Good Hope, but ended after three days when the ships' companies were informed that the sailors at Spithead had gained the concessions they demanded.

The very public execution of twelve sailors from The Nore fleet served notice that the Admiralty was not prepared to countenance any further collective disquiet in its ships. That the enemy fleets remained ignorant of the unrest on board the British ships was fortuitous. By the end of the year, perhaps the most tumultuous in British naval history, the British fleet had repelled the invading forces and the country's naval standing had increased, despite the instability on board her fighting ships.

The mutinies at Spithead and The Nore had two contrary outcomes. On the one hand, while the Lords of the Admiralty believed that they had maintained the desired standards of discipline and upheld the legal status of the crime of mutiny, the incidence of mutiny did not end. On 6 January 1802, John Mayfield and thirteen other sailors from HMS *Temeraire* were tried by court martial for 'using mutinous and seditious words, and taking an active part in seditious assemblies'. Twelve of the men were sentenced to death while another received 200 lashes. On 14 January, five more mutineers from the same ship were tried, found guilty and sentenced to death by hanging on board His Majesty's Ships. On the other hand, there was a belief among many British sailors that they could obtain redress for grievances through collective and resolute action.

Both the Spithead and Nore mutinies revealed to the Admiralty the awesome power of 'combination' which resided among sailors. This latent power was a reminder to the Parliament not to take the lower deck of the Navy for granted. And, indeed, the Nore mutiny was so potentially serious that it remained an encouragement to the Admiralty to care for sailors for many decades. The men had made clear in 1797 that they could only be pushed so far and only tolerate so much. Every man and group of men had their breaking point.

During the first twenty years of the colony of New South Wales a series of incidents occurred that received such widespread publicity that the Admiralty feared its authority, and that of its captains, was being more radically challenged. This had a bearing on the Navy's attitude towards mutiny throughout the following years, and on its reaction to those whose attitude towards authority carried even the faintest scent of insurrection.

3

The New South Wales Corps: were they really mutineers?

When the British Government resolved in 1786 that Botany Bay in New South Wales would be the site of a new settlement, there was universal recognition that the colony's Governor would need to possess absolute authority and the means to ensure his rule could be neither defied nor undermined. Thus, for nearly two decades the British Government turned to the Royal Navy in the hope of obtaining the services of officers experienced in the exercise of power. The first four governors were naval captains, each possessing a commission granting him civil and naval command. Given the distance of New South Wales from Britain and the remoteness of the settlement, any hint of mutiny would have endangered stable and effective rule, reduced the colony's financial viability, and weakened Britain's ability to ensure its sovereignty over the entire continent.

The small colony half a world away from the United Kingdom was originally composed of just two main elements: the convicts who had been transported for a range of crimes and the soldiers who were there to guard them. Because the duty of serving in a penal settlement did not carry much attraction for regular army regiments, a new unit was formed specifically for service in the colony—the New South Wales Corps. The Corps was filled with recruits who had been farm boys or the 'gaol-fringe' and officered by those who had neither the money nor the influence to purchase a commission in a more prestigious regiment. After the foundation of the colony in 1788, a third population group emerged and grew in number—discharged convicts, time-expired soldiers and a small but growing number of free settlers who saw opportunity in the Great Southern Land.

The colony as it developed hardly reflected a cross-section of genteel English society. Furthermore, life was complicated by climatic hardships and physical deprivations. There were shortages of all sorts of commodities, including a dearth of specie, or coinage, to lubricate the wheels of commerce and the greasy palms of innkeepers. One item was, however, freely available in a colony where there was such a high proportion of sailors and soldiers. Cargoes of rum were imported into the colony for consumption by military and civilian alike. Much of it was for the New South Wales Corps, whose officers issued rum regularly to the troops, who either consumed or bartered it in the manner cherished among soldiers since Caesar's time. The officers and quartermasters of the Corps also seized the opportunity to corruptly sell increasingly large quantities to civilian establishments. Rum became the constant companion of many.

It did not take long for the officers of the Corps to achieve a virtual monopoly on the supply and distribution of rum. At the same time, because it was readily available and coinage was not, rum became the common means of exchange in trade. Farmers traded their harvest to the commissariat in exchange for rum; workers accepted rum in lieu of wages and theatre owners put on performances where seats were purchased for rum. The first church in Sydney was built by workers who were paid in rum. Because the trade of rum became the main pursuit of the Corps' officers, the regiment itself became known as the 'Rum Puncheon' or 'Rum Corps'. The period between the departure in December 1792 of the first Viceroy, Captain Arthur Phillip, on the grounds of ill-health and the arrival of his successor, Captain John Hunter, in September 1795 proved to be disastrous for the Colony and its long-term administration. After nearly three years of rule by Lieutenant Governors—the two senior officers of the New South Wales Corps, Major Francis Grose and, briefly, Colonel William Paterson—the military had managed to gain economic and political ascendancy.[1]

When Captain John Hunter eventually arrived as Viceroy, the conditions existed whereby the Governor's authority could and eventually would be challenged. Hunter tried to break the power of the Corps by ending their monopoly on trade. Although the exercise of arbitrary authority was needed, Hunter failed to back this up in his personal approach to dealing with officers whom he generally believed, wrongly as it turned out, could be trusted to act honourably. Following unscrupulous denigration by the Corps, his reputation was further tarnished by critical letters sent back to Britain. His recall came as no surprise, not even to Hunter himself. The reputation of a gentle, humane and charitable man was destroyed by a group of men who had no respect for either Hunter or his office. He should have acted more decisively to enforce his authority and steadfastly refused to admit any challenge to his near-complete power to regulate the affairs of the colony. This was an instance in which a naval officer did not utilise the full extent of his prerogatives of command to fulfil the instructions given to him by Government. By allowing the Corps to achieve supremacy, legitimate authority had been challenged and the office of the Governor compromised. The legacy of Hunter's administration was a mutinous military which resented authority, especially when it resided in a naval officer.

The circumstances of Hunter's recall were the source of further humiliation for him. Lieutenant Philip Gidley King, who had earlier sailed with Hunter in HMS *Sirius*, arrived in Sydney on 15 April 1800 in HMS *Speedy* possessing a letter dismissing Hunter and appointing King his successor. Although Hunter remained until September, King set about making his own inquiries into the administration of the colony in preparation for assuming office. This soured relations between the two former friends.

From the outset, King tried to put a stop to the corrupt trade in rum but without an independent force of his own, reliant for military support on the very men who were the problem, he was powerless to curb the power of the Corps. Indeed, relations between the Governor and the Corps became so acrimonious that popular ditties and graffiti spread throughout Sydney, ridiculing King and his wife. In 1803, a frustrated King wrote to Lord Hobart, Secretary of State for War and the Colonies, complaining of 'the assassinating and dark attacks of those who dare not avow themselves, as well as the opposition and insults I have received in the discharge of my duties'. Conscious of his failure and its consequences for New South Wales, King wanted an inquiry into the affairs of the colony and his own conduct as Governor. Lord Hobart wrote to him in November 1803 deploring 'the unfortunate differences which have so long subsisted between you and the military officers of the colony'. He told King that a request from him to return to England would be granted 'as soon as the important trust with which you are charged can be placed in the hands of some person competent to exercise the duties thereof, free from the operation of the spirit of party which has reached such an alarming height'. Hobart's letter reached Sydney in June 1805. King explained publicly that he had been given leave of absence. In reality, he had been sacked.

The British government looked for another naval captain to

replace King. They sought the advice of Sir Joseph Banks who put forward the name of a man who knew the South Seas well and who, under his patronage, had collected breadfruit at Tahiti. He was a captain who had recently served well, commanding a line-of-battle ship at the Battle of Camperdown. He had also served under Admiral Nelson at Copenhagen. His ship, HMS *Duncan*, had been involved in the Spithead mutiny, although the ship's company had not considered him among the worst or more odious of the disciplinarians against whom they took action. The new Governor would have to be both temperamentally strong and administratively astute to succeed almost by sheer force of character where his two predecessors had failed. The nominee was Captain William Bligh. On securing the post, Bligh was issued with a commission from the Lords of the Admiralty as a post-captain of HMS *Porpoise*, and the right to hoist a commodore's broad pennant in any naval ship that happened to be at New South Wales.

Governor Bligh arrived in Sydney on 7 August 1806. He was received with all the honours due to him as Viceroy and Commodore, and was presented with an address of welcome from the colony's leading people. There were three signatures on the address, representing the three major groups within the 10 000-strong population. The first was Major George Johnston, acting commander of the New South Wales Corps, who represented the military. The second was Judge-Advocate Richard Atkins, representing civilian officials of the settlement. The third was John Macarthur, a former junior officer of the New South Wales Corps, a merchant and farmer who represented the free citizens.

Bligh came determined to impose his ideals of integrity and discipline on all within the Colony in order to clean up corruption among local traders. He could fall back on his experience of many years in command. The problem was that the practices of the quarterdeck were not easily transferable to the raucous and factious colony. He would not get much assistance. Major Johnston spent more time managing the Corps' corrupt trading than he spent on military duties. Judge Atkins was a corrupt drunkard with only a limited knowledge of the law he was pledged to uphold. John Macarthur, renowned as one of the founders of Australia's wool industry, was nevertheless the most villainous of the three.

Macarthur had once been apprenticed to a staymaker in England (and bore the nickname of 'John Bodice') but had taken the opportunity offered by a commission as a very junior officer in the newly-formed New South Wales Corps. Once in the new settlement, Macarthur seized every commercial opportunity that presented itself in the trade of rum and cattle. He had a natural shrewdness and energy that soon brought him substantial wealth and a quick exit from military life. It also made him unpopular. A number of free settlers soon complained to Bligh about Macarthur's signing the address of welcome. The decent settlers and citizens wanted to distance themselves from Macarthur and hoped for an end to the rum monopoly, the corruption it entailed and the misery it delivered. However, Macarthur had the twin advantages of personal wealth and influence with the Corps. He was an imposing figure.

Within a month, Bligh confronted Macarthur over the matter of a land grant of 5000 acres. Macarthur had lobbied the Secretary of State and the Privy Council to grant him the land so he could extend his grazing pasture and the size of his flocks. He argued that the garment manufacturers of England would benefit by a reliable supply of fine wool from an English colony instead of being reliant upon Spanish and northern European wool imports. However, Sir Joseph Banks had fully briefed Bligh on the matter before he left England and had told the Governor-designate that Macarthur had exaggerated the possibilities of the fine wool he said he could provide if given the land to do so. Once in New South Wales, Bligh refused to endorse the grant and Macarthur reacted angrily, although he took no precipitate action. Bligh also reacted angrily during this meeting with Macarthur. The Governor was not always able to keep his temper under control, a serious personality flaw which had certainly contributed to his troubles in *Bounty*.

During his naval career, Bligh had been able to get away with displays of temper on the quarterdecks of His Majesty's Ships, where most of the time his harassed ship's company had no avenue of protest or complaint, however, there was a world of difference between a warship and New South Wales. There was an even greater difference between sailors forced into obedience by the lash and ruthless traders who had become accustomed to getting their own way. Bligh evidently put the exchange with Macarthur into the past as he subsequently invited Macarthur, as a prominent citizen, to dine at Government House. Macarthur did not forget the exchange, however, but contained his resentment while he waited for the right moment to settle the score.

During his first year as Governor, Bligh worked hard at enforcing Philip King's regulations against corruption. His early success came from his personal energy and zeal. He was especially determined to stamp out the profiteering in rum which had led to so many other evils. But there was unrest in various quarters of colonial society and a growing sentiment of disloyalty. The conditions required for mutiny were created in the first instance by an incident involving *Parramatta*, a small ship owned by John Macarthur. A number of convicts had previously escaped in ships trading throughout the South Pacific. Often the ships' captains had assisted the men, either for financial gain or out of sympathy for their plight. In order to stop the practice, Bligh's administration issued a regulation that all ship owners guarantee a bond of £900 that would be payable if the administration could prove that a convict used the owner's ship to escape.

In December 1807, *Parramatta* carried an escaped convict when it departed Sydney. *Parramatta*'s captain allowed the man to leave at Tahiti and join a ship bound for England. Accordingly, the Government demanded Macarthur pay the bond of £900. He refused. The matter went to court. The court ordered that the guaranteed sum be paid. Macarthur still refused to comply. He was arrested and committed for trial before the Judge-Advocate, the incompetent Richard Atkins. While on bail, Macarthur demanded a copy of the indictment against him. When Atkins refused (an improper action in itself), Macarthur demanded that the Governor replace him with another judge. Bligh responded, with complete truthfulness, that there was no-one in the colony other than Atkins able to hear the case. The set-up of the colonial court was unusual in that six officers of the military (in this case the only military unit was the New South Wales Corps) sat with the Judge-Advocate as a tribunal. In the first in a series of calculated tactical moves, Macarthur used the period between his committal and trial to lobby his erstwhile fellow officers for support.

On 25 January 1808, Macarthur's case came before Judge-Advocate Atkins and six officers of the Corps. Macarthur immediately launched into a personal attack on Atkins. He stated that the Judge-Advocate was prejudiced against him and had been so disposed for several years. As a civil case involving the two men was also pending, Macarthur could readily protest his inability to receive a fair trial with Atkins presiding. The Judge-Advocate attempted to terminate the proceedings by telling Macarthur his case was to go to trial without delay. This was before the military officers intervened. The senior officer, Captain Kemp, told the Judge-Advocate that he (Atkins) rather than Macarthur should be brought to trial. Atkins hastily left the courtroom without taking his papers. The six officers, deliberating in his absence, supported Macarthur's objection. They wrote to Governor Bligh demanding Atkins' removal and replacement. Bligh responded that he had no authority to replace Atkins as Judge-Advocate and could not give any direction to the court on the conduct of its cases.

The exchange of letters continued. By now, Atkins had taken refuge in Government House. Bligh considered that the only way to restore calm and curb the officers' demands was to call on the commanding officer of the Corps and ask him to bring his men to order. Accordingly, the Governor wrote urgently to Major Johnston and asked him to attend Government House, waiting anxiously for his arrival. Johnston was then in his house (about seven kilometres away). He did not come, but sent a letter telling the Governor that he had fallen from his carriage the previous night while travelling home from a regimental dinner, that he was seriously incapacitated with a sore arm and had just received medical treatment (a session of bleeding), and that he was far too ill to come to Government House because such a journey might even endanger his life. There is no evidence that Johnston was acting in collusion with Macarthur and the other officers at this point. But given the Major was physically active the next day, it is probable that some coordinated plan of action had been agreed when Bligh sought his intervention. At the very least, Johnston was prepared to stand on the sidelines while waiting to see what would eventuate.

Evening came and the parties had reached a stand-off. On one side were Macarthur and the corrupt military officers opposed to the Governor's efforts to curtail their profitable trade. On the other side were the officials in Government House: the Governor, the Judge-Advocate and a small number of civil servants. There was some justice in the case that Macarthur had put before the court. Atkins was certainly a drunk and incompetent, while his actions in the courtroom were unacceptable. Yet he was the only person in the colony qualified to administer justice and should have been given an opportunity to hear some of the evidence before any impediment was alleged. Given his stern and unbending view of authority and regulations, Bligh naturally felt himself beholden to support the office Atkins held. Evidence suggests that the majority of free settlers in New South Wales also supported Bligh against the Corps.[2]

The next day was the twentieth anniversary of the founding of the settlement. To break the impasse, Bligh ordered an officer of the court, Provost Marshal Gore, to arrest Macarthur and take him to gaol. This Gore did. On hearing of Macarthur's arrest, the officers sought out Major Johnston. The next act in the escalating crisis was the release of Macarthur on the written order of Major Johnston. The release document was signed by Johnston as 'Lieutenant Governor', an office he did not hold. The title of Lieutenant Governor could only be conferred by a commission from the King. The Lieutenant Governor was actually Colonel Paterson, the commanding officer of the New South Wales Corps, who was absent in Tasmania on government duty.

Johnston's provocative use of the title Lieutenant Governor meant there could be no turning back from the course upon which he and the Corps had embarked. Its use implied assumption of authority and could be construed as a mutinous action in itself. It may have been Macarthur's plan to persuade Johnston to use the term so as to avoid any retreat by the Major. Johnston was not an overly ambitious man. He was popular with his men but easily persuaded, a serious weakness when Macarthur was the man ready to do the persuading. Macarthur was escorted by the Corps in a triumphant procession to the barracks. On arrival in the mess, Macarthur found Major Johnston had already arrived. The Major allegedly cried out: 'God's curse! What am I do to, Macarthur? Here are these fellows advising me to arrest the Governor!' Macarthur responded: 'Advising you! Then sir, the only thing left for you is to do it'. It reflected poorly upon the leadership quality of the New South Wales Corps that its acting commander was so lacking in initiative and resolve that he turned to a former junior officer for guidance.

Macarthur, of course, never lacked initiative. He sat down on a cannon in the regimental parade ground and penned a spurious appeal to Johnston, purportedly on behalf of other citizens, although few had any knowledge of what had occurred. He claimed all were in grave danger of their lives: 'The present alarming state of this colony, in which every man's property, liberty and life is endangered, induces us most earnestly to implore you instantly to place Governor Bligh under an arrest and to assume the command of the colony'. He added, in case that was insufficient to provoke Johnston to action, that 'they' would support the action with 'our fortunes and our lives'. Macarthur did not add that he was the only person whose property, liberty and life were endangered or that the threat to civic life consisted of Macarthur having to pay £900 for allowing a felon to escape on his ship.

Macarthur's move was a cunning one. At one stroke he pressured Johnston to act in his (Macarthur's) own personal interest while Macarthur would bear no legal responsibility for what transpired. He was 'merely' calling on the Major for protection and ensuring that responsibility for any subsequent actions would fall on Johnston. The event that was about to take place was, in legal terms, a mutiny by one man only. The Corps were merely following the orders of their legal commander. Citizens such as Macarthur were civilians and were clearly beyond the reach of military law in this case. At the time there was no law concerning incitement to mutiny by civilians.

With this scrap of paper seemingly enough to stiffen his backbone, Major Johnston immediately proclaimed martial law. In doing so, he undoubtedly initiated a mutiny because the Governor, as Commander-in-Chief, had overall military as well as civil authority. Martial law could only be proclaimed by the Governor. The Major then organised sufficient troops to march on Government House where Bligh was dining with a number of people, including Judge-Advocate Atkins. Also at Government House was Bligh's widowed daughter, Mary Putland, whose husband had died of tuberculosis two weeks earlier. Major Johnston had accompanied her to the funeral. Bligh and his guests had just finished dinner when the noise outside reached them. Atkins ventured out to see what was going on and returned with the news that armed troops were marching from their barracks towards Government House. Bligh said to him, 'Surely they dare not attack my person?' Atkins replied: 'I have no doubt they will'. Bligh must have had memories of another occasion when his men confronted him in arms. On that occasion, he had been rudely pulled from his bed. At least this time he had some warning. It says much for Bligh's courage that instead of following Atkins' example and seeking a hiding place, he poured a glass of wine, stood to attention, and proclaimed, 'The Health of the King!' Having drunk the toast, the Governor quickly left the room and went to his study to secure his official papers.

The troopers of the Corps came marching up to Government House with colours raised and the regimental band playing 'British Grenadiers'. Ominously, they had bayonets fixed to their muskets although they could hardly have expected much resistance. In view of the likely fighting qualities of the regiment, this precaution may have been just as well for their own sakes. At this point, an unexpected defender of constituted authority came forward. Waving her umbrella, Bligh's daughter came out of

Government House and blocked the path of the troops. She did not retreat, even as the soldiers marched up to her. When they were a pace away she called out: 'Stab me to the heart, but respect the life of my father'. Her bravery availed nothing. The troops did not assault her but she was pushed to one side as they spread out to surround Government House. They forced an entry through a side door and quickly apprehended Atkins and the others who had been dining with the Governor.

Bligh had meanwhile gathered some of his official papers and called upon his orderly to saddle a horse. He then hurried upstairs to put on his uniform. His long experience, especially of violent combat, had taught him that a gentleman and an officer ought to face his fate with dignity and in uniform. If he could have made good his escape on horseback and ridden to the outlying farming settlements on the Hawkesbury River, the settlers would probably have taken his side against the corrupt officers of the Corps. According to his own reporting, Bligh was at the head of the stairs when he heard the soldiers breaking in the side door. Realising that he could not escape by any of the doors, he made his way to a small room in the servants' quarters with a view to getting out through a window. He was kneeling by a window, stuffing papers into his waistcoat and trying to rip up others when an officer looked into the room. Bligh stated that he dropped down onto the floor near the window, in such a place that the bed hid him from the officer's view. The door closed again. Bligh thought he was in luck. He continued ripping up the official papers that he could not carry. However, the door burst open again and a sergeant and a lance-corporal tramped into the room.

By their version, they found Bligh hiding under the bed. Prodding him out at bayonet point, the lance-corporal dragged him to his feet by the collar. The officer said that there was dust on Bligh's collar and feathers on the back of his coat. According to Bligh's version, he was still by the window, about to escape when the door opened a second time. Bligh may have been concealing himself by the bed but there is no reason to suppose the man was a coward in trying to hide. His actions in drinking the health of the King and putting on his uniform were not the actions of a panicked coward. He was fully entitled to evade arrest by mutinous troops by every means at his disposal. Indeed, it was later established that there was insufficient clearance for a corpulent man such as Bligh to have secreted himself under the bed. When the soldiers dragged the Governor out of the room, he put his hand into his waistcoat. The lance-corporal waved his bayonet at the captive and said: 'Damn your eyes, if you don't take your hand out of there I'll whip this into you!'

Bligh protested that he was unarmed. He had been trying to protect the official papers pushed into his waistcoat. An officer calmed the men and led Bligh downstairs. Government House was engulfed by the Corps. Major Johnston was in their midst with Macarthur. Johnston led Bligh into the dining room where he had finished his meal only minutes before. He pulled out a letter which he had written and signed stating that the Governor was considered unfit to govern, and gave it to Bligh. Bligh was then searched and his official papers, including his commission from the King, were taken away. Apparently satisfied, Johnston, Macarthur and the soldiers left Bligh with his daughter, setting a guard of five men on their quarters. Johnston then issued a public proclamation that he had assumed control of the colony.

The next day, 27 January 1808, all those who had supported the Governor were removed from their posts and their places taken by cronies of Macarthur and the Corps. Major Johnston made another public proclamation with an odd texture of satisfaction and unreality. He announced that martial law had ended before expressing his appreciation of the citizens' support. He assured them that they deserved the protection that was his to offer. Macarthur was well-satisfied when Johnston appointed him Colonial Secretary. That position meant that he could arrange the dismissal of the charges that had been brought against him. It also meant that he could exercise de facto power in the colony. Bligh was kept under arrest at Government House for nearly a year. The armed guards of the Corps followed him wherever he went, even walking in the grounds with his daughter who was allowed to remain with him. Bligh later complained that the guards treated him in a 'most cruel manner'.

Bligh was able to send news of the affair to the British Government in May of that year with the aid of a London merchant. He also sent a coldly formal note to Johnston requesting permission to return to England in HMS *Porpoise*. The ship was still technically under Bligh's command because Johnston had chosen not to supplant his Admiralty commission as Commander-in-Chief and Commodore. The Major, however, was afraid that if Bligh had his freedom he might not return directly to England but rather remain in the area and make trouble for his illegitimate administration. Bligh was refused permission to leave. Lieutenant Colonel Joseph Foveaux, who had been Administrator of Norfolk Island and was technically Lieutenant Governor in the absence of Colonel Paterson, arrived in Sydney in July 1808 and assumed command but he did not release Bligh while he waited instructions from a superior officer. Colonel Paterson returned to Sydney from Tasmania in January 1809 in poor health. Instead of reinstating Bligh, however, Paterson judged that the legal situation was far from clear and decided to assume personal control of the administration. He did not release the deposed Governor.

A clash arose when Paterson ordered *Porpoise* to Norfolk Island to remove the settlers there. Bligh sent orders to *Porpoise*'s commanding officer that the ship was not to comply. In an odd choice of messenger, Colonel Paterson selected Major Johnston to go to Government House with a letter insisting Bligh allow the ship to proceed. It was the first time Bligh had seen Johnston since the day of the mutiny. The Governor refused to allow the ship to sail and reiterated that he was still legally entitled to give orders to its captain, adding that if anyone countermanded his instructions they would do so at their peril. Johnston replied that if Bligh would not agree, he had orders to confine him in the Corps' barracks. Bligh still refused. Johnston took the Governor against his will a second time.

Mary Putland heard that her father was being taken away to the barracks, and hurried after him. Reaching Bligh at the gate of the barracks, she went to his side and the two walked arm-in-arm into captivity. Their new prison consisted of two rooms with a bed in one and a sofa in the other. Entering the quarters, Mary collapsed on the sofa. That night, Bligh made up the bed for his daughter and slept on the sofa himself. After only six days, however, Colonel Paterson changed his mind about *Porpoise* proceeding to Norfolk Island. He decided to resolve matters by releasing Bligh and seeking an undertaking that he would return immediately to England. Once on board however, Bligh ordered *Porpoise* to sail to Tasmania, where he intended to stay until assistance arrived from the Government in England.

The British Government was preoccupied with other events overseas, such as the beginning of the Peninsular War, when word came of Bligh's problems in 1809. If such news had come at any other time it would have taken a much harder line with an illegitimate military administration, even on the other side of the world. Nevertheless, mutiny in any shape or form could not be left unpunished. The Government wisely decided that Bligh had to be reinstated, but having been returned to his post, he could not remain in office for any length of time. Therefore, Lord Castlereagh, the Secretary of State, appointed a soldier, not a naval captain, as the next Governor, and ensured that Bligh's replacement would have adequate force and loyal support in carrying out the necessary reforms. Lieutenant-Colonel Lachlan Macquarie of the 73rd Regiment (a Scottish infantry regiment) was appointed Governor. He would be accompanied by a battalion from the regiment under Lieutenant-Colonel Maurice O'Connell. The troublesome New South Wales Corps would be relieved. The new force was capable of suppressing the Corps by strength of arms in the event that its officers chose to maintain their mutinous stand. It may have been no coincidence that Lord Castlereagh chose Scottish soldiers to oppose the Englishmen of the Rum Corps.

Macquarie, now in the rank of Colonel, arrived with his regiment in December 1809 and landed without incident. Bligh, still at sea in *Porpoise* off Tasmania, heard of their arrival and immediately sailed back to Sydney where Macquarie proclaimed his reinstatement as Governor—but only for a single day. Macquarie then read his own commission as Governor.

Macquarie had orders to arrest both Johnston and Macarthur, the Major to be sent to England to stand trial for mutiny. By this time, however, both men had left New South Wales. No action was taken against other members of the Corps or civilians who had been involved in the mutiny. The public officials who were dismissed by Johnston during his turbulent days of power were also reinstated. The odious trade in rum was stamped out. Over the next twelve years, Macquarie's strong and capable government brought stability and growth to the colony.

William Bligh, now just another naval Post Captain, sailed for England in February 1810. His daughter did not join him this time, having married Lieutenant Colonel O'Connell. When Bligh arrived in England, he found both Johnston and Macarthur already in London, where they were busily lobbying for support. Despite his efforts, Johnston was tried by court martial in Chelsea on 7 May 1811. The court was composed of fifteen senior officers, including five lieutenant generals. The charge against Major Johnston was that on 26 January 1808, he did:

> begin, excite, cause and join in a mutiny, by putting himself at the head of the NSW Corps, then under his command and doing duty in the colony, and seizing and causing to be seized and arrested, and imprisoning and causing to be imprisoned, by means of the above mentioned military force, the person of William Bligh, then Captain General and Governor in Chief in and over the territory of New South Wales.[3]

This was the first court martial for a mutiny committed on Australian soil. Johnston's defence was that of necessity. He argued that Bligh was unpopular to the extent that ordinary people were ready to take arms to overthrow him and were encouraging soldiers to join them. Johnston claimed that his action had been the lesser of two evils. In arresting Bligh without bloodshed, he had prevented the loss of life and a more widespread rebellion. Macarthur gave evidence on Johnston's behalf. In the course of presenting their evidence both damned Bligh and muckraked through his previous life.

The defence was not accepted. It was clear to the court that Johnston should have supported Bligh's request for assistance on the day before the mutiny when events got out of hand in Atkins' court. Neither was the court convinced that the population was on the verge of open rebellion. Johnston was found guilty of an act of mutiny. The court sentenced him 'to be cashiered'. The judgment stated:

> The Court, in passing a sentence so inadequate to the enormity of the crime of which the prisoner has been found guilty, have apparently been actuated by a consideration of the novel and extraordinary circumstances, which, by the evidence on the face of the proceedings, may have appeared to them to have existed during the administration of Governor Bligh, both as affecting the tranquillity of the colony, and calling for some immediate decision. But although the Prince Regent [who was required to confirm the sentence] admits the principle under which the Court have allowed this consideration to act in mitigation of the punishment which the crime of mutiny would otherwise have suggested, yet no circumstances whatever can be received by His Royal Highness in full extenuation of the assumption of power, so subversive of every principle of good order and discipline as that under which Lieutenant Colonel Johnston has been convicted.[4]

Johnston's military career was over. It was coming to an end in any event as Johnston was prone to rheumatism and other complaints of age. He was allowed to return to New South Wales where he lived on his farm near Sydney, dying in 1826. The British Government rightly judged Macarthur to be a source of trouble. He was not granted permission to return to the colony (where his wife was managing his large landholdings) until 1817.

Bligh, not surprisingly given his explosive character, was bitterly disappointed in the outcome. He felt the trial had been unjust and his reputation had been unnecessarily sullied. His hope had been to see Johnston hanged and Macarthur banned from New South Wales with the 'other ringleaders'. He should have been thankful that he emerged from another controversial affair with his reputation intact, however, despite accusations of impeding the course of justice and of corruption. In June 1810 he was promoted to Rear-Admiral of the White and later, by virtue of seniority, Vice-Admiral of the Blue. He received a governor's pension in 1813 and died of cancer in 1817, aged 64 years.

Paul Brunton is perhaps closest to the truth when he notes that the 1807–08 mutiny was *not* about the control of rum.

> The rebellion was caused by the confrontation between two men: William Bligh and John Macarthur. Both were resolute and both were convinced of their own rectitude. Macarthur saw Bligh as the obstacle to the realisation of his vision for the Australian wool industry—a vision which included a central and lucrative role for himself. Bligh, influenced by his patron, Banks, saw Macarthur as an enemy of government who had vanquished his predecessors and who must be brought under control.[5]

The British Government acted swiftly to remove the conditions which had produced the mutiny against Bligh. From that moment, civil rule was secure and the threat of a *coup d'état*, which was a more accurate description of Johnson's actions than mutiny, given he did not usurp Bligh's position as Commander-in-Chief and Commodore, disappeared from the colony's political landscape.

The run of mutinies in ships and ashore involving naval personnel from 1790–1808 alerted British naval authorities to the need to heed the concerns and the grievances of the lower deck. That they were successful is, in part, evidenced by the absence of a single incident of mutiny in any RN ship in Australian waters for the remainder of the nineteenth century. But the Admiralty was less able to prevent unrest in the motley collection of naval ships operated by the various Australian colonial governments in the latter part of the nineteenth century. One such vessel was *Gayundah*, whose only claim to fame rested on a mutiny.

4

Mutiny in the Australian colonial forces

For most of the nineteenth century, the task of defending the Australian continent against foreign invasion was a matter of some concern for the British Government. The colonists were neither sufficiently well organised or wealthy enough to make their own independent arrangements for the security of the colonies or the seaborne cargoes that were their lifeline to the rest of the world. Happily for those living in Australia, the Royal Navy had given Britain unsurpassed supremacy of the seas. Following the Battle of Trafalgar on 21 October 1805, Britain would rule the waves for more than a century.

In 1815, the Royal Navy consisted of over 700 ships in commission manned by 140 000 men. Three years later, after a costly four-year war at sea with America, peace was secured on terms favourable to Britain, and the Navy was reduced to 130 ships and 19 000 men. Those who had been forced into the Navy were happy to be discharged. The men who remained were volunteers. The press-gangs were never used after 1815 nor were criminals sent to the Navy. Thus, for the first time, ship's companies consisted entirely of men who wanted to serve. Nevertheless, the Royal Navy's reputation for harsh discipline remained long after the misfits and troublemakers for whom it was needed were gone. While overall a much enlightened attitude flowed on from Lord Howe and like-minded colleagues who believed that after the Spithead incident in 1797—sailors responded more positively to compassion and respect than to harsh discipline—there remained captains who resorted to violence because they were bad-tempered, cruel, weak or incompetent. Men could still be flogged for minor offences and there were no avenues for appeal or redress.

Shore leave was another overdue innovation. With the constant threat of hostilities and a ship's company drawn from both volunteers and pressed men, captains had always been afraid of desertion. It was quite usual for a man to board a ship and be kept on board for several years. In place of shore leave, alcohol and prostitutes were conveyed to the ships. With the coming of peace and the stability of an all-volunteer Navy, captains began to allow shore leave and found their men could be trusted to return, albeit drunk. Trusted men were also allowed to have their wives on board with them.

The improved quality of food served in warships was another area of reform welcomed by sailors during the nineteenth century. There had usually been plenty of food in Royal Navy ships. Indeed, records suggest that sailors tended to have more to eat in the Navy than they could have afforded if employed ashore. The quality was sometimes suspect, though—the meat could at times be carved and polished like mahogany, and tunic buttons made from naval cheese were allegedly more durable than those made of metal or bone. The food was not ordinarily that bad, however, if boring. The standard weekly ration was seven pounds of biscuit, six pounds of pork and beef, twelve ounces of cheese, three pints of oatmeal, two pints of pease (dried peas), six ounces of butter and six ounces of sugar. On days when meat was not issued, each man received the ingredients for a huge plum duff: four pounds of flour, seven pounds of raisins and half a pound of suet. At this time, too, came the greatest improvement in sailors' food—'bully beef', issued in tins. This invention was originally a French idea, its name being the British sailor's version of *boeuf bouilli*. The tins were made in the Dartford Iron Works and began to appear in ships from 1813.

Another advance was actually a deprivation. The daily issue of a gallon of beer and half a pint of rum was universally considered to be excessive. It turned sailors into alcoholics and, not surprisingly, made the offence of drunkenness the most common charge brought against them. Previous attempts to reduce the issue had been resisted. While war was in progress, the Admiralty decided against reducing it. In 1824, however, the rum ration was halved and tea and cocoa were issued for the first time. Although the reduction met with anger, it was accepted. In 1850, it was halved again. One of the principal sources of shipborne trouble and strife had been greatly diminished.

All was not completely well, however. The daily round of shipboard life was arduous. And whereas the prospect of war provided some interest, peacetime life was often monotonous, boring and uneventful. War had also offered the prospect of prize money, absent during peacetime. Many remembered the occasion in 1803 when two frigates happened to capture an enemy ship that was laden with treasure: each sailor's share had come to nearly £500—more than a lifetime's pay! Such incidents had helped to focus the mind and add a spring to the step. In peacetime, there was no such encouragement and yet the work was still physically draining and had to be performed irrespective of the climate, the season or the weather. Working aloft in the rigging during a storm was the most dangerous task, because the driving rain and high wind made sails sodden and unmanageable, and even the most sure-footed sailor could be hurled out of the sail-tops in rough seas. Perched high above the deck with their legs braced precariously in foot-ropes, sailors often suffered ruptures as they tugged at the deadweight of wet canvas which they were trying to secure to the yards. The handling of heavy guns and huge water casks also caused many injuries. By the end of the nineteenth century, so many sailors complained of hernias that the Admiralty decided to issue those working in the rigging with trusses. About 3500 trusses were issued annually between 1808 and 1815. It is estimated that in this period one in every seven sailors suffered from a hernia. As for the ships themselves, they were neither heated nor well-ventilated. Maintaining hygiene was always a struggle. Disease was often rampant and sickness a constant companion.

But for all that, most accounts of the period suggest that the British sailor was largely content and happy with his life. Most men were proud of their personal skills and the standing of their ship. As always, however, the quality of shipboard life related directly to the character of the captain. A sailor serving in HMS *Albion* wrote in 1852: 'A week rarely passes . . . without some man receiving his three or four dozen lashes at the gangway'. Those punished in this way were usually guilty of insubordination. Threats to command and authority always met with this resolute response. As the correspondent from *Albion* also remarked: 'It was undoubtedly severe as the discoloured, raw-beef-hued appearance of the victim's back attested'. But not all captains used violence to reinforce their command. A sailor in HMS *Alceste* praised his benevolent captain. Whenever the ship was manoeuvred, 'the whole of the vast machine moved like clockwork, without jar or impediment'. How did he achieve this success?

His men were willing, because they found he wishes to be, would be, just; they put forth their strength, skill and cheerful alacrity because he was merciful and considerate in his discipline; he never irritated them by caprice, there was no . . . niggling in anything he ordered.

A Royal Commission on naval manning was established in 1858. It looked at training methods and the introduction of continuous service. For hundreds of years men had committed themselves to a specific ship for a defined period of service. Now they were invited to join the Navy, which would find a ship in which they could serve indefinitely. Sometimes sailors could even express a preference for where they served. In this way, the Navy became a career and sea-going skills could be enhanced and consolidated over time. Varied pay scales were introduced to reflect both experience and expertise. The retention of trained men was especially necessary after the advent of steam propulsion and the rapid intrusion of technological advances in all facets of naval warfare. The Navy also agreed to the introduction of uniform from 1857. The Admiralty had previously and somewhat mysteriously, always resisted the introduction of uniform clothing, but now it was decided that a formal standard of dress would be adopted along the lines of the unofficial 'uniform' sailors already wore.

The customs and traditions of the Royal Navy were transmitted directly to the naval forces established by several of the Australian colonies after the outbreak of the Crimean War in 1856. While there was never any thought of creating a separate or distinct navy for Australia, the colonists did begin to think seriously about the value of supplementary naval defence organised locally. In that year, reports came to Australia that a Russian warship was cruising off Cape Horn; four more were said to be heading for Valparaiso, and fourteen others were at Vladivostok. The Australians feared for the safety of inbound and outbound ships and cargoes, which were the colonies' lifeline with Europe. It was also a time of discovery, while the goldfields in New South Wales and Victoria were producing rapid changes in the economic and social environment. Rich stores of gold were being shipped to England or banked in Melbourne. The colonists feared the gold might attract a naval raider, so panic was never far below the surface. For the next 60 years, colonial naval defences developed in tandem; calls for an increased British presence in Australian waters were coupled with the efforts of individual colonies to form their own navies for the protection of local interests.

The Imperial Government appreciated the urgency of the colonists' fears and took action in 1859 to augment the naval force stationed in Port Jackson by establishing Australia as a distinct naval command separate from the East Indies Station. To this end, Captain William Loring RN in HMS *Iris* was authorised on 25 March 1859 to assume command independently of the Commander-in-Chief in India as Senior Officer of HM Ships deployed to the Australia Station. While Loring's flagship was a sail frigate, the screw corvettes *Pelorus* and *Niger* and the screw sloop *Cordelia* were also under his command. Although this was not a powerful naval force, it was a start and an improvement upon the previous Imperial provision. The ships which first served on the Australia Station were gradually replaced by more modern and powerful vessels, many of which were more suited to regional conditions and imperatives. Yet the Squadron was never viewed as an integral or balanced naval force. Obsolete sail vessels continued to serve with sail–steam types.

With time the Australia Station became a more important command in the view of the Admiralty, which appointed a flag officer, Rear-Admiral George Tryon CB, in command from January 1885. The colonists were still not convinced that the defence of Australia was assured and there was always the concern that some of the ships of the Squadron could be deployed elsewhere in the region in response to emergencies, effectively leaving Australian cities vulnerable to seaborne attack. To counter these fears the *Australasia Naval Defence Act* was passed in 1887, under which Britain agreed to provide a force of modern vessels in addition to those already maintained on the Station. In return, the colonies, including New Zealand, which was included in the Australia Station, agreed to pay 5 per cent of the establishment cost and an annual payment of £91,000 for the new ships. The Auxiliary Squadron, as it became known, would normally be based in Sydney and its ships would be deployed within the limits of the Station unless the colonial government authorised their use elsewhere.

In the same period the individual colonies created their own navies, following the passage of the *Colonial Naval Defence Act* through the British Parliament in 1865. For the first time there was legislation on the statute books providing for a definite colonial naval defence policy, which also granted the colonies the right to form their own navies, previously denied them. Victoria's navy, legally restricted to coastal waters, was by far the strongest, followed by those of Queensland and South Australia; New South

Wales relied in the main on Royal Navy ships based in Sydney; Tasmania possessed one torpedo boat while Western Australia had no sea-going navy.

The most important aspect of the Act was the right of the colonies to provide, maintain and use their own vessels of war under such conditions and for such purposes 'as Her Majesty-in-Council from time to time approves, and to place those vessels at Her Majesty's disposal when any such vessel would become to all intents a vessel of Her Majesty's regular navy'. The Act also allowed the colonies to 'raise and maintain seamen to serve in such vessels', together with volunteers and emergency volunteers 'so raised to form part of the Royal Naval Reserve'.[1] All the colonies strove to establish their navies on foundations which closely resembled the ethos and service conditions of the Royal Navy. Indeed, a great many of those who served in the colonial naval forces had formerly been members of the RN. While it was convenient to recruit trained naval personnel from the RN, it also created a number of problems, as the colony of Queensland was to find.

The colonial vessels *Gayundah* and her sister *Paluma* were two of the ugliest ships to ever serve in Australian waters. They were gunboats built mainly for coastal defence and, though small, were armed with an eight-inch gun forward and a six-inch gun aft. The weight of the forward gun meant its elevation had to be kept to a minimum to ensure the ship did not turn turtle. To give the weapon a reasonable field of fire the bow had to be cut down as low as was possible, leaving barely enough freeboard for safe sea-keeping. The funnel, which was thin and raked, was placed towards the stern. The end result was a ship which looked like a pylon on a floating steam iron. The ships formally entered service with the Queensland Colonial Government on 22 July 1886 after the passage of the *Queensland Defence Act* in 1884, legislation which enabled the colony to raise its own armed forces. The Admiralty drew up a warrant that put the services of the 'ship, *Gayundah*, belonging to the colony of Queensland' at the disposal of Her Majesty, under the direct command of the Rear-Admiral Commanding the Australian Squadron.

Unlike Victoria, the Queensland government wanted their ships to have a wider span of duty, including cooperation with Royal Navy ships on the Australia Station. This was not a straightforward matter, one of the substantive issues to be resolved being whether the two gunboats ought to wear the blue ensign and pennant of a colonial navy or fly the white ensign customarily displayed by Royal Navy ships. While this matter was considered, the ships' histories were marked by long periods of little activity interrupted by bizarre occurrences. *Paluma* was washed ashore by exceptional floods in 1893 and came to rest in the begonia beds of the Brisbane Botanic Gardens, while *Gayundah* featured in one of the oddest mutinies in any navy's history.

The only uprising in the history of the colonial naval forces centred on the gunboat's commanding officer, Captain Henry Townley Wright. He was born in England in 1846 and entered the Royal Navy on 13 September 1859. Promoted lieutenant on 3 April 1868, Wright was promoted commander on 9 March 1876 before retiring from the RN in the rank of captain on 17 September 1886. Appointed Senior Naval Officer and Superintendent of the Marine Defence Force of Queensland, and Commanding Officer of HMQS *Gayundah* from 1885 to 1888, Captain Wright was mercilessly pilloried by Queensland parliamentarians after he had left Australia. They circled like sharks. He was 'too big a man—we mean in inflated dignity—for these coasts. He is lost in this degenerate society'.[2] He was a 'modern *Bombastes Furioso*', a 'fiery little Captain', a 'dapper horse marine and Admiral of the Queensland Flotilla'.[3] The Captain's fall in the public esteem had not come about suddenly, however.

Early in his appointment, Wright apparently discovered that the salary of a Queensland gunboat captain did not meet his needs. In September 1887, attention was drawn to 'the continued bankruptcy of Captain Wright'. After an investigation, the Colonial Secretary of Queensland, Mr Boyd Morehead, found that Wright had appropriated Government stores and liquor allowances for his own use and refused to repay them when asked to do so. His conduct had been 'highly reprehensible and his management of his department most extravagant'.[4] Particularly irksome for the Colonial Secretary was the Captain's purchase of 'wines, etc'. at the rate of £15 each month. The Government made a decision to dismiss him as Captain (and Senior Naval Officer) but the decision was rescinded by a minute of the Executive Council on 16 November 1887. Wright's appointment was allowed to run its course to the end of 1888, although the authority to purchase ship's stores was taken away from him.

In mid-September of 1888, however, Wright asked for leave of absence until the end of the year (when the term of his appointment ran its course), and paid passage to England in the British–India mail steamer for both himself and his wife. The Executive Council agreed to his request. Captain Wright then drew a voucher to pay himself the full amount of his salary due to the end of the year. When the voucher came before the Colonial Secretary, Captain Wright was informed that, although on leave, his salary would be paid monthly in accordance with the terms of his appointment. There was an additional message that immeasurably hurt the Captain's pride. The Under Colonial Secretary told him that he was to hand over command of the gunboat and 'all stores therein' to his second in command, Lieutenant F. P. Taylor RN.

After taking a week to compose a reply, Captain Wright responded that his intention in seeking his pay in advance was simply to sever the relationship with the Colonial Government. However, he was offended that the government had chosen to communicate directly with Lieutenant Taylor while 'my pennant [was] still flying, and while I still hold the position of Senior Naval Officer and Captain in the Royal Navy under command of the Rear-Admiral Commanding-in-Chief'. According to Wright, this was 'an intentional slight on my official position which reflects on the service to which I have the honour to belong'.[5] He advised that he would report the Government's temerity to the Lords Commissioners of the Admiralty.

Captain Wright then ordered coal and stores for the ship without Government authorisation. The 35 tons of coal he acquired, in addition to twelve tons in the bunkers, would take *Gayundah* on a voyage of twelve days' duration. The stores embarked by the Chief Steward on Wright's instruction would last three months. Lieutenant Taylor, having informed the Under Colonial Secretary of the sequence of events, was then supplied with immediate authorisation to take command of *Gayundah*.

On the afternoon of 24 October 1888, Lieutenant Taylor confronted the Captain on the gunboat's quarterdeck and informed him that he was assuming command as prescribed in the Government's instructions. Taylor subsequently read his commission to the officers and men of *Gayundah* who stood in a circle around both men. The Captain ignored the Lieutenant. The reaction of the ship's company, bemused as they must have been, is not recorded. The next senior officer, Sub-Lieutenant Russell, continued loading the stores. This was an action that would later cost Russell his commission.

In Captain Wright's own words: 'On the following morning, after having most carefully considered the matter, I had no option but to place Lieutenant Taylor under arrest and owing to the peculiar circumstances of the case, I gave him a memorandum on the subject'.[6] The memorandum instructed the Lieutenant to 'obey all lawful commands from me as your superior officer, and comply in every respect with the regulations laid down for your guidance'. This was certainly the only 'mutiny' in history to be accompanied by formal memoranda between the participants. Wright's charge of mutiny against Taylor arose:

> by reason of his having intimated to me in writing that he proposed to take command of the ship out of my hands, at which time I held both Imperial and Colonial authority for holding my command, and by so acting Lieutenant Taylor committed a most serious breach of naval discipline.[7]

In other words, Wright was asserting that Taylor's mutiny was attempted in writing. This was a most unusual occurrence.

The Lieutenant, although under technical arrest, was not confined. The doughty Captain repaired to his cabin where he engaged himself in composing reports to everyone with even a marginal interest. He sent an appeal to Rear Admiral Henry Fairfax, the Commander-in-Chief of the Australia Station, asking him to restore his blighted honour. He also conveyed a protest to the Colonial Secretary. In both despatches Wright enclosed a copy of his memorandum to Lieutenant Taylor. Wright maintained the offensive:

> While I was for a short time in my office on shore, preparing a further protest, the Head Clerk of the Colonial Secretary's office came on board and endeavoured to seduce Lieutenant Taylor and Sub-Lieutenant Russell from their duty and allegiance to Her Majesty by rebelling against my authority, but I need hardly tell you that the attitude assumed by those officers frustrated such a questionable proceeding on the part of the government.[8]

The Captain then sat down to prepare an application for a court martial of the Head Clerk who had come on board his ship and, 'who has rendered himself liable under the thirteenth *Article of War*' for subverting the authority of the commander of one of Her Majesty's ships-of-war.[9] Then, apparently prepared to take on the whole colony of Queensland, he ordered the six-inch aft gun to be prepared for action. The forward eight-inch gun could not be brought to bear on the official buildings of the colonial parliament because the little gunboat was too low in the water and the quayside obstructed its line of fire.

The Colonial Secretary sent a message to the ship asking Lieutenant Taylor to attend the Government offices. Wright countered by stating that Taylor would be placed under close arrest if he attempted to leave *Gayundah*. Moreover, Wright threatened to take the gunboat to sea if further attempts were made to challenge his authority. His time was running out, however, the Queensland Government decided to end the matter as Wright later explained.

> The following day, whilst at luncheon on board, I received a communication from the Government to the effect that my action with regard to Lieutenant Taylor was considered as an open defiance of the Government and therefore His Excellency the Administrator had been pleased to dismiss me from the offices of Senior Naval Officer, Commander of the Queensland Gunboat *Gayundah* and Naval Superintendent in connection with the Marine Defence Force, with a copy of the *Government Gazette* notifying the date.[10]

A journalist with the *Brisbane Courier* also described events. He managed to capture the sense of farce enveloping the gunboat:

> 'Ho, then my little bark, we'll gaily sail; Pursue the triumph and partake the gale'. So hummed the Captain, but some Nancy Lee, grieved at the prospective loss of her Jack, 'blew the gaff', and ere he could slip his cables and bid a fond but mute adieu to the bothersome Colonial Secretary, the latter gentleman took the wind out of his sails. The Commissioner of Police, Inspector Lewis, and a score of fully armed constables were despatched to take possession of the *Gayundah*, and remove Captain Wright from the vessel, by force if necessary . . . The Under Colonial Secretary . . . also went on board and joined Mr Seymour in counselling Captain Wright to accept the situation . . . surrender his ship and quietly go ashore. At first the Captain metaphorically wrapped the white ensign round his epauletted shoulders, 'fire in each eye and pennants in each hand, he raved, recited, maddened round the quarterdeck'.[11]

The Captain, who seems to have faced his boarders undaunted, asked to examine the legal documents the party carried. The Commissioner produced an authorisation signed by the Colonial Secretary. However, 'he could produce no warrant in support of his proposed action'.[12] Captain Wright asked the men to leave his ship. The officials refused. Wright then asked the Commissioner of Police whether the presence of an armed party on board his ship meant that they were prepared to use force. The Commissioner replied that this was his intention. Wright reacted in his now usual fashion. He scurried away to his cabin and dashed off a written protest. He later told the Commander-in-Chief:

> I wrote a letter to the government (a copy of which I enclose) protesting against its action in removing me from one of HM ships by force, which I read, together with the warrant before referred to, on the Quarter Deck to the Commissioner of Police and the Under Colonial Secretary.[13]

The warrant he referred to was, in Wright's words, 'my warrant from the Lords Commissioners of the Admiralty informing me that the Services of the *Gayundah* together with the officers and men serving thereon had been accepted by Her Majesty . . . and pennants of HM Fleet to be worn thereon'. He claimed he pointed all this out to the 'influential gentlemen [in a] calm and dispassionate manner'. But this was to no avail. The 'influential gentlemen' wanted him off the ship.

Outmanoeuvred but with dignity intact and certainly unbloodied, the Captain summoned Lieutenant Taylor and released him from arrest. He then gave him formal orders to 'act as he thought fit' as soon as he (Wright) was removed from the ship. At about 5.30pm, Wright 'ordered [his] pennant to be hauled down' and left the ship, 'in company with the Police Magistrate'.[14] Sub-Lieutenant Russell was then informed that he also was dismissed for disobeying the orders of the Colonial Secretary. The Chief Steward, who had carried out the provisioning of the ship, met with the same fate.

Captain Wright, despite his voluminous writings, does not record where he was taken. It was evidently to some place equipped with pen and paper which afforded him the comfort of writing reports. His first letter was to Admiral Fairfax, informing him that he had only agreed to leave his ship 'until such time as I had communicated with you on the subject and received your directions'. Fairfax can hardly have been pleased but was probably not surprised to note that the Captain was 'preparing copies of all letters in connection with this case and forwarding an application for a Court Martial on Lieutenant Taylor under the terms of the fourteenth *Article of War*'.[15] He hoped the Admiral would 'approve' his actions and his 'best endeavours to uphold the dignity of the Flag'. Wright's next move was to seek some legal advice. He argued that his removal was 'unjust, unconstitutional and illegal'.[16]

The *Gayundah* incident was raised in the Queensland Parliament the following day. The *Brisbane Courier* remarked that 'seldom has there been such unanimity amongst all sections of the House as in the hearty approval of the course adopted by Mr Morehead'.[17] The Colonial Secretary based the legality of the Government's actions in removing Captain Wright on the *Colonial Naval Defence Act* of 1865. Captain Wright was not without his defenders however, Sir Samuel Griffith, a former head of government in Queensland, while agreeing that the Queensland Government had the power to seek the Captain's removal, argued that this should have been done through the office of the Commander-in-Chief rather than by authorising the Commissioner of Police to board the ship and physically remove him.[18]

Wright and his wife returned to England. Not surprisingly, he did not receive another command. The debate continued in Australia, where the last word was left to Admiral Fairfax. In a memorandum to the Secretary of the Admiralty, he stated that he could find no legal grounds for Captain Wright resisting his dismissal. Fairfax concluded that as Commander-in-Chief he exercised authority over the commanding officer of the *Gayundah*, but Wright's appointment as Senior Naval Officer and captain of *Gayundah* was at the pleasure of the Governor of Queensland. Consequently, it was Fairfax's opinion that Captain Wright would have to make his appeal through civil courts.[19] There is no record of such action ever being initiated.

Lieutenant Taylor was not court-martialled for his 'mutiny' in *Gayundah*. The only lasting effect of the incident was an increase in colonial parochialism. The *Brisbane Courier* expressed the attitude of most Queenslanders when it proclaimed in the midst of the controversy that 'we must not surrender a shred or tittle of control over our property and our servants—White Ensign or no White Ensign!'[20] On this somewhat defiant note, the only 'mutiny' in the colonial naval forces came to a close.

Although the only contribution made by the colonial navies to Imperial defence was the provision of the South Australian gunboat *Protector* and some naval brigades from New South Wales and Victoria during the Boxer Rebellion in China during 1901–02, their inactivity did not lead to indiscipline and mutiny. For the greatest part, the colonial navies were manned by part-time personnel who could terminate their service if they objected to any distasteful order or severe conditions of service. Most were pleased to be able to make a small contribution in return for the camaraderie they enjoyed. By the turn of the century, however, the colonial navies were run down and practically useless. The ships were old and many were operationally obsolete. With the proclamation of Federation in 1901, the Commonwealth Government 'inherited' the former colonial navies and on 1 March 1901, the ships and all personnel came under Commonwealth control. In fact, they continued to be administered under the provisions of existing State Acts and regulations until the proclamation of the *Commonwealth Defence Act* on 1 March 1904.

Australia was about to create its own navy. It would be a full-time professional force modelled on the command of the Royal Navy and the administration of the Admiralty. There was, however, one significant difference. The English class system, which had been harnessed so effectively by the Admiralty to promote and maintain order and discipline in the Royal Navy, did not exist in Australia. Rather, the strong commitment to egalitarianism among Australians had the potential to unsettle naval command and destabilise discipline. The clash of two distinct cultures within the one organisation would inevitably shape the evolution of an Australian navy, as the following chapters demonstrate.

5

A democratic navy

After the Australian colonies formed a Federal Commonwealth in 1901, the British Admiralty agreed to station and maintain an Imperial squadron of prescribed strength in Australian waters on the basis of a subsidy provided by the Commonwealth. New Zealand would continue to make its own separate contribution. But there were those in Australia who had long foreseen the need for an independent national navy. Foremost among them was William Rooke Creswell, an RN officer who came to Australia in 1879 after suffering a disability during his naval service and finding he was unable to live in England on half-pay. Not surprisingly, he soon became involved in Australian naval affairs at both an operational and political level.[1]

By 1901, Creswell had been involved in Australia's naval defence for two decades with a vision for a local navy which he was to pursue to realisation. As the first responsibility of government was the safety and protection of its citizens, Creswell argued that, as a sovereign nation, Australia should have its own navy. But there was more to his argument than a desire for some expensive expressions of statecraft. Creswell believed strongly that Australia needed an independent naval defence to secure its integrity and to protect its interests when these did not coincide with Britain's strategic or diplomatic priorities. For an island nation which keenly sensed its remoteness, an adequate navy was paramount. In 1902 he wrote: 'For a maritime state furnished without a navy, the sea, so far from being a safe frontier is rather a highway for her enemies; but with a navy, it surpasses all other frontiers in strength'.[2] Appointed the Director of Commonwealth Naval Forces in 1904, his task was to mould the various propositions that were raised by parliament and the people into a policy acceptable to both the Commonwealth and the Admiralty.

He had to strike a balance between Australia's responsibilities as a dominion of the British Empire and its operational and tactical needs as a nation at the foot of the Dutch East Indies Archipelago, far removed from Europe. This meant taking into account Australia's maritime geography and the internal and domestic political struggles of the day.

Achieving that balance would be the test of Creswell's skill and determination. There was no shortage of advice. In 1902 the First Lord of the Admiralty, Lord Selborne, stated that:

> it is desirable that the populations of the Dominions should become convinced of the truth of the proposition that there is no possibility of the localisation of naval forces, and that the problem of the British Empire is in no sense one of local defence. The sea is all one, and the British Navy, therefore must be all one.[3]

A contrary view was found in the writings of the American strategist Alfred Thayer Mahan, which were commanding great interest in Britain at that time. His remarks about Australia attracted immediate attention. Mahan wrote in 1902:

> What Australia needs is not a petty fraction of the Imperial Navy, a squadron assigned to her in perpetual presence. A continent in itself with a thriving population and willing apparently to contribute to the general naval welfare, let Australia frame its schemes and base its estimates on sound lines . . . recognising that local safety is . . . best found in local precaution.[4]

But against the might and persuasive power and prestige of the Admiralty, could local precaution prevail?

At the Colonial Conference held in London in 1907, Alfred Deakin, the Australian Prime Minister, and Sir William Lyne, Minister for Trade and Customs, put the case for the establishment of an independent Australian navy. The Admiralty's view was that Australia should have a naval force consisting of small coastal destroyers and a small submarine flotilla. Lord Tweedmouth, the first Lord of the Admiralty, in response to the Australian proposals, on 23 April 1907 stated that the Dominion would need to build locally 'the smaller craft which are necessarily incident to the work of the great fleet of modern battleships'. The First Sea Lord, Admiral Sir John 'Jacky' Fisher, also resisted the establishment of a dominion navy that did not meet Imperial needs. The Conference closed with the decision that the Admiralty would wait for formal submissions from the Dominion governments of Australia, Canada and New Zealand as to the form of assistance with naval defence that was desired.

A continuing close relationship between Australia and the Royal Navy made sense. After all, Britannia still ruled the waves and Australia could have no better example than the most powerful and professional navy in the world. There was certainly no doubt in the mind of Creswell, as Director of Commonwealth Naval Forces, that Australia needed as much help as it could get from Britain in building its own navy. In 1908, Creswell was concerned about the scheme of naval defence proposed by Prime Minister Deakin at the Colonial Conference. It consisted of six destroyers, nine submarines and two depot ships. It seemed to Creswell to be far too independent of Britain and to place too heavy a burden on Australia's ability and capacity, particularly in shipbuilding, to provide for its own needs. Creswell sought close collaboration with Britain and reserved his public judgment of emerging American naval power in the Pacific:

> With many it is a heresy to doubt the paramount supremacy of the Mother Country's great Navy over all and every conceivable enemy or combination with which it may be faced, or its ability to shelter us from aggression either now or in years to come. Yet but a few weeks since that distinguished Imperialist, the late Governor General of the Commonwealth [Lord Northcote] bade us, 'as men of common sense, to remember that there were Powers of greater population who were treading fast on the heels of Great Britain, and that there were other Powers nearer our shores'. Again, we have been recently reminded by English writers on defence that the time is fast approaching when the existence of Australia 'will depend on the goodwill of America and the politeness of Japan'.[5]

Creswell was more candid in his private correspondence. He wrote in a letter to Richard Jebb in 1908 that: 'The grand result is the spectacle of Australia appealing for *American aid in the Pacific*'[6] [emphasis added]. To hope the US Navy would assist in the Pacific should events inimical to the British Dominions develop was one thing, to think it would lead to a close and enduring naval relationship between the two countries was quite another. Australia wanted American help only for as long as circumstances were desperate or until the Royal Navy eventually arrived, as Australians believed it always would. The basis for this extreme Anglophilia, in naval circles at least, was the continuing importance of Britishness, a persistent attitude that Australian interests were little different from those of the Empire, and a dogmatic faith in the power of the Royal Navy against all challengers.

On 20 August 1908, the Admiralty advised that it had given careful consideration to Deakin's proposal for the establishment of a local Naval force as a substitute for the existing Naval Agreement of 1903. After explaining that the Admiralty was unsure of exactly what Deakin was proposing and why, the reply pointed out that the cost of the Australian naval proposal of six destroyers, nine submarines and two depot ships was £1,277,500. This was more than Australia could then afford.

Deakin's administration lost office at the polls in November 1908 and was replaced by a Labor government led by Andrew Fisher, the new government promising immediate action on naval defence. The cost and the conditions for sharing the overall responsibility for Australian naval defence became the subject of great debate over the next twelve months. Deakin's proposals had not met with much domestic support and the only action taken had been to earmark £500,000 of surplus revenue for naval defence. The new Defence Minister, Senator George Pearce, asked Creswell to produce some plans for a destroyer program. In clear defiance of the Colonial Conference of 1907, the design selected was an oil-burning, turbine-driven torpedo-boat destroyer of 700 tons. The armament was one four-inch gun and three twelve-pounders. The main capability was three eighteen-inch torpedo tubes. This destroyer was twice the size suggested by the Admiralty and featured a high forecastle to permit sustained speeds in heavy seas.

Much of the debate, however, was overtaken by the Imperial Conference on the Naval and Military Defence of the Empire held in London in July 1909. In calling this conference, the British government admitted that it had to reconsider the propositions of the dominions in a broader context. Thus, this Conference concentrated on finding the best means for dominion governments to participate in the burden of Imperial defence. The Admiralty's revised viewpoint was crucial to the creation of an Australian Navy and its eventual shape and form. The Conference adopted a general proposition that: 'Each part of the Empire is willing to make its preparations on such lines as will enable it, should it so desire, to take its share in the general defence of the Empire'. To that end, the Conference stated strongly that those dominions which wanted to create a navy should aim at forming a distinct Fleet Unit. As a minimum, the unit should consist of one armoured cruiser (of the *Indomitable* Class—a 'dreadnought' armoured cruiser), three unarmoured cruisers, six destroyers and three submarines with the necessary depot and store ships. The Admiralty claimed that: 'Such a fleet unit would be capable of action not only in defence of coasts, but also of the trade routes, and would be sufficiently powerful to deal with small hostile squadrons should such ever attempt to act in its waters'.[7]

A meeting was then convened between the representatives of the Admiralty and the Australian government on 19 August 1909, with the Australians provisionally adopting the Admiralty's suggestion of a Fleet Unit. The total initial cost of such a unit was £3,695,000 with the submarines, the C Class, costing some £55,000 each. The Commonwealth government would also pay approximately £750,000 to Britain for maintenance, pay and allowances for loan personnel, training and other associated costs.

The scheme was put to the Federal Parliament by the Minister for Defence, Joseph Cook, on 29 November 1909. Speaking in support of the proposal he said:

> We must remember, first of all, that Australia is part of the Empire, and that within our means we must recognise both our Imperial and local responsibilities. The Empire floats upon its fleet. A strong fleet means a strong Empire, and therefore it is our duty to add to the fleet strength of the Empire. Our first object is the protection of our floating trade and the defence of our shores from invasion or hostile attack . . . Should the motion which I am moving be carried, we shall turn over a new leaf in the book of our evolution. Our tutelary stages are past, our time of maturity is here.[8]

The motion was accepted and a *Naval Loan Act* was passed shortly afterwards to provide funds for the construction of the Australian Fleet Unit. The Admiralty would supply instructors for Australian recruits, and senior officers would be loaned to the new navy. Australia would pay Britain £750,000 to cover the costs of the RN personnel. Moreover, training would also be the same as that of the parent service so that both ships and men would be interchangeable.

On 9 December 1909 the Governor General, Lord Denham, despatched a cable to the Secretary of State for the Colonies at the request of Prime Minister Deakin. The Lords Commissioners of the Admiralty were asked 'to arrange for construction without delay' of the armoured cruiser and the three unarmoured cruisers. 'The destroyers and the submarines,' said the cable, 'would be the subject of special dispatch'. But the armoured cruiser as a class were to be replaced by a new class of battle cruiser; the 'Dreadnought' battle cruiser. Battle cruisers were heavily armed but fast and comparatively lightly protected ships, designed to support cruisers in their scouting operations, and also to destroy enemy cruisers. Their light armour made them unsuitable for action with battleships. They were designed to act as scouts for battleships and to attack light enemy forces. Light cruisers were also reasonably well armoured. Two light cruisers, *Sydney* and *Melbourne*, would be built in Britain. The third, *Brisbane*, would be built in Australia.

When Andrew Fisher became Prime Minister again in April 1910 he repealed the *Naval Loan Act*. His government resolving that the cost of the Fleet Unit would be paid from revenue. He also decided against accepting the Imperial government's offer of assistance with paying for the ships. Australia, he proudly stated, would meet the whole cost.

In 1911, the Imperial Squadron deployed in Australia consisted of the 14 000-ton 1st-class cruiser HMS *Powerful*, three 2nd-class cruisers, five 3rd-class cruisers and three survey vessels. To replace this force there was to be an Australian Squadron which consisted of ships owned and operated by the Commonwealth of Australia, after King George V granted the title 'Royal Australian Navy' to the Permanent Naval Forces and the title 'Royal Australian Naval Reserve' to the Citizen Naval Forces on 10 July 1911. The administration of the Australia Station by the Admiralty ceased in favour of the Australian Commonwealth Naval Board, created by the Commonwealth *Naval Defence Act* passed in 1910. At Melbourne in 1913 Admiral Sir George King-Hall struck his flag in HMS *Cambrian*, bringing to a formal end the Royal Navy's responsibility for the naval defence of Australia. It also marked the conclusion of a long and drawn-out effort to create an Australian Navy which could meet the burden of responsibility which had now passed to the Commonwealth Government. The ties that bound the new RAN to the parent service remained strong and, sometimes, inflexible, however.

The training of Australian junior officers in the British tradition was the means by which the RAN was to be placed and maintained on a sound professional footing. The Committee of Imperial Defence stated that 'the navies of each component part of the Empire must be trained to the same standards—the systems of tactics, gunnery, fire control, torpedo work, and signalling must be identical'.[9] It would also ensure that Australian ships could be interchanged with those of the Royal Navy in operations around the globe. The Navy and the nation held high hopes for what the young Australian officers would achieve. The *Sydney Morning Herald* remarked in 1914 that 'the son of an Australian boundary rider today may be the Commander-in-Chief of the British Fleet in the Pacific tomorrow—for all one knows he might be a second Nelson who will some day preserve the British Empire'.[10]

The RAN for many years would have been more aptly titled the RNA—the Royal Navy in Australia. The RAN would effectively develop not as an independent Navy but as the local manifestation of the Royal Navy. The RAN was initially led by Royal Navy officers on secondment to Australia and finely modeled on the way things were done in England with minimal departure for local conditions. So imposing, so well developed and so effective was the Royal Navy and its system of administration and organisation for operations that it permeated almost every facet of Australian naval affairs. The traditions of the Royal Navy were forged across several centuries and were thoroughly ingrained in the RAN from the day that every boy joined the navy as a young officer cadet.

The RAN College was an institution unparalleled in Australia and certainly more British than the most elite non-Government schools. Young boys at age thirteen were taken from varied family backgrounds and inducted into a very rigid English public school outlook with all its implied social prestige. The College staff was British; the curriculum was totally imported from Dartmouth. In recalling the earlier years of the RAN College, one Australian admiral remarked: 'Really it was an institution designed to turn small Australian boys into Englishmen'. For Australian naval officers and sailors the three great victories of Nelson and his commanders formed the basis of tradition. This was emphasised by the Governor General, Sir Ronald Munro Ferguson, in addressing the first graduating class of cadet-midshipmen from the RAN College in 1916:

> You, who are of the same blood, have been trained here in the traditions of a race which for three hundred years and more has never lost its hold on the sea . . . Your bearing, good manners and conduct testify to the high tone maintained in the College, and we may confidently expect that you are qualified to exhibit that character and personality which, from Nelson downwards, has ever distinguished the British sea officer. All at home are anxious to see what Australia has made of her cadets . . . But after the first few months you will soon cease to discriminate between Australian and English born, and you will remember

only that you belong to the greatest of all British Services—that of the sea.[11]

It was deliberate policy to limit the differences between Australian and British naval officers. Australian officers were to spend long periods of service in Royal Navy ships or under Royal Navy commanders or captains. The two services and their officer groups were to be virtually interchangeable. The only differences were that Australian officers were innately more egalitarian in outlook, seldom had private incomes and could not rely on the famous names of their forebears for assured or rapid promotion.

The 1909 Naval Agreement also ensured that disciplinary matters in the new Australian Navy should be dealt with in the same manner as they would be in the Royal Navy. When the RAN was created, personnel serving in the new navy were made subject to the Imperial *Naval Discipline Act* (NDA) (see pages 6, 69). Under the NDA, a ship or unit commander had the power under law to punish sailors without formal court martial. A sailor charged by an officer or senior sailor would be brought before the Executive Officer, who could issue minor punishments such as loss of leave, loss of pay or extra duties for minor offences including exceeding leave and breaches of uniform requirements. More serious offences would be referred to the Commanding Officer, who had the power to demote and imprison members of his ship's company. Reduction in rank had consequences for a sailor's pay and future career prospects while those imprisoned did not accumulate any pay.

The means by which this British legislation was made to apply to the Australian service was straightforward. As Brian Beddie has explained, the British Act was

> incorporated in Australian legislation 'by reference'; that is, by naming, but not reproducing either the text or the content of, the British Act. If (and for long this was the practice) the name of the British Act was not followed by a date which served to specify its provisions at a precise time, future amendments to the Act made by Parliament at Westminster would automatically apply to the Australian services.[12]

Section 36 of the (Australian) *Naval Defence Act 1910* made the provisions of the Imperial NDA apply locally in Australia. The Royal Navy supported the wholesale incorporation of the legislation as it would create a common disciplinary code for the RN and the RAN which would be vital in time of war and make the interchange of RN ships and RN personnel with those of the

RAN much more straightforward.[13] Admiral Creswell believed that the case for a uniform disciplinary code was 'unassailable'.[14] This was, surprisingly to some, not a view held throughout the Australian Navy.

In addition to the two light cruisers being built in England for the RAN, two destroyers, *Parramatta* and *Yarra*, were being built there. Detachments of Australian sailors were sent to England to crew the vessels. A legal question emerged when two men named de Wardt and Richardson refused to take up their duties. The two, who had been stokers in the Victorian colonial navy, complained about being taken into the new RAN and formally objected to coming under the *Naval Discipline Act*.[15] By their refusal to obey a directive, it may be that these two men became the first RAN mutineers—even before a single new ship was commissioned. The Naval Board dismissed the men as being unfit for duty and the matter was referred to the Crown Solicitor for appropriate action. His opinion was that de Wardt and Richardson were within their rights and that men who had joined under former provisions could not be forced to go to England to man the new RAN vessels.[16]

There were wider concerns within Australia about the rights of RAN sailors obliged to serve under British officers and Admiralty service conditions. A Labor senator, Arthur Rae, believed that the class-based discipline of the Royal Navy was inappropriate for Australians and feared that Royal Navy officers would not fairly handle RAN sailors.[17] The possibility of 'mutiny' was suggested in the Australian Parliament by a Queensland Anti-Socialist Party senator, Thomas Chataway. He expressed his anxiety that there was a standing state of 'virtual mutiny' among men who had served in the former colonial navies and who, like de Wardt and Richardson, did not want to come under the Royal Navy's disciplinary code.[18] A New South Wales Labor senator, Allan McDougall, commented:

> It is hard to bring Australians down to what men have to stand in the navy of the Old Land and other navies. It is hard to break the spirit of the Australians. But let him know he is in exactly the same position as the best on the vessel though holding a humbler position in life, let him know that one man is as good as another, and you will find that the Australian will be ever ready to take his place in the front fighting line, not only on the land, but at sea.[19]

The linking of the disciplinary code with the British social class system was a persistent lament among Labor politicians. They believed it would lead to recruiting difficulties, excessive discipline and poor morale. Hyslop is right when he concludes:

> As with the personnel system generally, the principles and practices of the disciplinary code were thus British in origin and they made no concession to Australian patterns of behaviour which were rooted in different social conditions. Certain it is however that an Australian navy, created at least in part as an expression of Australian nationhood, was within itself United Kingdom-British rather than Australian-British. It was essential to the Australian navy that this was so, but the adjustments that had to be made were not easy, and the disciplinary troubles in the Navy immediately after the War of 1914–18 were reactions not only to a post-war let-down but also to a disciplinary pattern that many could not endure. Prospective recruits by then had fair warning of what to expect in the navy and only those prepared to accept the situation offered to join. The departure from the scene of recalcitrant original and wartime sailors meant a cleansing of the barrel and thereafter there was an acceptance of the disciplinary code as a reasonable concomitant of naval life.[20]

Public debate spread from naval discipline to conditions of service. Another Labor politician, James Mathews from Victoria, told the Australian parliament that he had received no less than 107 complaints from RAN sailors about conditions of service.[21] Mathews was subsequently supported in parliament by Labor colleagues, James Fenton, who discussed the comparative pay of officers and men and the limited avenues available for the expression of grievances,[22] and Alfred Ozanne, who laid before parliamentarians details of the basic diet of Australian sailors in the destroyers *Parramatta* and *Yarra*. Breakfast was bread and butter and porridge; lunch was roast meat and potatoes only and supper was bread and butter and tea. There was pudding twice a week.[23]

The question of rations and their potential to prompt a mutiny came before the Parliament again in 1914, this time in relation to the new cruiser HMAS *Sydney*. Robert Howe, Labor member for Dalley, stated that the men in *Sydney* complained that they were given bad meat, rotten tinned sardines and no butter during the voyage out from Great Britain.[24] The supply officer in *Sydney* had not spent all the money allocated for the men's food, spending only four pence out of the daily allowance of one shilling and four pence, thereby making savings for the administrators at the expense of the men.[25] Besides the problems with food, there was a quandary with the conditions on board the vessels. The mess decks in the battle cruiser *Australia*, for example, were designed for northern conditions, not the warmer climes of the south. The ship had poor ventilation while the mess decks were crowded, with only fourteen inches of space (350 mm) for each man to hang his hammock when the ship was fully manned. The same space also had to serve as the men's dining and recreation area.

Victorian Labor member James Fenton drew attention to inequities in pay scales. While senior officers had the power to set their own pay rates, he asserted that 'men who do some of the most important work lower down the ladder have to make request after request before being listened to'.[26] Other politicians received complaints about both the quality and quantity of food served in sea-going ships. At issue was the lack of variation in the sailors' diet, with the same menu appearing day after day. There was also irritation that there was too little variation in the vegetables served and that the offer of dessert was too infrequent. The heart of the problem seemed to lie in the Australian system of making an allowance for each man on board each ship. If the Accountant Officer was incompetent or indifferent to the needs of the ship's company, the allowance could be poorly spent or even misappropriated. There was also the difficulty of recruiting cooks prepared to make use of the restricted and sometimes antiquated naval galleys.

Inconsistencies in leave entitlements and disparities in arrangements for social functions on board also caused problems, as did inconsistency and hypocrisy in official responses to misconduct. Officers returning on board their ships drunk would be escorted discreetly to their cabins while sailors were usually charged with drunkenness. The Naval Board was indifferent to the criticisms and complaints, and oblivious to the concerns behind them. As Hyslop observes, there was an inbuilt gulf between the Navy, the Government and the Nation.

> The foremost characteristic of the Naval Board was its essentially British nature. Most of its members were British officers and it took its style from that of the Board of Admiralty. In the period 1905–1939, the twenty-one ministers responsible for naval administration were Australians either by birth or by adoption, and of the seven finance and civil members all except one were Australians. However of the twenty-seven naval members of the Board, all had been initially trained in the RN and only six of the twenty-seven were RAN officers at the time of their appointments to the Naval Board.[27]

Of course, it made sense for the Commonwealth to borrow wholesale from Britain. Naval law was complex and complicated, and the British legislation seemed to have served the Royal Navy well during the previous half century in which the NDA had been in operation. It also allowed an easy and convenient sharing of personnel with both RN and RAN sailors subject to the identical disciplinary code. The incorporation of the NDA into Australian law had prompted little comment or controversy for these plain and practical reasons. Within the Federal Parliament there was nonetheless an element of concern about Australian service personnel being subject to a law their legislators did not enact. Beddie notes an element of disdain for the social origin of the Imperial Acts: 'They were said to be the expression of a highly stratified society which produced individuals who, in the mass, were different from and inferior to Australians in character, initiative and intelligence'.[28]

There was also anxiety about the effect of some portions of the NDA, especially the power of a court martial to impose the death sentence. This was dealt with in Section 98 of the Commonwealth *Defence Act* (1903):

> No member of the Defence Force shall be sentenced to death by any court-martial except for mutiny, desertion to the enemy, or traitorously delivering up to the enemy any garrison, fortress, post, guard, or ship, vessel, or boat, or traitorous correspondence with the enemy; and no sentence of death passed by any court-martial shall be carried into effect until confirmed by the Governor General.

However, section 54 of the *Defence Act* stated that Australians serving 'on board any ship of the King's Navy on the Australian Station' would be subject to the NDA without modification. In other words, they would serve without the benefit of the provision in Section 98 and be treated as though they were RN sailors.

When the Commonwealth *Naval Defence Act* was passed in 1910, the Defence Minister George Pearce commented that the NDA was neither unduly harsh nor 'out of keeping with modern thought'. He went on to explain that the RAN would be subject not only to the NDA but to the 900-page *King's Regulations and Admiralty Instructions* (KR & AI) as well, and that these would apply during peacetime and in war. The *Naval Defence Act* also expanded the range of situations in which the NDA would apply without modification. When the Governor General transferred 'all vessels of the Commonwealth Naval Forces, and all officers and seamen of those vessels' to the King's Naval Forces on 10 August 1914, and three months later placed all Australian ships in commission at the disposal of the Admiralty, it meant that all RAN personnel were subject to the NDA *without modification.* While there did not seem to be any direct criticism or resentment of the NDA and its operation during World War I, the continued operation of the NDA without modification in 1919 was to cause a parliamentary controversy and the most serious rupture in the politico-naval relationship in Australia's history. (This incident is considered in Chapter 7.)

Despite the debate over discipline, nothing detracted from the grandeur accompanying the ceremonial entry into Sydney Harbour of the Australian Fleet Unit on 4 October 1913. It was by far the proudest moment in Australia's short history. Enormous crowds gathered from dawn right around the harbour to gain a good viewpoint. To mark the occasion, all schoolchildren in New South Wales were granted a special holiday and given a small silver medallion commemorating the event. Rudyard Kipling wrote a short verse for the arrival:

> Carry the word to my sisters,
> To the Queens of the North and the South.
> I have proven faith in the heritage.
> By more than word of mouth.

Within a year the young nation of Australia and the Fleet it had striven so hard and so long to acquire would be engaged in naval combat. On 1 August 1914, Germany declared war on Russia, which had mobilised her army in response to the Austrian declaration of war on Serbia. Russian troops crossed the German frontier and German soldiers entered Cirey in France. By 3 August, the mobilisation of the British Fleet was complete. At 11am on 4 August 1914, Britain declared war on Germany.

The mobilisation of the British Fleet was just as efficient as that of the German Army. The Grand Fleet was comprised of three Home Fleets, which consisted of battle squadrons and flotillas. Abroad there was the Mediterranean Fleet, the China and East Indies Squadrons, the Australian Squadron, and a West Atlantic, South Africa and West Africa Squadron, in addition to a flotilla based at Gibraltar. Britain boasted 20 dreadnoughts, 40 pre-dreadnoughts, 9 battle cruisers, 34 armoured cruisers and 74 cruisers. Germany had 13 dreadnoughts, 20 pre-dreadnoughts, 4 battle cruisers, 9 armoured cruisers and 41 cruisers. Germany's coast was immediately blockaded, her commerce progressively swept from the seas, and most of her Navy was reduced to impotence in the North Sea river estuaries. The Royal Navy would cut off supplies to Germany from abroad and make safe the transportation of troops and supplies from one Allied country to another.

Australia would clearly enter the war as part of its strong commitment to Imperial Defence. Australia's Prime Minister, Joseph Cook, had already told his countrymen: 'If there is to be a war, you and I shall be in it'. This position had bipartisan endorsement, the Opposition leader, Andrew Fisher, having pledged that Australia would 'stand beside the mother country to help and defend her to our last man and our last shilling'. The Australian Fleet was embarked on its annual winter cruise and was off Queensland when news of imminent war was received. The Minister for Defence was campaigning for the next election and Rear Admiral Creswell, now titled 'First Naval Member of the Naval Board and Chief of Naval Staff', was taking some leave. The tranquillity of Australian life was shattered by the ominous news of 26 July:

> A great crisis had developed in Europe, owing to the action of Austria in issuing an ultimatum to Serbia and demanding a reply by 6pm yesterday . . . Early in the evening it was definitely announced that the ultimatum had been rejected . . . The best informed circles in Buda-Pest consider that war is inevitable . . . The Austro-Serbian differences are the first symptom of a gigantic Slav-Teutonic struggle.[29]

The prospect of war in both eastern and western Europe caused enormous concern in London. On 30 July the Admiralty sent out a warning to Australia that preparation should be made for an outbreak of war and that Australian naval vessels should begin to move towards their war stations. By an arrangement agreed to at the 1911 London Imperial Conference, the Australian ships would be controlled by the Australian government while in home waters but the entire fleet would be placed at the Admiralty's disposal in war. The fighting ships of the Service comprised the battle cruiser *Australia*, the light cruisers *Melbourne* and *Sydney*; the torpedo-boat destroyers *Parramatta*, *Warrego* and *Torrens*; the cruiser *Encounter*; the small cruiser *Pioneer* (a gift from the Admiralty); and the old ships of the colonial navies, *Protector*, *Paluma* and *Gayundah*. Three thousand eight hundred men were serving in the Permanent Naval Forces in August 1914. Of these, around one-fifth were Royal Navy officers and sailors on loan to Australia. Command of the Fleet was vested in Rear Admiral Sir George Patey RN, who had assumed command in 1913. Patey was promoted Vice-Admiral on 20 August 1914 and remained in command until 1916 when he was appointed Commander-in-Chief of the North American and West Indies Station.

The main threat to the Australian continent when the war broke out was the German East Asiatic Squadron of Admiral Graf von Spee, the last known position of the armoured cruiser *Gneisenau* having been Nagasaki in Japan. Nothing was known of the whereabouts of the other major naval menace, her sister ship *Scharnhorst*. The Australian Fleet immediately sailed north. At Sandy Cape off Fraser Island in Queensland an Australian Naval and Military Expeditionary Force exercised and prepared for an operation to capture German New Guinea. But the opening phases of the war were marred by what would become a constant problem in Australia's naval use of ships—mutiny.

Although this book does not focus on mutinies in the merchant naval service, the merchant steamer *Kanowna* was involved in a naval operation at a time when simmering unrest exploded into mutiny among the crew. The *Kanowna* affair is also significant in being the only mutiny recorded in Arthur Jose's official history of the Australian Navy in the Great War, although there were several other such incidents. Jose's account is noteworthy in that the stated motivation for the mutiny, that *Kanowna*'s crew did not want to leave Australian waters, does not appear to be accurate.[30]

Kanowna, part of the New Guinea Expeditionary Force despatched from Australia at the end of August 1914 to occupy German territory in New Guinea, was loaded with around 1000 soldiers, including 500 infantrymen. There were provisions for a voyage of three weeks and stores to last the troops one month ashore. The ship was chided for a late sailing from Townsville on 8 August, which the captain put down to the difficulties of receiving troops, stowing cargo and delays due to the tide. Further incidents made the ship's departure even later. *Kanowna* was anchored near Thursday Island until 16 August before resuming the passage north with the Force. Provisions began to run low. On 8 September, the captain informed all on board that there was a shortage of fresh water and until further notice the allowance per man per day would be one gallon of water for all purposes. Around the same time, rations had to be drawn from the stores that were meant to support the troops after they had landed. *Kanowna* finally arrived in Port Moresby after a 29-day voyage.

The crew expected relief from their deprivations but there were inadequate stores available for the ship in Port Moresby. *Kanowna* took on salt beef and potatoes from other ships in the port (including HMA Ships *Sydney* and *Encounter*). The ship's records note that only 96 tons of water (valued at £27) were taken on board, including 30 tons from *Encounter*, water that had already been in the cruiser's tanks for weeks.

On 7 September, the ship sailed with a convoy of other storeships and transports for Rabaul, on the same day encountering strong head winds that reduced *Kanowna*'s progress and made it obvious to all on board that the voyage to Rabaul would be a lengthy one. The troopship fell behind the rest of the convoy, drawing tart criticism from the senior naval officer. *Kanowna*'s firemen, men who maintained the boiler fires in the heat and stench of an old stokehold in the tropics, demanded more than the one gallon a day water allowance. Not only did they sweat profusely in the stokehold but of all the crew on board they needed to wash off the black coal grime that coated their skin after their work. Their request for an extra water ration with which to wash was refused, even though the firemen had pointed out that condensed water available in the engine room could be used for washing. Their demands ignored, the men refused to work. *Kanowna*'s master had evidently reached the end of his tether as well. Despite the presence of several hundred armed soldiers on board, the master raised a despairing signal, calling for assistance from the convoy commodore in *Sydney*: 'Crew in state of mutiny'.[31] The commanding officer of the troops on board volunteered to have his men keep order. A second message was sent: 'The firemen have mutinied and are in custody of an armed guard'. Rear Admiral Patey ordered *Kanowna* back to Townsville. It arrived on 10 September and the firemen were placed under arrest and later tried.

The Naval Board was not directly responsible for the mutinous firemen, even though the incident took place while *Kanowna* had been commandeered for naval service. Nonetheless, the Board conducted an inquiry into the circumstances of the mutiny, concentrating on the shortages on board the ship that had led to the incident. The inquiry noted that Colonel Holmes, the commanding officer of the troops, had inspected *Kanowna* at Port Moresby on 6 September and been very critical of the state of its stores. The military equipment was inadequate, especially medical supplies. The inquiry was told that the ship was 'completely out of stores' and required replenishing.[32] Stores had had to be drawn from other ships and warships to provide a minimum ration for the crew and troops in *Kanowna*.

The problem was found to lie in inadequacies in the local administration at Port Moresby. In preparing for the expedition, the port had been put under naval control and a senior naval officer appointed, although 'matters were in a state of chaos there for some time'.[33] There were insufficient stores and replenishment facilities available to cope with the convoy. The Senior Naval Officer in Port Moresby with responsibility for re-victualling ships was Commander Claude Cumberlege. Although he was praised for his work in organising 'patrolling and boat services'[34] and was not directly criticised in the inquiry report, there may have been a perception that his work in Port Moresby had not been adequate and could have contributed indirectly to the mutiny in *Kanowna* and its subsequent return to Australia with troops embarked. It had been a messy affair and proper attribution of blame was a complicated undertaking. Certainly the difficulties of operating in tropical waters could not be ignored. Thankfully, the *Kanowna* mutiny did not detract seriously from the war effort.

With the removal of the German naval threat in the Pacific by the end of 1914, the RAN's ships were scattered across the globe as part of a comprehensive Imperial strategy that met with complete support from the Naval Board and Commonwealth Government. This support was not without its price, however. Some of the naval ships lent to Australia during the war by the British Government were obsolete and ill suited to operations in tropical waters. This led to sailor unhappiness and mess-deck unrest. Further difficulties were created by the inadequacy of arrangements for the payment of RAN personnel serving abroad. The Naval Board would quickly learn the whereabouts of the Australian sailors' breaking point.

6

World War I

When King George V bestowed the title Royal Australian Navy on the Permanent Naval Forces on 10 July 1911, he also granted the title RAN Reserve to the Citizen Naval Forces. Reserve personnel were formed into a single RAN Brigade shortly before the outbreak of World War I. By mid 1914, the RAN Brigade (RANB) consisted of some 1646 officers and men who could be mobilised for war service. Mindful that their training was limited and opportunities for combatant service few, the Naval Board decided against sending the RAN Brigade to sea. Other than a few hundred officers and men lent to the RAN, most of whom were formerly full-time RAN or RN personnel, and the 110 sailors who saw service in requisitioned merchant vessels as telegraphists and gun crew, the vast majority of the RAN Brigade served ashore throughout the Great War.

The RANB manned the Merchant Ship Examination Service as well as signal and lookout stations. As part of its harbour and dockyard patrol duties, the Brigade undertook minesweeping operations and supervised detention of captured enemy vessels. Two units were formed for overseas service. The first was the RAN contribution of 500 Naval Reserve personnel to the Australian Naval & Military Expeditionary Force (ANMEF), formed on 15 August 1914. The task of the ANMEF was to expel any German forces from New Guinea before capturing enemy wireless stations. These were considered vital facilities which would assist in the deployment of Vizeadmiral Graf von Spee's squadron. The naval personnel were organised into six companies under Commander J. A. H. Beresford. They were all volunteers whose period of service would not exceed six months. Overall command of the Force was vested in Colonel William Holmes, previously Officer Commanding 6th Infantry Brigade of the Citizens' Military Forces. The

ANMEF embarked in the P&O ship *Berrima* and sailed from Sydney on 19 August. The vessel was escorted north to the Queensland coast and then to Port Moresby by HMAS *Sydney*. The escort was deemed necessary as the Naval Board was still concerned about the whereabouts of the German ships *Gneisenau* and *Scharnhorst*. After occupying the German possession of Samoa, a sizeable naval force including *Australia*, *Sydney*, the cruiser *Encounter*, a destroyer flotilla (*Warrego*, *Parramatta* and *Yarra*) and the two submarines (*AE1* and *AE2*) was available to support the ANMEF attack on the German headquarters at Rabaul and the wireless stations (there were thought to be two) on the island of New Britain.

On 11 September, the ships secured the area before the ANMEF was landed. The total 'enemy' force consisted of 52 Europeans supported by 240 New Guineans commanded by nine German officers—two of whom were members of the permanent army while another two were reservists. In the ensuing operation, two naval personnel were killed—Lieutenant Commander Clive Elwell RN and Able Seaman John E. Walker. Elwell was shot through the heart and died instantly while leading a charge on a German position; Walker (who served under the name John Courtney) was hit by a sniper's bullet and died later. The radio station, which was actually located at Bitapaka, was captured. The masts had been wrecked in anticipation of the Australian attack but the equipment appeared to be in working order. Admiral Patey directed the German Governor to surrender the entire German dependency to Colonel Holmes who would assume responsibility for local administration. With the occupation of Bougainville in the Solomon Islands on 9 December 1915, the ANMEF's specific objectives had been achieved and the unit was no longer required.

With the return and subsequent disbandment of the ANMEF in January 1915, the Naval Board found itself in the curious position of having enthusiastic naval personnel with some experience of combat standing idle and advised the Australian military authorities of the RAN Brigade's availability for service overseas. Colonel J. Gordon Legge, Chief of the Australian General Staff, had been made aware that there was an increasing need for engineering units on the European Western front as fighting had become bogged down in trench warfare. These units, called Bridging Trains, were deployed to construct pontoon bridges across rivers and canals where bridges had been destroyed or were non-existent, and to carry out *ad hoc* engineering tasks. After preliminary discussions, it was decided to form a Naval Bridging Train from the RAN Brigade which would be offered for service in France. In choosing to have the unit composed entirely of Naval Reservists, the Naval Board remarked that 'a Naval rating would be fully qualified to undertake the technical work connected with such an arm of the service, observing that the calls made upon the Royal Engineers for field companies had absorbed all available personnel in the British Army'.

In a formal communication with the Imperial War Council on 15 February 1915, the Commonwealth Government offered 'a Bridging Train in accordance with Imperial War Establishments, including personnel and their equipment, vehicles and horses. Personnel will be RAN Reserve and trained in bridging'. The unit would consist of seven officers and 285 sailors and would operate under the administrative control and operational command of the Royal Naval Division which had been raised in accordance with a pre-war plan in August 1914. The Australians were desperately needed after severe British losses in the opening phases of the war in France.

The Admiralty anticipated mobilising over 30 000 Royal Navy Reserve personnel although there would be no opportunity for these officers and sailors to serve at sea. These men would be formed into three brigades (two made up of Naval Reserves and one from the Royal Marines) and be engaged in either home defence or in the seizure and operation of an enemy naval base on the continent. With the commencement of hostilities, the Reservists were mobilised and formed into the RN Division. Notwithstanding pre-war plans, the Division was undergoing only preliminary training when hastily despatched to Belgium, where it acted as an infantry division deployed for the defence of Antwerp and Ostend from German invasion. Not surprisingly, the Division was ill-prepared for this sort of action and suffered heavy casualties. Indeed, a whole brigade was lost to the Allied effort when the men were forced to retreat into neutral Holland where they were interned. Following the fall of Belgium to the advancing German Army, the RN Division returned to Britain in October 1914. An Australian Bridging Train would add to the depth of resources and capabilities available to the RN Division.

The Commonwealth Government's offer was accepted on 18 February. Ten days later, the 1st RAN Bridging Train was officially created, the designation '1st' reflecting the desire of the Naval Board to establish another Bridging Train if the first proved effective. Despite their naval background, the men's training included several long route marches and basic drill that was apparently both irksome and frustrating for old navy men, some of whom had held the rank of Chief Mate or Chief Petty Officer. Those who enlisted in the unit were rated AB Driver, and considered the equivalent of Able Seaman. Two officers who had recently returned from German New Guinea were selected to command the unit. A permanent service officer, Lieutenant Leighton Seymour Bracegirdle RAN, was placed in command and promoted shortly afterwards to the rank of lieutenant commander.

During initial training, fifteen men were discharged on disciplinary grounds, either as a consequence of insubordination or repeated drunkenness. Another fourteen men deserted, five on the eve of the Bridging Train's departure from Australia. Several other men stated that circumstances prevented their departure from Australia and they were discharged on compassionate grounds. Another three men of the unit were despatched to naval prison for theft. Lieutenant Commander Bracegirdle had to report to the Commandant on 12 May 1915 that 'considerable dissatisfaction exists' in the unit.[1]

Nearly 90 per cent of the men were married or had nominated a partner to be allocated four shillings per day from their pay. Throughout March and April, the unit records include several complaints from the men that their nominees had not received any money since their enlistment. On 24 March 1915, a deputation consulted Bracegirdle and reported that many families were still not in receipt of their allocation. The unit's records reveal further complaints, with a number of men stating on 4 May that their wives had not received any money for five weeks. It is unclear who was to blame for the men and their spouses not receiving the money that was due. While the unit did not have a dedicated paymaster officer, Lieutenant Bond, a qualified accountant in civilian life, had accepted responsibility for the coordination of the Bridging Train's pay and allowances. Considering the many tasks involved in preparing for overseas service, it is probable that Lieutenant Bond had limited time to ensure the timely payment of monies due. The problem of late payments was to re-emerge as a more serious issue early in 1916, although it appears that the problems reported in March and April 1915 were overcome by mid May.

When the troopship *Port Macquarie* weighed anchor and sailed out of Port Phillip Bay at 7.30am on 4 June 1915, the officers and men of the 1st RAN Bridging Train were finally bound for war.

On arrival at Port Said in Egypt on 17 July, Bracegirdle reported to Vice Admiral Richard H. Peirse, Commander-in-Chief of the East Indies Station. At this meeting, Bracegirdle was informed that the Admiralty's intentions for the Bridging Train's deployment had changed. Rather than proceeding to England for further training and deployment on the Western Front, the Bridging Train would be transported to Mudros Island in the eastern Aegean Sea and prepare to participate in the British landings at Suvla Bay, to the north of Anzac Cove. The Allies had landed on the Gallipoli Peninsula on 25 April 1915, after two failed naval attacks, in an attempt to end Turkey's involvement in the war on the German side. The landing at Suvla Bay was made to give relief to the troops at Anzac Cove and to open another advance against the Turkish defence of the Peninsula. The campaign had been under way for more than three months when the Bridging Train learned of their planned participation.

While the Australians prepared to depart from Port Said, shore leave was restricted to officers. However, 35 men managed to leave the ship by hiding away in Arab dhows and coal barges. Their absence without leave was short and all returned to *Port Macquarie* before the ship sailed the following morning. The passage to Mudros took two days. Three days later, *Port Macquarie* was ordered to Imbros, another Greek island, closer to the Gallipoli coastline. Finally, the fate of the Bridging Train was made known. The unit had been transferred from Admiralty control to the British Army. The Australians would be attached to the 11th Division IX Army Corps under Lieutenant General the Honourable Sir Frederick Stopford. Their immediate superior was Colonel (later Brigadier) E. H. Bland of the Royal Engineers.

There was further news. The Bridging Train's principal task was to be the construction and control of pontoon piers, an undertaking for which they had received no training at all. Nonetheless, the unit's equipment was unloaded and transported ashore on rafts made from the pontoons. By the time seven vehicles had been unloaded, an order was received from General Stopford's staff to retain all vehicles on board *Port Macquarie*. Communication between the command and the Australian unit was very poor and morale in the Bridging Train was depleted as a result.

At 2am on 8 August, the Australians left Mudros embarked in transports for the eighteen-mile journey to Suvla Bay. During the Bridging Train's first month on the Peninsula, fifteen Petty Officers and sailors of the unit were recommended for decorations 'for exceptional devotion to duty during the operations of erecting piers at various beaches, the landing and despatch of trench stores to the front. Daily exposed to shell fire'.[2] General Bland, who commanded the engineering units at the Dardanelles, wrote of the Train and another engineering unit: 'Both these units set a fine example of endurance, good organisation and discipline'.[3] Clearly, there was nothing wrong with the performance of the unit in action, but morale deteriorated as discontent grew over conditions, especially the monotonous diet and the poor preparation of food. The Bridging Train's senior officers were aware of the dissent because all letters sent home were screened by the unit's censor. The cumulative effect of the dissatisfaction led to indiscipline which reached a climax on 7 December 1915. During a still cold night, a drunken brawl broke out involving two chief petty officers, Bruce Holman and Harold Lingard. The latter had to receive hospital attention for his wounds. Both were charged and dealt with summarily by Bracegirdle. One of the defendants claimed he had saved 'a couple of tots' of his rum ration which had led to his intoxication. Owing to a head injury sustained during earlier naval service, he had reacted badly to the alcohol and had become unexpectedly violent.[4] The excuse did not impress Bracegirdle, who recommended the dismissal of both senior sailors from the Navy. In a report to Captain Edward Unwin RN, the naval officer in charge of the Suvla area, Bracegirdle complained that his unit suffered frequent 'serious breaches of discipline' that made it 'impossible to carry on with such CPOs' who had been 'severely punished for similar offences'. He wanted them dealt with so as to 'have a deterrent effect upon the remainder of the unit'.[5] The men were sent back to Australia and dismissed from the Navy. Happily for Bracegirdle, not all the members of the unit were fractious. At least two, Drivers Langdale and Brass, were recommended for commissioned rank. Langdale had been a chief mate during prior merchant navy service. Thankfully, the end of the campaign was already in sight.

Following the visit of the Minister of War, Lord Kitchener, to Gallipoli, including a trip to Suvla Bay on 14 November, the British decided to evacuate the Peninsula and conclude the whole Dardanelles Expedition. In contrast to the initial Allied landings on 25 April, the final withdrawal was a stunning success. The men departed at night, measures having been taken to fool the Turks into believing that all the Allied positions were still occupied. The main body of the Bridging Train rowed out to the transport HMT *El Kahira*, which sailed from Suvla Bay bound for Lemnos Island at 2am. When a detachment of 50 men commanded by Sub-Lieutenant Charles Hicks destroyed the Allied supply dump at Suvla, the Bridging Train had the dubious honour of being the last Australians off the Gallipoli Peninsula on 20 December 1915. After the withdrawal, a party of Bridging Train men was detached from Mudros for varied port duties in Egypt. This included the control of tugs and lighters in the Suez Canal. The remainder of the unit stayed at Mudros to assist in the loading and unloading of ships. The unit's official historian remarked that for most of the Bridging Train 'this was a peaceful and healthy, but very monotonous period'.[6] He makes no mention of any discontent.

Away from enemy action, problems of indiscipline within the Bridging Train resurfaced. But concerns about discipline went beyond a lack of self-control among ordinary ranks. At the time, the Commander-in-Chief distributed a general notice complaining that not only were officers not being saluted but that officers were noted outside the camp confines without gloves or sticks. He ordered that stricter standards be maintained. In late December, an old problem appeared again when men received mail from their families containing complaints that their pay was overdue. This was partly due to the hectic events of the evacuation from Gallipoli, but the problem persisted well after then. For wives in distant Melbourne and Hobart, not only was Christmas spent without their spouses but those at home faced the season of gifts and revelry without money. On first inspection it appeared that the non-payment of allotments to families was a consequence of the outcome of the Bridging Train being under sailing orders while stationed at Mudros. It was customary for units under such orders not to be paid until they reached their intended destination.

In early January 1916, the men were directed to undertake numerous route marches in addition to rifle exercises and squad drill. It was thought that physical activity might counteract the growing boredom, but it was difficult to generate any enthusiasm for seemingly pointless training in men who had spent the previous five months fighting a war. Morale was most affected, however, by the long-running disputes over pay and allowances. Disagreements about pay rates had begun even before the Bridging Train left Australia. Those who had joined the Bridging Train from the RAN Brigade had arrangements for their pay and allowances transferred to the new unit. However, the local Military District was actually responsible for their pay at AIF rates. As the Bridging

Train was recruited and transported across state borders, District Naval Officers in each state were required to notify the military of the relevant rates of pay and details for payment. The system was cumbersome and many naval wives found that their allotments had ceased without warning or explanation.

On arrival back at Mudros on January 4, the men found there was still no pay ready for collection. Unknown to them, it was being held by the paymaster of the ANZAC forces at Mudros. Presumably because the Bridging Train was technically part of the 1st Division of the AIF, communications from the paymaster's office had gone astray. To add to their chagrin, local people were selling fresh fruit and vegetables, luxuries that the Bridging Train personnel had not seen for months, but which few of the men could afford to buy because they had not been paid. In the absence of Bracegirdle, hospitalised with jaundice, it appeared that none of the other officers took any interest in the worsening situation. By 13 January, the men of the Bridging Train had had enough. Driver R. Thompson recorded: 'One night, someone came along and lifted the flap of the tent and said, "We're not going on parade tomorrow", to every tent he went. To this day no one of us told who that man was'.[7] Clearly, there was a ringleader although his identity was never disclosed.

At 9am, when a bugle called the men to Divisions for the day, 189 out of nearly 300 men refused the order, including 60 out of 78 Drivers who appeared to be at the centre of the dissatisfaction. Lieutenant Bond was initially nonplussed. He summoned the Petty Officers and gave them orders to go to every tent of the unit and tell the men that their action in refusing to parade was mutinous. He would allow 30 minutes grace for the men to think carefully about their response. At 9.45am, the bugle again sounded the call to Divisions. Again, the majority of the men did not respond. Instead, the lieutenant was confronted by a deputation of twelve men led by Driver Langdale, the sailor recommended for commissioned rank a month earlier. The message was simple: the men had no intention of 'busting up the show', but until they and their families were paid, they would not work. Lieutenant Bond made no effort to argue the merits of their case but left to confer with his superiors. Within an hour he returned with naval police, threatening the men with immediate arrest unless they returned to duty without delay. A third time they refused. Believing he had no other option, Lieutenant Bond placed all of them under open arrest pending charges of mutiny.

The naval police collected rifles and ammunition from the unit and withdrew.

An awkward hiatus ensued. The 'arrested' men stood around in small groups and some drifted back to their tents, unsure of what would happen next. Bond retreated to his office and had the clerk check the pay situation. It was then he discovered that the Bridging Train men had received nothing since 18 December, the week before Christmas. Receiving an undertaking from the ANZAC Field Cashier at Mudros that the money was on hand, and could be calculated and paid within four days, Lieutenant Bond called Langdale and two other 'spokesmen' for the mutineers into his office. They discussed the matter of the pay and the men went back to report the contents of the meeting with the rest of the unit. On the promise that their pay would be forthcoming, the men reluctantly resumed their duties. Lieutenant Bond reported to the naval command authorities on Mudros that the men would 'push on in a straightforward way' and take whatever punishment was forthcoming for their actions.

Naval command was alarmed by the event and thoroughly concerned about its wider consequences. A preliminary inquiry into the circumstances of the Australian servicemen 'deliberately refusing to obey the orders of their commanding officer' was held by Rear Admiral (later Admiral) Arthur Christian, the naval officer in charge at Mudros, on board HMS *Agamemnon* on 15 January 1916.[8] The inquiry, which heard from around a dozen men as well as officers and senior sailors, concluded that there was no 'malice' involved in the refusal of duty nor were there any 'cliques' behind the actions. It was obvious that no large-scale insurrection was brewing. Admiral Christian instructed the unit to prepare for operations elsewhere.

Pending further legal proceedings, the RANBT was ordered to Egypt. There was urgent work to be done in the Canal Zone where the army was preparing for action against the Turkish forces in the Sinai. Bridges had to be constructed over the Suez Canal. Lieutenant Bond's request that the men prepare for disembarkation without malice was unnecessary. Most were enthusiastic about the prospect of leaving Mudros and returning to active service. The Bridging Train gathered its equipment and personal effects and loaded them into *Empress of Britain*, a bloodstained former hospital ship, which proceeded initially to Alexandria. Lice infestations on the lower decks made the passage uncomfortable. Worse was to come, however. On arriving at Alexandria, the men boarded a cattle freight train and proceeded to Ismailia, where the Mudros mutineers were placed under an AIF armed guard. By this time the Board of Inquiry had concluded that the cause of the mutiny was solely attributable to the men of the Bridging Train. Neither the conduct of the officers nor the effect of any external circumstances, such as the non-payment of their wages, was considered in mitigation. On 23 January, an order reached Lieutenant Bond from Vice-Admiral Peirse, to prepare a list of all those involved in the mutiny and indicate 'ten to twenty of the men who you consider to be the ringleaders of the outbreak with a view to their trial by court-martial'.[9] Bond prepared two lists of all the men then under his command and headed one 'Loyal' and the other 'Defaulters'. On the Loyal list were eighteen sailors and 44 other ranks. There were 60 on the Defaulters' list. Bond placed a cross adjacent to the names of twenty men whom he described as 'only a shade worse than the others on the list'. Among those immediately charged and placed under close arrest without pay were Langdale and Brass. Bond sent the list to Vice Admiral Peirse on 25 January and busied himself preparing for the courts martial.

The courts martial were scheduled to start on 1 February in HMS *Agamemnon*. On 28 January, before any evidence was heard, Vice Admiral Rosslyn Wemyss succeeded Peirse as Commander-in-Chief. Three days later Bracegirdle left hospital, scheduled to rejoin his unit on 31 January. The two met at the railway station in Alexandria to travel on the same train to Ismailia, a rendezvous which was providential for the accused Bridging Train men. Wemyss and Bracegirdle used the opportunity to devise a common-sense resolution to what could have been an enormous humiliation for the RAN and an international embarrassment for Australia. By the end of the train journey, Wemyss had postponed the courts martial and given Bracegirdle four days to discover the full story of the mutiny and the men's reasons for taking such drastic action.

Bracegirdle arrived back at his unit and wasted no time in interviewing the men involved. After rigorous inquiries he came to the opinion that their actions at Mudros could be justified because 'no officer came to the troops and explained that there was no pay due to sailing orders'. He believed the men would have paraded if the situation had been explained to them. Bracegirdle reported the outcome of his deliberations to Wemyss, who agreed to consider his views and later that day informed Bracegirdle that he had decided to erase any record of the incident. All charges were dropped.

In a further unusual move, the Commander-in-Chief ordered the Bridging Train to parade, where he addressed them on issues of discipline, inspected the unit and congratulated them on their gallantry at Gallipoli. With that, the parade was dismissed and the men were granted leave. Wemyss then had a private meeting with the officers of the unit, including Lieutenant Bond. He informed them of his opinion that the mutiny was largely their fault because they had not been attentive to the grievances of the men under their command. He was also critical of them for letting the situation drift to a point where the men saw no alternative course of protest but through mutiny. Wemyss shared the belief that if men mutinied the fault lay mainly with their officers and flawed leadership. Fortunately for the Bridging Train, the men did not maintain a grudge against either the Navy or their officers and reaffirmed their commitment to undertake any work given to them in the future.

Given the arduous nature of their work and the uncomfortable and difficult conditions in which they laboured, the Bridging Train deserved better officers. For his part, Bracegirdle placed blame for the mutiny entirely on Bond's shoulders. Bond could and should, Bracegirdle contended, have investigated the source of the problem and obviated a situation where the men were virtually forced to mutiny. For the sake of the Bridging Train's future operations and Bond's own standing as an officer, he was transferred to the Naval Intelligence Unit at Alexandria on 22 March 1916 at the direction of Wemyss and General William Birdwood, commander of the Anzac forces. Bond was promoted to the rank of Lieutenant Commander and saw out the war in the Middle East. He returned to Australia in 1918 and was eventually placed on the retired list in the rank of commander. Drivers Langdale and Brass were posted to England for commissioned officer training. Although an embarrassing international incident had been averted, the Bridging Train gained for itself the ignominious honour of being the first RAN unit to stage a mutiny. They would not be the last.

Despite a sensible resolution to the mutiny, the future of the Bridging Train was uncertain. On 15 March 1916, the Commander-in-Chief sought a report on options for the unit's future, including disbandment or absorption into the Royal Navy. On 26 March 1916, the Bridging Train was 'returned for use ashore' and placed under the command of the lieutenant general commanding the ANZAC forces. There was, however, continuing discussion of the unit's future deployment. In November 1916, the

Acting Secretary of Defence told the Secretary of the Navy that the Bridging Train men were 'very desirous of going to the front to take part in the actual fighting'.[10] A memorandum from the Department of Defence dated 11 December 1916 authorised the transfer to the AIF of any Bridging Train men who volunteered for alternative service. Those wanting a transfer would be given infantry training, including eight weeks of 'Route marching, entrenching, physical training and Battalion and Company drill'. Not surprisingly, when the time came to volunteer for service with the AIF, less than 100 men stepped forward. More than 200 sought discharge and return to Australia.[11]

The Bridging Train was formally disbanded on 18 February 1917.[12] Bracegirdle was promoted to commander and appointed Acting District Naval Officer in Hobart. His service was recognised by the award of the Distinguished Service Order. In World War II, by then in the rank of captain, Leighton Bracegirdle served as Official Secretary to Lord Gowrie, Governor-General of Australia. He left his personal papers to the Australian War Memorial. Among these documents are comments he wrote on 8 July 1917 reflecting on the disciplinary problems of the previous year.

> A certain amount of discontent always exists where-ever sailors or soldiers on active service are not actually engaged in the strife [and their commander] has great difficulty in forcing men to see the necessity for the interests of the Public Service having preference over those of individuals.[13]

These comments sum up much of the character of ordinary Australian servicemen. While in action, they will accept and endure all the rigours of service life. Out of action, they are not so readily persuaded of the need for strict and traditional discipline. However, the full story of the 1st RAN Bridging Train must remain incomplete. Among the final entries on the official files is a note from the office-in-charge of naval records in Melbourne lamenting the loss of files and correspondence.[14] One suspects that some of the documents generated by the mutiny were among those lost to posterity.

Just as the problems with the Bridging Train faded into the past, a new outbreak of unrest confronted the Naval Board. This was the first of many incidents in which sailors took action to protest the physical conditions they were obliged to endure for the sake of the Navy and the nation. In December 1917, the Prime Minister of Australia, Billy Hughes, received a letter which he referred immediately to the Naval Board:

I have the honour to humbly solicited your assistance in the present case. I am a Frenchman naturalised Australian since ten years, leaving on this country more than twelve years.

My son, Maurice Henry Monin, about twenty months ago (eighteen years old then) had asked me to enlist in the Australian Navy. I give him my consent and after a stage of seven or eight months as stoker at Williamstown, my boy was forwarded on the HMAS *Fantome* patrol duty in the Pacific Ocean, I think. I received from the boy good news from the first months, but from July last, I don't know just what have happened, but the boy who had then less than twenty years, must have left himself misleading by the other stokers, as by a letter I have received from him on these terms:

'The 26/8/17 on the morning we went to division as usual at 9am, and was told to do drill. We refuse on account of the hard working, also the food, which have been something very bad, and a mutiny was join on the stokers side. We had a Court Martial in HMS *Suffolk* and was sentenced to two years detention, twelve of us. I am certainly very sorry for that, but can't be help as I will be against the other stokers'.

Since then, Hon. Prime Minister, my son have let know that he is at Goulburn Gaol. My son, are now very anxious to go to the front, do his bit, as himself are very sorry for what he have done and very repentant. Myself and my wife (both are French) are very sorry for what the boy have done, and my wife are not well since we have received that very sad news.

I have always done the best I could for your Government. I have been rejected for military service on account of Rheumatism and weak heart by the French Government, also by the Australian authority. I have three brothers on the fighting line in France, and many nephews and cousins on that terrible war, and my father seventy-five years old (ex Commandant Superieur on the French Administrature in Paris).

If Hon. Prime Minister, you will have the kindness to permit the boy to be released and allowed to enlist for service in France, my wife and myself we will be very thankful to you. The boy are young and have a good heart, and I am sure you will never regret it as the boy will do everything he could on the future. Excuse me, Hon. Prime Minister for the trouble I give you, and be sure of the assurance of our deep gratitude.

I may say that I have written first to the Hon Premier Mr Holman, who advise me to write to you, sir, as it is a question of the Commonwealth Government. Incluse letter from the Comptroller General's of Prison and a letter from my son.

Monsieur Monin's letter prompted action. The Naval Board reconsidered the sentences of twelve men found guilty of mutiny after an incident in the sloop *Fantome*. Captain John Glossop, then Senior Naval Officer in Sydney, advised that the men were contrite and model prisoners, worthy of leniency. The Board reduced the sentences from two years' imprisonment with dismissal from the RAN to one year's imprisonment, after which they could resume their service. Maurice Monin was released from Goulburn Gaol to continue his RAN service. But why did this impressionable young man join a mutiny?

Fantome was one of many ships that undertook the arduous and routine tasks of war for months and years on end. The official military historian, Charles Bean, includes two references to *Fantome* in his summary volume on the war. Both reflect the unexciting although necessary work of the ship. 'In mid-1915, Australia sent, first, the small cruiser *Psyche* and sloop *Fantome* (two old British warships lent to the RAN) to patrol together with some British ships the Bay of Bengal'.[15] Clearly, it would be onerous work involving a threat to the physical safety of the men embarked. *Psyche*'s sister-ship, HMS *Pegasus*, was earlier engaged and sunk by the German cruiser *Konigsberg* off East Africa in a one-sided action. The second reference to *Fantome* discloses a key factor in the decision of the ship's company to mutiny.

> *Fantome* and *Psyche* patrolled in Indian and Malayan waters for more than two years—a trying task, in very great heat. The entry of America into the war made possible their return to Australia in September 1917. Both badly needed refitting; their speed was very low.[16]

The official historian does not record any hint of action or excitement in the wartime service of the two old vessels. Both were involved in monotonous patrolling in 'very great heat' and both were old, worn-out ships in need of refit and repair. Of the two, *Fantome* was the smaller and more crowded. These ingredients led to mutiny in August 1917. It is probable that the insurrection and the likelihood of further trouble in the ships led to their recall to Australia, not simply, as Bean has it, because of America's entry into the war.

For the earlier part of its Australian service, *Fantome* was technically on loan to the Australian Squadron. The ship was not designed for cruising in the tropics nor did it have a capacity to accommodate an enlarged wartime ship's company. Conditions were obviously appalling.

> The mess decks are very cramped . . . there is not sufficient stowage for bags . . . The bathing accommodation is very small

> . . . No bathing arrangement is made for seamen-ratings . . .
> There is no part of the superstructure or upper deck which could
> be made into a comfortable crew space . . .[17]

There was not enough space for everyone to sling their hammocks and some had to sleep on the upper decks despite frequent rainstorms. The ship's company had limited fresh food. Most meals consisted of 'salt provisions'. Like many ships of that era, *Fantome* was probably overrun with cockroaches and vermin which were impossible to eradicate permanently.

In 1916, the ship was swept by influenza. The illness proliferated in the crowded and fetid conditions ideal for the spread of disease. At one stage, only twelve seamen and seven stokers were fit for duty.[18] The ship's company normally comprised 107 men—51 seamen, 37 stokers and engine room staff and nineteen other ranks. Much of *Fantome*'s patrol work was carried out off the coasts of Burma, China and Indochina, areas not known for conditions conducive to good health. Typically, a patrol would involve a cruise of ten to twelve days followed by two to four days in a port like Rangoon.[19] *Fantome*'s consort, the old cruiser *Psyche*, also faced problems with illness. On one occasion the ship lost 27 personnel who were considered unfit for duty and landed at Hong Kong.[20] The ship had to recruit fifteen 'natives' to stoke the boilers and keep the ship at sea.[21]

At their court martial, the men accused of mutiny in *Fantome* made a desperate plea for leniency. They explained that they

> suffered unduly from the heat, rain and bad accommodation. . . .
> Sleeping or rest in the mess decks has been practically impossible
> owing to the great heat, the number of men and the consequent
> bad air through absence of ventilation . . . Owing to prevailing
> sicknesses the engine room staff . . . have nearly always been
> undermanned, causing extra work to those who are able to carry
> on. The general heat of the stokehold is 122 degrees [Fahrenheit]
> or more . . .

The stokers had to work all day, including Sundays, 'most frequently' at night and even in port, in order to keep the ship at sea. They endured protracted duty periods of four hours on-watch and four hours off-watch.

Acting Commander Lewis Tobias Jones was *Fantome*'s commanding officer. His permanent rank was that of lieutenant. Although a strict disciplinarian, he possessed a poor knowledge of disciplinary regulations. In 1915 he was advised (although not officially reprimanded) that he had overstepped the mark in having one of the ship's boys, Edward Hughes, given six strokes of the cane for being insolent. Physical punishment of this nature had been banned by the RAN in 1914.[22] Technically, Jones was guilty of common assault, but no further action was taken in regard to this incident. In 1916, however, the Naval Board was moved to examine Jones' record in maintaining discipline. After deliberating on the evidence, the Naval Secretary informed Jones that he had imposed excessive punishments, including some which were beyond those permitted by regulation for officers of his rank. Jones had frequently dispensed sentences of detention although his predecessor in command of *Fantome* during 1914, Lieutenant G. Fitzgerald, had awarded very few.

One part of the ship where there appeared to be major deficiencies in discipline was the engine room. Although having more than 30 stokers *Fantome* was still considered too small to have an officer-in-charge of the engine room. The overseer of the engines, boilers and stokers was a non-commissioned officer, Chief Stoker Charles Bushell, an RN senior sailor who transferred on loan to the RAN in 1912. He was 45 years of age, far older than most of the young Australians who worked under his direction. The cramped and noisy machinery spaces of the boiler and engine rooms were an environment that modern Australians would find difficult to imagine. The Chief Stoker had his position on a starting platform, surrounded by steamy valves, dials and pressure gauges. Men moved about the heaving engine with oil-cans, watching the vibrating machinery for over-heating, working in sprays of fine oil and water. In the boiler rooms, the half-naked stokers shovelled coal down bunker chutes into ever-hungry furnaces which gaped at them, red and hot within. There was the constant stench of sweaty bodies working in the cramped spaces.

Off-duty, the men had little chance to get clean owing to the '4 on–4 off' watchkeeping routine in force. They often threw themselves into hammocks that were still damp and odorous as they tried to sleep in mess decks that seldom welcomed fresh air unless wind-scoops could be fitted in the calmest of waters. In a tropical port like Rangoon, there would be the business of coaling ship and only a few hours in which to rest or take a minimum of recreation. No wonder there was a high incidence of drunkenness when men were granted brief periods of shore leave.

It was also no wonder that there were incidents of unrest in *Fantome*'s engine and boiler rooms. In December 1914, two stokers received extra duties for an offence recorded as: 'did make an improper remark to Chief Stoker Bushell'.[23] In January 1915, another stoker, William Thompson, was demoted despite a good conduct record for using obscene language to the Chief Stoker. Another stoker received 90 days imprisonment for refusing one of Bushell's orders.[24] The start of 1917 saw the number of insubordinate incidents multiply. In April of that year, seven men were charged with 'disobeying a lawful command'—one step short of mutiny. Owing to the seriousness of the offence, they were brought before a court martial.[25]

Under disciplinary provisions, when men are tried at a court martial, they are entitled to have an officer act on their behalf and present their defence. None of *Fantome*'s officers would act for the men, but an officer in the *Eclipse* Class light cruiser HMS *Venus* agreed to speak on their behalf. Despite a shortage of time to prepare for the trial and an unfamiliarity with the vessel and the ship's company, it was argued in the men's defence that they had no knowledge of either the *Naval Discipline Act* or the *Articles of War*. This was, not surprisingly, rejected as a defence and the men were sentenced to twelve months imprisonment. In response to the defence case, Acting Commander Jones was instructed to make the regulations available for inspection and dissemination among the ship's company. The sentences of those convicted of insubordination were later reduced to four months.

After the experience of the court martial, Jones decided in July 1917 that the ship's company needed smartening up. In addition to their usual duties, he believed the sailors needed more parade ground 'drill'. This was precisely the wrong time to impose extra and unnecessary duty in a ship that was already short-staffed after a number of sailors had been invalided ashore with illness. To make up for manpower shortages, Chief Stoker Bushell ordered the remaining stokers to work four hours on-watch before having four hours off-watch. In other words, the men were being ordered to work twelve-hour days in the sweltering engine room compartments. After Divisions on 24 July 1917, Jones ordered the off-watch stokers to fall-in for drill. They complied, but later in the day a deputation went to the Captain and made a complaint that 'under present conditions of steaming it constituted a hardship'.[26] The Captain dismissed the complaint. He told the complainants that he considered that the drill was necessary, and 'their alleged hardship' was 'overrated'.

There was no drill on 25 July as the ship's company were involved in 'general evolutions'. On 26 July, after divisions at noon, the sailors were ordered to perform drill with small firearms. The off-watch stokers were fallen-in and ordered to commence marching practice on the quarterdeck. Five men paraded as ordered. Another eight refused. At the same time, the stokers rostered for the first dog watch announced they would not go below to begin their watch until the drills were 'washed out'. Acting Engineer's Mate Davies ordered the stokers to their place of duty. He singled out the two nearest men, Stokers O'Donnell and Barr, and directed them personally to proceed to the engine room. They refused. Stoker Gilmour was ordered to go on-watch. He too refused. Stoker Morris was ordered to begin the dog-watch. He also refused, stating that he 'did not intend to do any more work until the drill was washed out'.

The Executive Officer was summoned. Acting Lieutenant Roskruge then repeated the order for the stokers to perform their duty. Once again they refused to obey unless the marching drill was cancelled. To elaborate their stand, they asserted their willingness to do the drills while the ship was in port but considered them 'unjust' while the ship was at sea. The presence of the Captain was requested. In his own words, Jones 'pointed out to them the serious nature of their offence, that they were destroying the efficiency of the ship and thereby directly assisting the enemy'.[27] The men still refused to return to duty. The eight men who had refused to do drill and the additional four men who had refused to go below for the commencement of the dog-watch were placed under arrest. Jones immediately reported to the Commander-in-Chief of the China Station that there had been a mutiny on board his ship and that twelve stokers had been charged with that offence.

Fantome proceeded to Singapore where all twelve men were tried by court martial. Each was sentenced to two years' imprisonment with hard labour. At the trial, they were found guilty of mutiny even though there was no direct evidence of conspiracy. It was clear that they had disobeyed a direct order but it was not clear whether they had conspired together to do so. This crucial element was lacking. On completion of the court martial, the men were transported back to Sydney in *Pysche*. They were then conveyed to Goulburn Gaol to serve their sentences. There were pleas for clemency, by Monsieur Monin and others, particularly on the basis of the arduous service the ship's company had endured in the tropics, especially the engine room staff. Eventually the sentences were commuted. In addition, the Admiralty admitted the overtaxing nature of the stokers' duties in *Fantome* by declaring the ship should have an additional ten recruits to assist the stoker-ratings—a custom in other ships of the class. Jones was also informed that:

> their Lordships have noted with displeasure the two outbreaks of collective insubordination which have occurred on board his ship during a period of five months, and which show that the handling of the men under his command has been injudicious.[28]

While the Admiralty admitted there was some justice in the sailor's complaints, it was also obliged to acknowledge that the mutiny was due in part to the atrocious living conditions on board the sloop. Jones' decision to impose marching drill on overworked stokers had not been helpful.

Fantome remained an unhappy ship. In 1918, it was converted to undertake surveying duties. The ship continued in this role after the war. The sloop's first lieutenant at that time was Lieutenant Commander Rice. He was a difficult man. Even the captain, Commander Scott, commented that Rice 'possesses an imperious and intolerant manner in dealing with subordinates'.[29] During a long cruise in 'a hot climate and congested living conditions', Rice's manner contributed to a long list of offences and infractions. Mess deck overcrowding was the principal source of discontent. When designed, *Fantome* was intended to accommodate 113 personnel. After its conversion for surveying duties, the ship's company was increased to 134. That number should have included no less than 41 sailors for general seaman duties. However, a shortage of seaman branch sailors in the RAN after the war meant that *Fantome* had only 27 sailors embarked for seaman duties. These men were, of course, seriously over-worked.

During 1920, whenever the ship returned to its base at Cairns, the Master-at-Arms had his hands full. There were twenty charges during one short period. Most related to Able Seamen Moir and Ackell ('Broke out of ship and [returned] drunk four times') and Able Seamen Wylie and Lawless ('deserted' but returned to the ship by Queensland Police). Moir and Ackell were the cause of particular anxiety. It was noted at the time: 'These two men though troublesome were never actually violent consequently charges against them were never of a nature to warrant summary imprisonment'. The two sailors were renowned for 'cunningly seizing opportunities' of breaking out of the ship while it was alongside a wharf, despite the presence of marine guards, and finding somewhere to get themselves drunk. Commander Scott lamented that he had difficulties in dealing with some of his men who had a propensity for going absent without leave. He concluded that 'the only reliable resource is the irons'.

On 17 November 1920, after a three-month absence from its home port, *Fantome* returned to Cairns. When the ship's company was granted shore leave, the men hit town apparently determined to make up for the hardships of the cruise. Their enthusiasms resulted in a 'drunken orgy' which ended up with seven sailors charged with court martial offences. To make matters worse, another nine personnel deserted. When Scott sought the courts martial of so many of his ship's company, all of whom were from the seaman branch and would be hard to replace, the Naval Board realised there were serious problems to be faced. The Board decided to hold a court of inquiry into the whole matter of *Fantome*'s disciplinary problems.

The officer chosen to conduct the inquiry was Captain Claude Cumberlege, assisted by two commanders of the Royal Navy. The three officers found that there were no obvious reasons for excessive indiscipline other than the presence of 'a number of very chequered characters'. However, they had to conclude that 'whereas ordinarily decent men can and do put up cheerfully with discomforts', *Fantome* was simply too small, too crowded and too old for its assigned duties. Although the inquiry found that there was 'no blame attributable to Commander Scott and his officers', the Board, guided by a report produced by Commodore Dumaresq, decided to allow Scott to retire. Five sailors were dismissed. In a decision long overdue, the old *Fantome* would be replaced by a more modern vessel. Ironically, *Fantome*'s replacement, HMAS *Moresby*, would suffer similar problems for not dissimilar reasons.

During World War I, mutinies were suffered in a number of other navies. The most calamitous was the mutiny of the German High Seas Fleet at Wilhelmshaven and Kiel in the period October–November of 1918, which set in motion a sporadic but short-lived revolutionary movement across Germany.

Following the Battle of Jutland in May 1916, the High Seas Fleet had sortied only three times: in August and then October 1916, and again briefly from 23–25 April 1918 in search of two British convoys. The inactivity, poor food, left-wing propaganda and the dispersal of the best sailors to the U-boat fleet had left those serving in the capital ships dispirited. There had already been one mutiny in the summer of 1917, suppressed with the execution of two of the mutineers.

In August of 1918, Admiral Franz Von Hipper, who had commanded the German battlecruisers at Dogger Bank and Jutland, succeeded to the command of the High Seas Fleet. In October he planned to take the fleet to sea in a last desperate raid on the Straits of Dover and the mouth of the River Thames. The sailors saw the scheme as nothing more than a suicidal foray with minimal chances of success. On 29 October, the ships' companies at Wilhelmshaven refused to take their ships to sea. Their example was followed by the fleet at Kiel. By 3 November, the sullen resistance of the men broke out into armed insurrection. The sailors of the U-boat flotillas remained loyal and, for a brief period, there was a possibility that the submarines might be used against the battleships of their own fleet.

Events elsewhere overshadowed the mutiny, however. The German government was on the point of collapse. In Hamburg and Bremen, 'soviets' of workers and sailors were formed. Bavaria declared itself a socialist republic on 7 November. Two days later the Kaiser announced his abdication. Admiral Hipper retired after being overwhelmed by the mutinous spirit within the fleet. The new Provisional Government appointed Ludwig Von Reuter in his place. Admiral Von Reuter restored discipline in the fleet by transferring disloyal sailors ashore, but still he had to raise his flag in the light cruiser *Emden*, of whose loyalty he was assured, rather than in the former fleet flagship *Friedrich der Grosse*.

Admiral Reuter later took part in an action that may have been the most destructive mutiny in recent naval history. On instruction from the Provisional Government, Reuter sailed from Germany with eleven battleships, five battle cruisers, eight light cruisers and 50 destroyers, ten days after the Armistice of November 11, surrender his ships to the Grand Fleet which was waiting in the Firth of Forth. The High Seas Fleet anchored for the last time in the British naval base of Scapa Flow. The ships remained moored there while the peacemakers at Versailles debated their future. Already demoralised by the years of inactivity in their home bases, the German sailors suffered further through months of isolation and privation. Reuter complained frequently about the quantity of rations his men received and the effects of being confined to their ships. By June it appeared that the discussions at Versailles would result in the fleet being distributed among Germany's former enemies. On 21 June 1919, two days before the

German government had agreed to surrender the ships, Reuter defied his own superiors and ordered the High Seas Fleet to be scuttled. British boarding parties were too late to prevent most of the ships settling on the bottom of Scapa Flow, where they remained until broken up for scrap. Von Reuter and his men were treated as prisoners of war and were repatriated in 1920.

In the same month as the scuttling of the High Seas Fleet, another mutiny took place half a world away in Western Australia, in one of the battle cruisers that had once been part of the fleet that was Germany's nemesis. But their reasons could not have been more different.

7

Mutiny in whose flagship?

The RAN Flagship HMAS *Australia*, from the time it was brought into service in 1913, had never been a happy ship. The percentage of *Australia*'s sailors facing charges during World War I was among the highest of any ship in the Navy. The imposition of severe punishments improved neither discipline nor morale. This was evidenced on one occasion by the response of 100 stokers when several of their number were placed in irons for something they regarded as a minor offence. *Australia*'s captain met a delegation of sailors and agreed that restraining their messmates in this fashion was unnecessary. The stokers resumed their duty but earned for themselves the ill will of officers like Lieutenant George Williams, who was amazed by his captain's attitude: 'It was something unique in the annals of naval history for part of a ship's company to present an ultimatum to their superior officer and that during a war [on the success of] which depends the fate of the Empire'.[1] This was not really true, but poorly informed officers were numerous and widespread.

On 12 June 1919, *Australia*'s ship's company received a 'hearty welcome home' after the war from the citizens of Melbourne, as they marched through the streets in the early morning, although it was noted that the crowds were not as large as those which had greeted the return of the Anzacs not so long before.[2] Thirty officers and 450 petty officers and sailors were greeted by crowds that included many young women, waving placards, cheering and applauding. Flags were carried and field guns were drawn along by horses as a tribute to the naval gunners who had served ashore. The march wound along Flinders and Swanston Streets to the Town Hall where the banner of the Navy League decked out a speaker's rostrum.

The Lord Mayor and the Acting Defence Minister expressed

the 'heartfelt welcome' of all present and commented that the country would undoubtedly have been raided by the Germans in the early days of the war if it had not been for the presence of the battle cruiser—owing to *Australia*'s presence the warships of the Kaiser's Navy 'did not dare to come too near'.[3] The ship and the men had then gone on to serve with distinction in the Grand Fleet. A fine tradition had been maintained, even if a minor collision had prevented *Australia* taking its part in the biggest naval engagement of the war, the Battle of Jutland. Yet there was a discordant note in the speeches. The Lord Mayor, Alderman W. Cabena, hoped that the men would uphold fine naval traditions, do their duty and remain in the Navy. He acknowledged that there was discontent in the ranks, especially over the matter of deferred pay and the maintenance of severe punishments for acts of indiscipline. The men were praised for being steadfast and repudiating the actions of the men who 'held up' *Australia* at Fremantle. Journalists did not record the reaction of the sailors to these dark references. As the speeches concluded, *Australia*'s ship's company were marched away to the drill hall at Eastern Hill where the Commonwealth Government entertained the men to lunch.

Later in the day, one journalist circulated among the sailors and recorded that they were 'generally discontented about naval regulations which were unduly severe, and exceeded the bounds of reasonable punishment'.[4] They spoke of one celebrated case of an Australian sailor who had overstayed his leave on the night of Armistice celebrations and was charged with desertion on his return. The man was imprisoned for three months and forfeited all his accumulated pay. Other men complained they had not been paid the shilling a day that should have been accruing to them as deferred pay. They acknowledged that at least the food was plentiful but alleged its presentation was unsatisfactory and the quality often poor. There was tension between Royal Navy sailors and locally-enlisted Australians, who complained that as most of the senior positions were held by Royal Navy men, Australians had fewer opportunities of advancement. Engineers and artificers in particular planned to leave the Navy at the earliest opportunity for civilian service. All agreed that reforms were needed but, in the words of one man, the 'Fremantle incident [had] put back by years our hope of making any change in the present state of affairs'.[5] What, then, was the notorious 'Fremantle incident'?

In April 1919, HMAS *Australia* was detached from the Grand

Fleet of the Royal Navy and proceeded home to Australia. Many of the ship's company had not seen their homes during the four years since *Australia* had sailed as part of the covering force for the Anzac contingent in 1915. There were a number of issues which had contributed to a low morale in some sections of the ship's company. The period in late 1918–19, when the ship had been part of the guarding force that watched over the surrendered German High Seas Fleet had involved long and monotonous duty, either on patrol in the North Sea or at anchor near a quiescent and defeated enemy. Earlier, *Australia* had missed the largest sea battle of the war when the Grand Fleet engaged the High Seas Fleet for a darkening afternoon and evening on 31 May 1916. A few weeks before, on 22 April of that year, the battle cruiser had rammed her sister-ship, HMS *New Zealand*, during exercises in fog, and had been further damaged while entering dry-dock. Some of *Australia*'s men did see action, however, even though their ship did not, in April of 1918, when a party of volunteers joined men from other ships in a daring raid to cripple the U-boat base at Zeebrugge. The attack was a success and the harbour entrance was choked when blockships were deliberately sunk in the canal. The action was hard-fought and British casualties were high. Six Victoria Crosses were awarded and a number of Australian sailors also received awards for gallantry. Among them was Stoker Dalmorton Rudd.

Australia's ship's company had other causes for dissatisfaction while on overseas service. There were high rates of illness, several men dying of measles and its complications during 1915. There had been limited leave in the United Kingdom and what leave there was had been restricted by a lack of cash. The fixed-service enlisters expected to be paid a sum related to their deferred pay on the expiry of their term although their enlistment had been continued to the end of the war. This payment was delayed for reasons that were not clearly understood by those affected. There was also the tedium of maintaining a strict shipboard routine on the cessation of hostilities, when there seemed to be less need for the rigour of wartime discipline. Australian frustrations were escalated by British sailors being promoted faster and occupying the leading positions on the lower deck. The British personnel had a perception of naval tradition and discipline that was not wholeheartedly embraced by many of the young Australians who had only enlisted when war was declared and their country seemed in peril. All these dissatisfactions and relative inactivity led to disciplinary problems. Patsy Adam-Smith writes that on the lower deck, the men of *Australia* did not toast the Crown with the cry 'God Save the King', but rather called out 'Bugger the King'.[6]

The concerns arising from wartime service were put in the past during *Australia's* voyage through the Mediterranean and the Indian Ocean to its home waters. The ship's commanding officer was Captain Claude Cumberlege, an RN permanent service officer from London on loan to the RAN; he was then 41 years old. Also on board was the Commodore Commanding the (Australian) Fleet, Commodore John Saumarez Dumaresq. Commodore Dumaresq came from a family with strong naval traditions and, although born in Sydney in 1873, had left Australia to join the Royal Navy at thirteen. He commanded HMAS *Sydney* during the latter part of the war, and had been promoted to commodore and command of the Australian Fleet only some two months previously.

When the battle cruiser arrived in Fremantle it was met with a rousing welcome and extensive hospitality. There was an 'Open Day' for the local citizens and thousands of people visited the ship. The stay was, however, a comparatively short one of just three days. This led to the frustrations of many among the ship's company coming to the surface again. It was also unfortunate that *Australia* arrived in the midst of a dockyard strike that had become the centre of a nasty confrontation between authorities and workers, with a clash between strikers and 'scabs' on the waterfront the day after the warship's arrival. This was an unfortunate first experience of home for many impressionable young sailors who had left the country several years before as teenagers. Representatives of the ship's company went to Captain Cumberlege and asked if the ship could delay its sailing by a day so that the men could have a full weekend of leave. They reminded him that this was their first visit to their homeland after four years of war service. The extra day would also give some an opportunity to travel from Fremantle to Perth where they had family and friends. The captain replied that the request could not even be considered because *Australia* had to comply with a strict timetable of port visits.

After leave and some partying on the Saturday night, *Australia* prepared to sail early on Sunday morning. By 10.30am, the ship was standing by ready to proceed to sea. There were dutymen on the forecastle while parties of sailors hoisted the ship's picket boat and prepared to secure the gangways. The Engineer Commander reported that steam was raised and all was ready in the engine and boiler rooms in preparation for getting under way. Cumberlege was thus startled to see between 80 and 100 men emerge from the mess decks and assemble on the quarterdeck in front of 'P' gun turret where they could face, and be seen from, the captain's position on the bridge. While some were still in full uniform, having recently returned from their leave in Fremantle, the captain reported later that:

> I noticed that many of the men wore the rig of libertymen, and they straggled on to the quarterdeck, that is to say, they did not march on to the quarterdeck, and formed up there with more or less even front; but no attempt at an orderly formation was made. It was, in fact, what may be termed a mob rather than an orderly deputation.[7]

Cumberlege had clearly never seen the like in nearly 30 years' service. He sent his executive officer to find out the reasons for the extraordinary assembly, who returned to advise his commanding officer that the men were requesting that the ship's departure be delayed so that they could have further leave ashore. The captain reacted somewhat indignantly, immediately adopting a strict legalistic tone, referring to tradition and the hard rock of legal authority upon which many a poor man's bark had foundered, adding that it was 'no ordinary request preferred in a legitimate manner in accordance with the customs of the service and the *Articles of War*'. He went to the quarterdeck and addressed the men directly, speaking quietly and slowly. He told the sailors that their 'request' amounted to a demand to delay the ship's sailing. Because of other commitments it was impossible for him to agree to such a demand. He allowed no further comment from anyone and peremptorily ordered the men below decks. While there was no argument from the men and they immediately followed orders and dispersed, there was clearly dissatisfaction. Cumberlege noted: 'While they were moving off the quarterdeck, a number of ejaculations of an insubordinate nature were being made by them, and certain persons, obviously fomenting trouble, were noticed, and their names were taken'.

The captain may have congratulated himself on rapidly dispersing an unauthorised assembly, and noting the ringleaders for subsequent retribution. The assembly in itself probably did not constitute a mutinous assembly as the men accepted the orders they were given. However, a more rigorous interpretation of the *Articles of War* may have judged their insubordinate remarks and even their use of an unorthodox channel of complaint as a mutinous action. Unexpected actions were to follow.

The ship was ready for sea and waiting for the Commodore to come on board, Dumaresq having also taken the opportunity to go ashore and appreciate the hospitality of Fremantle after years of wartime service. He arrived alongside and was piped aboard. Cumberlege was probably relieved that the squadron commander had not witnessed the short and embarrassing episode on the quarterdeck and gave orders to let go the aft lines. At that very moment, he received an urgent telephone message from the engineer commander. The stokers, the personnel responsible for feeding coal into the furnaces and maintaining steam pressure, had left the boiler rooms *en masse*. *Australia* could not maintain sufficient steam to get under way. Immediately after the assembly on the quarterdeck, a number of sailors had apparently masked themselves with black silk handkerchiefs and gone to the boiler rooms where they had persuaded or intimidated the on-watch stokers to leave their posts.

The situation was now becoming awkward. The delay was obvious even if its cause was not. A large number of notable public officials from Fremantle and Perth had assembled to farewell the RAN flagship. Clearly they could see that all had been secured ready for sea and groups of men were at their stations on deck. The party at the stern had prepared to cast off the lines still securing the battle cruiser. There followed a period of inactivity as the men waited for further orders. The captain gave instructions that the ship's chief petty officers and petty officers were to assemble immediately in the engine and boiler rooms, where they were to stoke the boilers to regain steam and enable the battle cruiser to leave harbour. With the combined efforts of the petty officers and men on duty drafted from other parts of the ship, *Australia* cast off and steamed out of port only an hour behind its scheduled departure time. Out at sea, the stokers returned to duty and the rest of the crew resumed their normal sea-going duties. Midway through that Sunday afternoon, the Captain had all off-watch personnel mustered on the quarterdeck where he read them the *Articles of War* and emphasised that it was a serious matter for any member of the crew to refuse duty. The mood of the gathering was quiet and there were no comments before the men were dismissed. The captain and his officers then held an urgent inquiry into the incident.

To the names taken as the men left the quarterdeck were added the names of other sailors who had been observed in discussions in the mess decks, encouraging and persuading their messmates to assemble on the quarterdeck to request that

Australia's departure be delayed. Thirty-two men who had refused orders in the boiler rooms were put under arrest. Of the 32 men, 27 were sentenced to 90 days in cells for refusing duty. Cumberlege made his formal report to the Fleet Commander and charged the remaining five men, whom he considered instigators, with mutiny. The charge was that 'being persons subject to the *Naval Discipline Act*, [they] joined in a mutiny, not accompanied by violence, on board the *Australia* on 1 June 1919'. The charge sheet carried the commanding officer's comment: 'The act of mutiny committed by the accused consists in the fact that a body of men . . . resisted my lawful authority inasmuch as they prevented me from taking my ship to sea'. The accused were Stoker William MacIntosh, Stoker Dalmorton Rudd, Ordinary Seaman Wilfred Thompson, Stoker Leonard Rudd (Dalmorton's brother) and Ordinary Seaman Kenneth Patterson. The latter was charged for his actions while among the assembly on the quarterdeck. The stokers and Ordinary Seaman Thompson were cited for encouraging other men to refuse duty in that they went to the boiler rooms and 'caused the boiler rooms to be quitted'. Patterson and Dalmorton Rudd were considered to have been among the instigators because they were seen conferring in the mess prior to the assembly on the quarterdeck. All were RAN personnel. The charges carried penalties of imprisonment. It is significant that none of them was accused of being the ringleader—a charge which carried the death penalty. The ages of the five accused ranged from 18 to 22 years. One of the accused, Dalmorton Rudd, had volunteered for the Zeebrugge raid in April 1918 and been awarded the Distinguished Service Medal. Rudd had been a well-respected member of the ship's company until his wife, whom he had last seen in 1915, died in early 1918. Rudd's behaviour had changed as he grieved. He faced several charges involving alcohol and had recently been disrated from leading stoker to stoker.

The five were tried when *Australia* arrived in Sydney three weeks later. The entire ship's company was sent on leave and the ship was closed to public inspection, the Naval Board stating that the influenza epidemic then present in Sydney posed a risk to any public assembly. At the time the port of Sydney was also suffering serious disruption due to a strike by merchant seamen. The day of the court martial, 20 June 1919, there was a large parade of the Returned Soldiers & Sailors Ship and Wharf Labourers' Union. The sound of their brass band as they marched by the quays of the port was heard out on the harbour. The court martial was convened by Commodore Dumaresq in the cruiser HMAS *Encounter*. Its president was Commodore John Glossop, the next senior naval officer in Australia after the Fleet Commander. A court martial had a minimum of five officers and a maximum of nine with one of that number designated presiding officer or president. The president had to have the minimum rank of captain, while the involvement of any other officer could be challenged by the accused. Besides Commodore Glossop as president, the other members of the court martial were Captains Brownlow and Robins, and Commanders Brabant and Feakes. The court thus had the minimum five members.

The proceedings were conducted in open session. The accused were entitled to the presence and participation of a representative, usually termed a 'friend'. This was often an officer from the accused person's ship. In this case, due to the seriousness of the charges, a civil lawyer, Richard Orchard, appeared as the 'friend' of four of the accused. Orchard was also a Commonwealth Parliamentarian. A Judge Advocate was also appointed. His role was to assist the court on points of law but, unlike a prosecutor, he could not call for any sentence to be passed on the accused. The Judge Advocate was Paymaster Commander Cooke.

None of the five sailors charged with mutiny denied any of the facts, or challenged the jurisdiction of the court or the validity of the indictment. They pleaded guilty to the charges and asked the court for leniency. Thus the majority of the proceedings concerned submissions for reduced sentences. Richard Orchard stated how all the accused, despite their youth, had served for periods ranging from three to five years, principally in the testing conditions of North Sea combat operations. They were looking forward to the return to Australia. The hospitality of the people of Fremantle had been overwhelming. It was commonly understood among *Australia*'s ship's company that they would remain in port until Monday and that Sunday would be an open day when local citizens would be able to visit the vessel and the ship's company could 'show our gratitude' for the 'many kindnesses shown to us' and 'all the good things that had been done for us'.[8] When the off-duty sailors returned to the ship early on Sunday and learned that *Australia* was to sail almost immediately, there was a great deal of resentment among the Australian nationals in the ship's company. Orchard argued that the men were still feeling the results of their festivities and did not understand the seriousness of the actions they contemplated nor, he asserted, were they aware that those actions would be considered mutiny.

The sailors pleaded that they 'had no desire to be disloyal to our officers or to bring discredit on our ship' and asked for clemency from the court.

Lieutenant Philip Bowyer-Smyth RN and a lawyer named Elliott appeared as advocates for Kenneth Patterson. Patterson's story was more involved than that of his four co-accused. He had joined the Navy and first gone to sea at the age of fifteen. During passage in an unnamed merchant vessel to join his assigned warship, the cruiser *Psyche*, Patterson had witnessed a disturbance among the merchant seamen. Then, while serving for a year in *Psyche*, he had seen the twelve men from *Fantome* brought back to Australia for punishment after the mutiny in that ship. This meant the young Patterson had:

> twice come into contact with serious trouble of a disciplinary nature before reaching the age of sixteen years, [and] . . . had not had the opportunity to gain that sound conception of discipline which was given to the majority of youngsters entering a naval service.[9]

Some character witnesses were then called. All agreed that the accused sailors were not of a 'criminal tendency'.

The representations on behalf of Patterson seemed to have influenced the court because he and Thompson received the lightest sentences—imprisonment for one year. Leonard Rudd received eighteen months' imprisonment. The other two men were dismissed from the Navy and sentenced to imprisonment for two years with hard labour. The court martial was closed and the prisoners were led away to Goulburn Gaol where the *Fantome* mutineers had also been imprisoned. With the trial over, differences in public and official opinion started to emerge on the outcome. Some thought the sentences were too lenient. Others described them as 'vicious and cruel'. There was no debate on whether the men's actions constituted a mutiny—it was the question of appropriate punishment for their actions and their culpability that provoked bitter disagreement. The key issue as far as the Australian public was concerned was the severity of the sentences and the timing of the punishments. The mutiny occurred at the end of May 1919—some six weeks before planned peace celebrations and eight weeks prior to the return of the RAN to Australian control (1 August 1919). In the four months from July to October 1919, debate raged in the popular press and in Federal Parliament about the severity of the sentences and the necessity of the Admiralty retaining operational control of the RAN well into 1919.[10] The Nationalist Government of Billy Hughes, obliged to respond to public anger before the general election at the end of that year, was placed in an embarrassing position by the dispatch of the relevant documents of the case to London, as *Australia* was still under Admiralty control. Hoping for some goodwill to be exercised in response to the Commonwealth's unconditional support for the war at sea, the Australian Government asked the Admiralty to send copies of all papers connected with the trial to Melbourne and to exercise leniency when it confirmed the sentences imposed.

Richard Orchard, who had appeared at the court martial as 'prisoner's friend', returned to Parliament disappointed by the outcome. On 26 June 1919, he raised the possibility of an appeal by the prisoners against the severity of their sentences. The Acting Prime Minister, W. A. Watt, responded that there was no right of appeal against the decision but hinted that the sentences would be reviewed. In the course of parliamentary discussion, the sentences were widely criticised with one senator referring to them as 'savage'. The court martial process and the sentences were raised in the Commonwealth Parliament on more than 25 occasions between July and October 1919.[11] The Government was under pressure not just from the Labor Opposition but from Government members as well. During the peace celebrations on 19 July and again after the Commonwealth assumed control of the Australian Fleet from the Admiralty on 1 August, there were requests for clemency to be extended to the mutineers. In the period to August, the Government pointed out that it was powerless to act and that such requests had to be directed to the Admiralty because *Australia* was still under Admiralty control. Finally, on 10 September 1919, the Admiralty advised that the sentences of the mutineers would be halved. This did not satisfy the Australian Government.

On 11 September 1919, Sir Joseph Cook, Minister for the Navy, was asked whether the Government was considering a request to the British for further reduction of the sentences. The Minister responded:

> I will say this in general terms, at whatever cost, the discipline of the Navy must not be interfered with. The constant agitation for the release of these men does not help these men at all. I suggest that in the interests of discipline, and of the men themselves, members leave this matter at rest with my assurance—
> *(Interjection):* No fear. It was a vicious and cruel sentence.

Minister: All the statements members may make in the House will not influence the Navy one way or the other.
(Furious interjections) Mr Page: It is a pity someone does not sink the blessed ships in Sydney Harbour.
Minister: A very strange suggestion.
Mr Page: It is what I would do in any way.
Minister: May I complete my sentence?
Mr Page: That is what you would do for the men.[12]

The ships were not sunk but the strong statements made in Parliament did have their effect. The controversy continued. On 19 September, there were statements in the Senate concerning the 'need of having a regard for Australian ideals and sentiment' and also 'the need for impressing upon Imperial officers that it was the Parliament of Australia, and not the imported officers, who had the last say in the administration of the affairs of the navy'. The conflict between Australian nationalism and traditional British discipline was out in the open.

Senator Keating stated that 'just as crimes could be committed in the name of liberty, so . . . tyranny could be practised in the name of discipline'. He added that 'Australians were not encouraged by the imported officers'.[13] There were growing differences of opinion between the Government and the Commonwealth Naval Board on the matter, with the Board opposed to giving any leniency to the convicted mutineers while the Government was still seeking to reduce the sentences.[14] On 6 November, the Government bypassed the Naval Board and communicated directly with the Admiralty, expressing the hope that all the men would be released by Christmas 1919. The Admiralty agreed. The sentences of each of the men would be reduced as an acknowledgment of the gallantry and service of the Australian forces during the war.[15] The Government made the announcement on 21 November 1919. Cook told the House that the sentences would be remitted as from 20 December 'on account of the youth of the prisoners and good previous records'. When the men were released in December, their sentences had amounted to six months' imprisonment.

The Government's actions outraged the Naval Board, whose members were appalled that it should have listened to public criticism of the trial and its outcome, and angry that the Minister for the Navy did not make known to the Board the contents of its 6 November cable to the Admiralty. The Chief of Naval Staff, Rear Admiral Percy Grant, and Commodore Dumaresq, as Commodore Commanding the Squadron and president of the court martial, threatened to resign. In the meantime they refused to sign the official orders that would release the men. Eventually the formalities for their release were completed at Goulburn Gaol and the men walked free. The debate over naval discipline, however, continued unrestrained. Dumaresq believed strongly that 'The Australian . . . did not realise, as did the Britisher, the necessity for strict discipline. In the Navy discipline was more essential than it was in the Army, . . . [although] Discipline did not mean tyranny'. There was a great deal of truth in this. However, there were genuine problems of perception that the Naval Board seemed almost powerless to understand or overcome. As Hyslop notes:

> In Australia, it was difficult to get the rationale of naval discipline across to the public, with the result that there was a suspicion on the part of the public of what they saw as British class-consciousness, while they discounted its value in maintaining good conduct. At the time of Federation in 1901, many people in Australia were disillusioned by British failures in conducting the campaign in South Africa even to the extreme of being prepared to excuse any form of conduct on the part of an Australian and to mistrust any form of controlling action on the part of a British officer. There was a conviction, widely held in Australia but not shared by naval officers, that Australians would not readily fit into the pattern of the strict discipline typical of a British man-of-war.[16]

Dumaresq believed that the maintenance of discipline was directly linked with 'the happiness and contentment of the officers, petty officers and men'.[17] Not surprisingly, Dumaresq considered the Government's reaction to be quite inappropriate, and advised the Government that they would have his resignation if the sailors were released in December. If the men were released, he said, the Government's action was

> fraught with grave danger to the future discipline of the Navies of the Empire and particularly to that of a Commonwealth which is already in an acutely adverse strategical position accentuated by social tendencies and political temptations highly adverse to discipline.

True to his word, Dumaresq submitted his resignation on 19 December. Grant did likewise. As the senior naval officer in Australia, Grant's controversial decision was discussed by the Minister for the Navy and the Naval Board. On 17 December the Prime Minister asked Grant to withdraw his resignation. Instead, Grant re-submitted it on 21 December. It was only withdrawn on

16 February 1920 after the Minister promised Grant that his views would be taken into account in all future representations with the Admiralty and the Commonwealth Government. However, the damage had been done. The Government agreed to a general notice being issued throughout the Australian Fleet in 1920 stressing the Government's deep regret at the defiance of authority which had marked *Australia*'s return home and affirming that in future it would 'fully support all just and proper actions taken by the constituted authorities to maintain the discipline of the Fleet'.[18] As historian Neil Primrose explains, 'this was the only occasion in the history of the RAN in which Flag Officers submitted their resignations on a matter of principle'.[19]

Dumaresq was a man of firm but not unrelenting principle, as his December 1920 report into the troubles on board *Fantome* revealed (see page 94). While he accepted that those in *Fantome* had reasonable grounds for complaint given the sloop's obvious inadequacies, no such mitigation existed in relation to the Flagship in 1919. Despite the personal wishes of some among the ship's company, it was necessary for *Australia* to resume operations to avoid the appearance that 'the ship's company . . . have succeeded in stopping a programme and obtaining a return to Sydney'.[20] Such an action was 'very important for general discipline in ships of the RN and RAN'. The hard line taken by Dumaresq and Cumberlege would set the tone for official responses to mess-deck dissatisfaction in the coming decades.

Nevertheless, much was learned from the mutiny in HMAS *Australia*. The Commonwealth Government wanted to avoid any repetition of the unfortunate incident. While Australian legislators were keen to amend those sections of the *Naval Defence Act* which incorporated the NDA into Australian law, the British officers then commanding the RAN consistently alleged that a different disciplinary code would 'render cooperation and interchange with the Royal Navy almost impossible'.[21] Although this was an exaggeration their veiled threat served to strangle debate on the need for legislative reform. If anything, Australia and the RAN were more closely tied than ever to Britain and the Royal Navy as a consequence of the Great War. This is evident from a comment made by the Minister for the Navy, Sir Joseph Cook, in December 1918:

> The war has shown us that every part of the Empire can make an effective contribution to the common cause of Empire defence. Australia counts herself fortunate that she was able to contribute in the great war by both sea and by land. The RAN has been working in and with the Royal Navy. During the war it has therefore been relatively easy to work to a single standard. It is fundamental to the idea of Empire naval defence that there should be a complete standardisation of personnel and ships and equipment and that this should be to the level of the best. Only the best is good enough for any navy in the British Empire.[22]

He went on to announce that Admiral Sir John Jellicoe, former First Sea Lord at the Admiralty, would be undertaking a mission to Australia to advise on post-war naval defence requirements. However, the *Australia* mutiny provided ample evidence that reform of the letter and operation of the disciplinary code was urgently required. The challenge for the Australian Government was the development of legislation which both reflected Australian social realities and preserved the nation's vital link with the Royal Navy.

8

The turbulent twenties

The period after the Great War was marked by widespread political instability that caused unrest in many navies around the world. The Royal Navy experienced several mutinies in the first decade of peace. The first was in the cruiser HMS *Vindictive*, which was deployed for operations against the Bolsheviks in June 1919. The ship was overcrowded with extra personnel embarked to replace men in ships already serving in the Baltic. Over 1000 men were crammed into a ship designed to accommodate 700. The ship was delayed in reaching its destination after suffering a grounding and persistent heavy weather. While the ship was in port sheltering from a storm, a group of stokers was caught interfering with the ship's equipment in an attempt to disable the propulsion system. An officer dispersed the group although two of their number were subsequently charged and convicted of mutiny.

There were continuing problems related to the RN's anti-Bolshevik operations. Most sailors believed they had accepted their fair share of hardship between 1914 and 1918 and were dissatisfied with the prospect of continuing warfare in the frigid northern latitudes in a confused political conflict. In the cruiser HMS *Delhi*, during October 1919, a group of reluctant sailors locked themselves in their mess decks. Their actions resulted in convictions for 'joining a mutinous assembly'. When the destroyers *Velox*, *Versatile* and *Wryneck* were ordered to the Baltic, more than 100 sailors deserted, while another 50 were prepared to march on the Admiralty in London. They were arrested by police. Ten were imprisoned and dismissed from the service after being found guilty of mutiny.[1]

The navies of other countries saw more serious incidents than those involving the British sailors. There was a mutiny in the French Navy during 1919. In April of that year, the battleship *France* had been away from its home port for eighteen months. The ship's company was disaffected, disillusioned and susceptible to influence from political agitators. While off the Crimean port of Sevastopol, 400 sailors refused orders to coal ship and raised the red flag of revolution. A group went ashore to join a political demonstration. Six men were killed when Greek soldiers, commanded by a French officer, restored order. Although 23 men were convicted of mutiny, the French public was tired of military conflict and less than enthusiastic about the maintenance of naval discipline. This climate ensured the men received short jail terms instead of the threatened death penalty.

Several years later there was a mutiny in the Brazilian Navy involving the battleship *Sao Paulo*. The *Sao Paulo* mutiny was unique in that it was not driven by discontent among ordinary sailors but by a sense of revolutionary fervour among a small group of junior officers.[2] On 4 November 1924, when the captain and most of the senior officers were ashore, six young lieutenants seized command of *Sao Paulo* and hoisted a red flag. After encountering some difficulty firing-up the ship's main engines, the would-be revolutionaries sailed from the harbour, exchanging fire with shore batteries. The idealistic young officers soon discovered that their dreams of setting a navy-wide revolution in motion were not meeting with the response they expected. Uncertain of what to do, they headed south. In the meantime, the Brazilian Minister of Marine had boarded the *Sao Paulo*'s sister ship, *Minas Geraes*, and set off in pursuit. The episode ended when the *Sao Paulo* entered Uruguayan waters and the mutineers asked for refuge and asylum on the grounds of political persecution, a request granted by the authorities in Montevideo. The six junior officers were joined by another officer and 250 sailors taking the opportunity to land in Uruguay. The remainder of the battleship's complement, numbering around 200, took the ship to sea again to accompany the *Minas Geraes* back home.

By far the most serious post-war naval mutiny was in Russia, where the Bolshevik revolution was yet to run its full course. The chaotic and turbulent conflict in the former Russian Empire continued after the Allies finally withdrew in 1919. Over the winter of 1920–21, the sailors of the Kronstadt soviet who had assisted the Bolsheviks in the early days of the revolution became disillusioned with the Bolshevik cause, convinced that the new regime in Moscow had become tyrannical. Four battleships and some smaller vessels, with around 16 000 sailors, were at this Baltic base. A deputation came from Moscow in an attempt to mollify the sailors but at a rowdy gathering the sailors declared that they would be their own masters. Leon Trotsky, the leading figure in the new government, decided the mutinous sailors needed to be confronted. On 8 March a contingent of 25 000 Soviet troops attacked the base across the Baltic ice. They were met by around 1500 sailors turning the warships' guns against the Red Army. There was little more they could do as the ships were frozen at their anchorages. On 16 March, a second attack was made by a larger number of troops. On this occasion the defenders, with ammunition running low, began to desert their positions. Around 600 mutineers were killed while thousands were captured. A substantial number also escaped across the ice to Finland.

It was against such uncertain political and social backgrounds that all the world's navies attempted to operate in the 1920s.

In the absence of impending war, preserving order and discipline in the RAN was also difficult. What became known as the 'Fremantle incident' (see chapter 7) took place at a time when defence and naval affairs were in the forefront of public attention. Admiral of the Fleet Jellicoe, former First Sea Lord and British commander at the Battle of Jutland, arrived in Australia on 23 June 1919 for discussions on Imperial defence strategies. It was an embarrassment for the Navy, and also for the government, that heated debates concerning naval discipline were taking place at the very time the Australian authorities were planning their long-term role in the naval defence of the British Empire in Asia and the Pacific. The Prime Minister asked Jellicoe for his opinion on the discipline problem and also what he thought of a popular notion that 'Australians were not amenable to the kind of discipline necessary in a naval service'.[3] Jellicoe reported to the Australian government that he did not agree that 'the incident had been caused by Australian independence rebelling against press-gang coercion'.[4] He felt, with some shrewdness, that provided Australian sailors understood the reasons for discipline, and provided that discipline was fairly applied, they would respect it. Later, however, Jellicoe reported to the Admiralty that the disciplinary situation in the Australian fleet was grave. He recommended that the RN send out some of its best officers to bolster the standards of the RAN.

Jellicoe's report reinforced the fears of the Admiralty, which had followed the debates on the *Australia* mutiny in the Commonwealth Parliament with some alarm. Whether these fears were accurate or otherwise, the Admiralty was concerned about the reliability of Australian sailors and their ability to accept naval discipline. Of course, the political fallout from the *Australia* mutiny had harmed relations between the RAN and the Admiralty. The Admiralty did not have full confidence in the RAN, despite the predominance of British officers on the Naval Board, as a partner in Imperial defence strategies.

In Australia, the politicians and the admirals gradually became even more suspicious of each other. For its part, the Naval Board had not been sufficiently aware of the political ramifications of the *Australia* mutiny. What was worse, neither the Government nor the Naval Board seemed to learn from the three mutinies which had already marred the RAN's record. In the course of naval financial planning in the 1920s and 1930s, the politicians were not sufficiently aware of the consequences to the Navy of Depression-driven cost-cutting measures, while the Board was too feeble or perhaps too diplomatic in its response. Retaining old and obsolete ships on the grounds that the Australian Government did not have the funds to replace them meant that sailors endured conditions that could hardly be justified in a peacetime service. The case of HMAS *Geranium* was an example of political ignorance and Naval Board indifference.

HMAS *Geranium* was a small Flower Class sloop of 1250 tons launched in 1915. There were 56 ships in the class. All were named after flowers although *Geranium* was later nicknamed the *'Gerger'* while in Australian service.[5] *Geranium* was one of three vessels deployed by the Royal Navy after the war to clear the minefields laid by the German raider *Wolf*. For these operations, *Geranium* was joined by two other ships of the same class, *Marguerite* and *Mallow*. Sweeping just one mine off the Victorian coast near Cape Everard on 8 September 1919, they achieved minimal results for what was painstaking and dangerous work. The three ships were transferred to the RAN on 18 October 1919. Because the rigs of the minesweepers made them suitable for handling the small boats and gear used in surveying, *Geranium* was assigned to surveying duties in northern Australia. In their favour, the ships of this class were described as 'good sea-boats' although as coal-burning sloops they were unable to exceed a maximum speed of 15 knots.

The reputation for good sea-keeping was taken into account when, like its sister ship *Fantome*, *Geranium* was converted for surveying operations,[6] although, also like *Fantome*, *Geranium* was cramped with the extra equipment and crew needed for the specialised survey work. The conversion was not entirely successful, for while the equipment fitted to the ship was suitable for its assigned duties, *Geranium* itself was never designed for extended cruises in warm climates. Ventilation was poor and the mess decks were crowded. The fact that *Geranium* was a coal-burning vessel meant two extra hardships for the ship's company. First, they would face the frequent and onerous duty of coaling ship in hot weather. And second, the boiler-room staff would have to endure the heat of fireboxes while tropical conditions made temperatures soar.

'All hands to coal ship' was one of the most unpopular orders issued by the sloop's first lieutenant. The work consisted of shovelling coal from hoppers on the quay-side into large sacks which were then carried into the ship and down gangways before being emptied into coal bunkers situated in the crowded corners of the boiler rooms. The weight of the sacks was a nominal hundredweight (around 112 pounds or 50 kilograms). The men in the coaling-ship party had to negotiate narrow gangways and ladders while dodging 80 other men doing the very same thing. *Geranium* carried a maximum 250 tons of coal—the equivalent of 5000 sacks. A rough calculation suggests that if 80 men were carrying sacks of coal while others were filling the sacks, each man would have to make in excess of 60 journeys from quay-side to boiler-room bunkers with a 50-kilogram weight on his shoulders—all in Darwin's tropical heat.

Everyone involved in coaling ship, even the officers supervising, became grimy with soot and dust which made the eyes sting. The black dust gathered in every crevice of the body and as the sweat ran, so the dust irritated and rubbed the flesh raw. Encrusted salt on deck fittings, and salt water, added to the irritation. The men wore sacking flaps to protect their necks and shoulders but the flecks of coal lodged in the coarse weave of the flaps acted like sandpaper. Many men cast them aside and endured the pain of the hard-lumped sacks grinding on their shoulders. The grime from the coal dust could not be washed out for days afterward.

While at sea, even when boilers had to maintain only enough steam for peacetime cruising speed, the heat of the boiler and engine rooms was debilitating to stokers and engineers alike. Not for nothing was the boiler-room staff known as the 'black gang'. They would sweat continually, and this, combined with condensation and the spray of fine engine oil, ensured that the men found it difficult to keep themselves clean.

It was little wonder in these conditions that most sailors preferred to sleep above decks if they could (technically a breach of naval safety regulations). There was limited room even for this relief, however. Crowded as the small ship was with extra hands and the specialists required for surveying duties. *Geranium* was carrying ten officers and 103 other ranks, whereas its designated complement, when it was designed for minesweeping duties in the North Sea, was a total of 77 officers and men—around two-thirds of the number required for surveying.[7] The extra bodies had to be accommodated somewhere, in quarters designed for North Sea cold, not Australia's tropical heat. While conditions on board were barely tolerable, there were opportunities for groups of sailors to go ashore on deserted northern beaches where they could relax around a hastily constructed barbecue. Other opportunities to let off steam arrived when the ship came into harbour to replenish stores. Time in port was brief but the men had the chance to take shore leave. The *Geranium* men became well known in hotels and bars from Broome to Darwin to Torres Strait to Cairns.

From the commencement of its Australian surveying career, *Geranium* had an eventful time on the north and north-west coastline of the continent. In 1920, the ship's company was drafted ashore to help quell the rioting between Japanese and Javanese in Broome. Then there were survey tasks around Bynoe Harbour, Broome and Darwin. In 1921, *Geranium* accompanied a sailing vessel carrying Swedes and Americans from Broome to Wollal to observe a total eclipse of the sun.[8] For the rest of 1922, the ship was involved in lengthy survey deployments, the long weeks away from port eventually affecting the morale of the ship's company. Their pay was not available to them, and even if it had been, there were limited opportunities for leave and the chance to spend it. In the heat of the tropics, fresh food quickly spoiled and the men had to exist on canned food, while the drinking water became putrid. Only the use of chlorine could hide its smell and render it drinkable.

Later that year, the ship returned to cooler climes when assigned to complete survey work off the south-west coast of Tasmania. The months from December to February were not generally suitable for survey operations involving small ships in the northern coastal waters because of the risk of sudden changes in the weather, especially hazardous to men embarked in the survey tender vessels. The bulk of the survey work had to be done by men in the ship's boats or tenders, rowing through coastal waters while depths were measured by a leadline (a lead weight on a marked line cast into the water to measure the depth at regular intervals). Another task was to measure the fall of tide by setting up a pole with measurements and recording the levels periodically. The journey south also provided an opportunity for the ship to undergo refit and for the data collected to be collated and charted by the RAN Survey Service, established in 1921.

In early 1923, *Geranium* was ordered to return north under the command of Commander Harry Bennett RN. Reaching Cairns, *Geranium* took on coal and fresh provisions. On completion of 'store ship', most of the ship's company were granted liberty, another name for shore leave. Not unexpectedly, a number of sailors became drunk. *Geranium*'s second in command was Lieutenant J. P. Dixon RN. As first lieutenant, Dixon was responsible to the captain for the ship's discipline. While the obligatory imposition of punishment was not in itself likely to make an officer popular, Dixon was notably unpopular and thoroughly disliked as a human being. He was described as 'an RN man who insists on discipline and will have things just so. Some of the men do not want things just so'.[9] Considering *Geranium*'s size and the crowded conditions, it may not have been the ideal ship for a strict disciplinarian to exercise his leadership.

In Cairns, Commander Bennett and Lieutenant Dixon went ashore and came across a party of *Geranium* sailors. Under the influence of alcohol and perhaps feeling less restrained because they were ashore, a number of the sailors expressed their opinions of the two officers in somewhat colourful language. Lieutenant Dixon, as was his responsibility, upbraided the men for insolence and disrespect. That done, the respective parties went their way. When Dixon returned to the ship, he discovered that his cabin had been soiled by oily rags and peanut shells. There was no clue as to the identity of the culprits. The next day, the ship's company were ordered to parade and the captain delivered a stern warning about the consequences of indiscipline. It had some effect in that there were no further incidents as the ship continued its journey until, at Bynoe Harbour near Darwin, *Geranium* stopped to embark Rear Admiral Clarkson for the final run to Darwin. That evening, the Admiral had dinner with Commander Bennett in the commanding officer's cabin. Halfway through their dinner, the ship's power supply failed and the lower decks were plunged into gloom. The two senior officers waited in the cabin for power to be restored. This was neither a quick nor an easy job.

On the other side of the cabin door, they heard several sailors begin singing. The words of one song penetrated the wooden door: 'Oh my, I don't want to die—Iiieee want to go home!'[10] The

Captain ordered the men to disperse. They did not. Embarrassingly, the response was yet another song. Technically it was a mutiny, as the men acted together in refusing the direct order to discontinue singing. The difficulty, of course, lay in identifying the sailors in the darkened ship. The noise brought some of the ship's petty officers to the scene who, on the captain's orders, restored some order amid the confusion of the mess decks. Commander Bennett was clearly concerned about the discipline of his men. Fearing more serious events he ordered the petty officers to secure the ship's arms.

Geranium had been armed with two four-inch guns for war service but these had been removed in the refit for survey duties. The sloop still carried a number of small arms and rifles for ceremonial use and for shooting sharks which threatened surveying operations. The firearms were removed from the gunner's store and taken to the captain's cabin. When electricity was restored a semblance of discipline returned. The ship arrived in Darwin the next morning after a tense night. Commander Bennett was unable to lay any charges as no-one had been clearly identified in the dark, chaotic and crowded conditions below decks. To defuse the situation, a section of the ship's company was granted shore leave. One of the men again fell victim to insobriety and refused to return to *Geranium*, instead going on board the steamship *Montoro* which maintained a regular Darwin—Sydney service, and locking himself in a cabin. When *Montoro*'s crew discovered the absconding sailor, he refused to leave, adamant that he wanted to stay on board and go back to Sydney. It took two hours to persuade him to vacate the cabin and return to his own ship.

Despite the reluctant attitude of the ship's company, *Geranium* sailed from Darwin for survey duties in the Gulf of Carpentaria. The work had an early setback when a survey team went ashore on the Sir Edward Pellew Islands and became lost in mangroves. It took them a full day to find their way back to the ship. A little more than a week later, the ship had completed its day's work and prepared to anchor near Vanderlin Island. The captain was asked if soundings should be taken as *Geranium* neared the island. He said it was unnecessary as the ship had been in the area before. An able seaman on watch on the bridge explained what followed:

> The Captain then told me, 'Go aft and tell Number One we will be anchoring in five minutes'. So I left the bridge and made my way along the boat deck and down the ladder to the quarterdeck

and just as I said, 'Compliments of the Captain, Number One: we are going to anchor in five minutes', when all of a sudden we hit this reef. She rolled to starboard then to port and straightened up with her snout in the air and her stern partly submerged. Number One said, 'Fowler, I think we are well and truly bloody anchored'.[11]

Geranium had struck an uncharted reef and the ship's company had to take desperate measures to prevent the vessel sinking. The pumps were put to work and all heavy gear that could be moved was jettisoned. Two anchors were manhandled into the survey tenders, taken out and dropped some distance from *Geranium* to enable the winches to pull the ship off the reef. One anchor cable parted under the strain but fortunately the other held and the ship slid off the reef. *Geranium* was leaking badly through several holes the reef had punched in the hull plates. These were hastily plugged with the cement that was carried for the purpose of making survey markers.

The ship slowly got under way and made a safe though slow passage to Thursday Island where the temporary repairs were strengthened. *Geranium* limped down the coast to Sydney and went into dry dock for permanent repairs. When the work was completed, *Geranium* sailed under a new captain, Lieutenant Commander Vaughan Lewis, and commenced surveying off the Barrier Reef. On 12 October 1923, *Geranium* assisted *Montoro* when the steamship ran aground on Young Reef. The officers and ship's company were commended by the Naval Board for 'the promtitude [sic] and sailorlike manner in which the operations were carried out'.[12]

Geranium grounded again in 1924 while working in the McArthur River, once again needing extensive repairs. But all was not entirely well when the repairs were completed. The men complained of not receiving their pay regularly, in addition to a number of other grumbles about conditions on board. In the course of the survey work that followed, some of the sailors negligently lost valuable equipment overboard, and the Naval Board found cause to censure *Geranium*'s captain. Later, perhaps anxious to ensure that the ship's company had the benefit of firm direction, the Naval Board removed Lieutenant Commander Lewis and replaced him with a more experienced officer. Acting Commander K. McKenzie showed a firm hand immediately upon joining the ship, sending a number of the more fractious sailors ashore in Darwin and directing that they be put on board the old auxiliary steamer *Biloela*, returning to Sydney for scrapping. For the other sailors he arranged payment of outstanding pay and also seven days extra leave on account of their service in isolated areas of the tropics.[13]

Commander McKenzie was a good leader and surveyor. Morale in *Geranium* recovered almost instantaneously. The ship proceeded to complete further survey tasks and was the first survey vessel in Australia to conduct surveys assisted by an aircraft, a Fairey IIID float plane. In May 1927, *Geranium* featured in another sea rescue, on this occasion coming to the aid of the passenger steamer *Tasman* which struck a reef off Clarke Island. Shortly afterwards, *Geranium* was decommissioned, an eventful life finally over. *Geranium* was broken up at Cockatoo Island in 1932 and the stripped hulk sunk off Sydney Heads on 24 April 1935.

Even before the collapse of the New York stock market and the onset of the Great Depression in October 1929, the decade after peace was concluded at Versailles had not been happy for the RAN. In addition to a shortage of trained personnel, allocations from the Commonwealth had declined to the extent that the Navy was reduced to four operational warships and a mere 3200 men. Most of those remaining were pleased to have employment, although they appeared to lack the means of opposing a succession of government decisions, cutting the Navy's budget and their allowances in the cause of financial restraint. Another potential crisis was in the making. History had already shown that sailors were rarely passive when they felt exploited by parsimonious or uncaring governments.

9

Depression disputes

The Great Depression ensured the continuation of the 1920s dissatisfaction and unrest in many navies into the 1930s. Indeed, it was impossible for navies to be shielded from political instability and agitation while the financial stringencies of the Depression kept most ships in harbour. The number of commissioned officers in the RAN was reduced by 26 per cent between 1929 and 1932. The number of sailors shed by the Navy was even greater—around 40 per cent. Many of the sailors were discharged 'Services No Longer Required'. This meant the men forfeited their deferred pay, the contemporary equivalent of superannuation.[1] There were regular complaints about food among those kept on. In ships without refrigeration fresh food could only be obtained while in port. And the curse of dry stores—weevils—were just as much a problem for sailors of the 1930s as they had been for sailors a century before. Tuberculosis was also common. A fleet general signal in 1932 referred to its spread due to crowded accommodation and poor ventilation and humidity.[2] Not all was well in either the RAN or in the ships of Australia's neighbours.

The new decade opened with a mutiny on the eastern shores of the Pacific. The flagship of the Chilean Navy was the modern British-built battleship *Almirante Latorre*. Following a refit in Britain, during which time authorities claimed the ship's company was 'infected' with Communism, the ship was lying off the port of Coquimbo. On 31 August 1931, while many of the officers and men were ashore, a group led by the petty officers took over not only the battleship but the elderly armoured cruiser *General O'Higgins* as well. There was some minor violence but no deaths. The mutiny spread to several destroyers and also to the naval base of Talcahuano. It was resolved in a way that reflected the changing nature of warfare—aircraft threatened and then bombed the ships into submission, fortunately without any casualties in the ships or in the planes, some of which were hit by anti-aircraft fire from *Almirante Latorre*. The ringleaders of the mutiny, arrested and sentenced to death, received a reprieve when a change of government brought a more liberal regime to power.

At the same time that the Chilean mutiny was being reported in British newspapers, Britain's own fleet had erupted in the most extensive mutiny seen in the Royal Navy since the uprisings at Spithead and The Nore in 1797. The trouble began at a fleet anchorage near the town of Invergordon in Scotland. The cause, once again, was pay, the government under economic pressure having decided to cut the pay of all service personnel. The decision reached the 12 000 sailors of the Atlantic Fleet through newspaper reports. Three hundred sailors gathered in the naval canteen in the small town to discuss their situation. More sailors joined them in the course of the meeting and similar gatherings were held on board ships in the fleet, notably the battleships *Nelson* and *Valiant* and the battle cruiser *Repulse*. The men resolved that no ship would go to sea until the government reviewed its decision.

The next morning, however, *Repulse* proceeded to sea as usual. *Nelson* was slow to follow. The captain cleared the lower deck and addressed the ship's company. Poorly chosen words about their wives being able to take in washing to support their families infuriated the men. The captain retreated to his cabin and the ship was immobilised. From the cruiser *Norfolk* loud cheering could be heard. The same sound was repeated from one ship to another. In some ships the strategy was to close the hatches leading to the forecastle so that anchors could not be raised. In *Valiant*, a crowd of sailors gathered on the foredeck and sat down on the cables so the ship could not raise its anchors.

By mid morning, *Repulse* had returned to the anchorage and Rear Admiral Wilfred Tomkinson, temporarily commanding the Atlantic Fleet,[3] informed the Admiralty that discipline could not be restored without a revision of the new pay scales. The Admiralty prevaricated. Their Lordships promised only to review cases of hardship. This was not enough to satisfy the men. Hardliners in the government, including Mr J. Thomas, the Secretary for the Dominions, who apparently saw in the protesting sailors images of Kiel and Kronstadt, wanted strong and immediate action taken to put down the 'sailors' soviets'. Although the sailors were well-behaved, Admiral Tomkinson was afraid that precipitate action would result in the situation getting out of control. The Admiralty ordered the ships to return to their home ports where it was hoped they could deal with the mutinous ships' companies separately. The men reluctantly returned to their duties and the ships proceeded to sea. In *Valiant*, the captain threatened to have the detachment of Royal Marines fire on a group of sailors still clustered on the foredeck.

While the Atlantic Fleet was being dispersed, political events were overwhelming the Chancellor of the Exchequer, Austen Chamberlain. The value of the pound had crashed when news of the mutiny reached the newspapers. Political pressure prevented the Admiralty taking any harsh disciplinary measures with the mutineers. The government reviewed its pay decision and reduced the extent of the pay cuts. Although the sailors accepted this compromise, discontent remained. No mutineer was punished but Admiral Tomkinson was relieved of his post some five months later.

While the incident in South America had hardly affected naval thinking in Australia, the events at Invergordon alarmed the Naval Board and made senior officers attentive to any suggestion of rebellion on the lower decks. As in Britain, political decisions had created a climate of dissatisfaction but wherever it became obvious, naval administrators and commanders either denied there was a problem or censured those involved. The RAN needed a thoroughgoing audit of the effects of expenditure reductions on its operating capacity and the well-being of its personnel. This was unlikely to take place.

While the strategic situation was benign, the Commonwealth Government reduced defence expenditure to a level which was certainly inadequate for operations at even the lowest contingency levels. In 1927–28, defence spending was 1.04 per cent of national income. This figure dropped to 0.6 per cent in 1932–33, rising to 1.09 per cent in 1936–37. Although this level of spending was higher than in the other Commonwealth Dominions, it was less than half that of Britain, expressed in terms of expenditure per head of population.[4] It was not until the years following the Great Depression, and in the wake of Japanese aggression in Manchuria and Northern China, that Australia increased its defence spending, a move welcomed in London.

Despite relinquishing operational control over the RAN during World War I, and the legacy of the 1919 *Australia* mutiny the Admiralty continued to exert considerable influence over naval affairs in Australia. As Macandie observes, the Royal Navy was 'the fount of advice, the provider of senior personnel and a wide range of services for the Australian Navy, and the controlling authority for Australia's ultimate naval bastion'. For its part, the Royal Navy encouraged the Dominions to feel dependent on Britain for their naval defence as the Admiralty strengthened its centralising policy. While Australia was a loyal member of the Empire, the Admiralty wanted to ensure it retained maximum peacetime control over the Dominion navies which would come under its control in wartime. In his pioneering study of Australian naval administration, Hyslop notes: 'The Admiralty influence was further strengthened by the existence in Australia of a Navy Office moulded on Admiralty traditions and methods, and by its own undoubted effectiveness as an administrative and political organisation'.[5]

There was no major change in operational policy after 1919. The pattern of Fleet deployments throughout the 1920s and 1930s reinforced the exclusiveness of Australia's Imperial relationship. The need for such close links with the Royal Navy was formally outlined in a memorandum from the Secretary of the Naval Board to the Minister for Defence in 1936. It pointed out that the RAN had achieved its operational efficiency through a close relationship with the Royal Navy, particularly in the areas of training, naval materiel—construction, acquisition and supply, and intelligence. In considering personnel the Secretary said the Admiralty had made an undertaking

> to consider Australian naval officers for appointment in due course on their merit, to the highest commands in the Empire Navy. This undertaking is made practicable only because the training of RAN officers is identical with that in the Royal Navy and it is essential, in order that this opportunity shall remain open to Australian officers, that full co-operation between the two Navies is maintained and that qualifications for promotion, including seniority, should continue, as at present, to be the same in each Service.[6]

That such an understanding was desperately needed is apparent from a scathing article published in 1939 by journalist Tyler Dennet in the American periodical, *Foreign Affairs*: 'For many years New Zealand and Australia have resembled the radical sons of wealthy parents. In both countries one heard the sort of petulant expressions that are associated with children who have been overindulged'.[7] He criticised those Australians 'who habitually sneer at British Imperialism but they demanded the protection of the British Navy both for themselves and their mandated territories'[8] but noted that: 'Persons in government positions in Australia and New Zealand have been careful to refrain from any statements which would appear to imply that the US has made any commitments in the Pacific'.[9]

This careful approach to Britain was evident in the speech made to Parliament by the Defence Minister, Brigadier Geoffrey Street, in 1937: 'The people of Australia have the fullest appreciation that British seapower is the essential basis of the security of the Empire . . . If Britain were confronted with an alliance, there is no reason to believe that she would lack powerful allies'.[10]

Nevertheless, in early 1939 Britain asked the United States to transfer quietly a fleet from the Pacific to the Atlantic.[11] This is the background against which a number of small dramas would be played out.

HMAS *PENGUIN*, OCTOBER 1932

Throughout 1931 and 1932 there were signs of heightening unrest on the lower decks of RAN ships, including incidents of sabotage in a number of vessels. The engines of the seaplane carrier HMAS *Albatross* were damaged in November 1931, and again in September 1932. Naval authorities put these problems down to the re-entry into the Navy of men 'whose associations have tended to give them extreme views'.[12] In other words, it was not the fault of the Navy or its leadership but of regrettable influences exerted by people such as Communists in the outside world. But the problem would not go away if it was simply ignored.

In 1929 the basic wage of an able seaman was cut from seven shillings per day to five shillings and eightpence.[13] At the same time, the Naval Board secured exemptions for officers from various cost-cutting measures, although an offset was required in the form of reduced allowances, with increased workloads demanded elsewhere. While a greater proportion of sailors than officers was retrenched during the Depression, curiously the number of flag officers increased in the same period. This prompted a parliamentarian to comment that in 1930 the Navy had more admirals for four commissioned ships than it had in 1920 when the RAN operated 30 vessels.[14]

The quality of leadership also led to unrest. In the peacetime Navy, officers sometimes issued orders just to keep the lower deck busy, rather than to advance their skills or abilities. Some of the odder exercises have been noted by Spurling:

One of the most ridiculous instructions was, 'Officers' cook to flagship with fried egg', which involved an egg being fried, then taken in the pan by boat to the flagship where it was inspected by the Admiral. One of the cruelest orders was, 'Raise the anchor by deck tackle'. One of the most peculiar orders, 'Officers' stewards to Garden Island to bring back ten cats'. The cats were wild and difficult to capture. The stewards returned with four cats, sporting severe scratches and torn clothes.[15]

In October 1932 there was a mutiny at HMAS *Penguin*, a depot ship permanently based at Sydney. There are no official reports concerning the event because the commanding officer was sympathetic to the complaints of his men and had agreed to convey their grievances to the Naval Board after giving an assurance that he would not lay charges against them. He was criticised by the Naval Board for his generous attitude, the Board considering that the men's grievances were 'subversive of discipline'. The matters at issue were not even considered.[16]

Evidence of trouble comes from Welfare Committee requests made to *Penguin*'s commanding officer from the early 1930s. Essentially, the sailors believed they had no proper avenue for airing their grievances. The principal complaint was that their pay and conditions had been eroded. They asserted that the Naval Board 'have shown that they are apparently unable to ensure that members of the Lower Deck shall receive humanitarian treatment'.[17] The men had no-one to speak on their behalf or to embrace their cause. Consequently, their pay had, by default, been 'reduced beyond that required for bare necessities'.[18]

It was no wonder that the sailors' welfare committee in *Penguin* complained that 'those in authority' were 'dictators' who cut the 'sustenance and living' of members of the naval service.[19] It is perhaps also no wonder that the Naval Board refused to consider the men's complaints and instead chose to admonish their commanding officer. The Chief of Naval Staff expressed regret that the Board could not apply punishment to the men because the officer had given his word that they would not be punished and his word had to be respected.

The details of the mutiny at *Penguin* are sketchy because of the lack of official reports. Technically there was a mutiny, as the sailors refused to carry out an order, but on the basis of their commanding officer's undertaking to convey a document outlining their grievances, they returned to duty. The Naval Board admitted: 'In regard to the letter from the Captain Superintendent, Sydney, there is no doubt that an act of mutiny occurred', and it had been the duty of *Penguin*'s commanding officer to take disciplinary action 'as required by the *Naval Discipline Act*'.[20] Moreover, the Board wanted to make it very clear that the 'Government is determined to dispense with the services of any men who refuse duty'.[21]

What the reaction of the *Penguin* sailors was when they were informed that the Board would not consider their complaints has not been recorded. The Board did, however, recognise that ordinary sailors were disadvantaged by pay cuts and it resolved to approach the government over the need for 'early amelioration of the men's financial condition'.[22] It is evident, however, that there was continuing unrest on the lower decks of Australian warships. This untreated anxiety resulted in three more mutinies in close succession.

PRINCE'S PIER, NOVEMBER 1932

The events on Prince's Pier, Melbourne, during November 1932 were, in the words of one politician, 'a dastardly plot to create disaffection'. In the opinion of the *Age* newspaper, they were 'an attempt to incite . . . mutinous conduct'. The judgment of the Fleet Commander was quite different. The reports were all a 'damnable lie' concerning the 'loyalty of the Australian Navy men to the great British tradition'.[23]

The facts of the case were straightforward. In November 1932, the new County Class cruisers *Canberra* and *Australia* (flying the flag of the Fleet Commander, Rear Admiral G. Francis Hyde RAN), together with the seaplane carrier *Albatross* (which had had the problems with engine sabotage noted earlier) and the destroyer *Tattoo*, undertook a training cruise to the Bass Strait area. There was dissatisfaction among the sailors concerning rumours of a further pay cut on top of the reduction made three years before. On 1 November sailors serving in units of the New Zealand Squadron had their pay reduced by 10 per cent. This was reported in Australian newspapers on 3 November. Sir George Pearce, the Minister for Defence in the United Australia Party Government, told Federal Parliament that it was inaccurate to say that sailors 'had issued an ultimatum to the Government'[24] concerning reductions in armed forces pay. It was a 'gross reflection on the men of the Navy to suggest that insubordination existed among them'. It was all 'propaganda in the newspaper [sic] . . .'[25]

At the time, the big news story was the 'Emu War' in Western Australia. A Major Meredith had claimed that the most cost-effective way of eliminating the birds was with machine guns using obsolete ammunition—at a cost of only £50 for 10 000 rounds! Correspondents reported that the birds 'beat a retreat' under withering fire from Lewis guns mounted on the backs of trucks.[26] The newspapers did not necessarily seem to be involved in beating up any issue concerning naval pay, and there were only brief reports when the Australian Squadron docked in Melbourne on Tuesday, 8 November 1932. The next day, however, there were more extensive reports that 200 men 'had walked off the ships in Melbourne and after refusing duty had carried a resolution to leave their case in the hands of the Naval Board'.[27] A subsequent newspaper article which reported and commented on the affair was to result in Australia's only trial of a civilian on a charge of inciting a mutiny.

Most reports of the incident confirmed that a large number of men did congregate on Prince's Pier and express their concerns about wage reductions. There were also misgivings about the operation of lower-deck welfare committees, which were the official avenues of complaint to senior officers. It also seems that the sailors sought some advice from union movements on the best way to advance their cause. However, in the words of the Leader of the Government in the Senate, when the ships were made open to the public they were boarded by Communists 'directing the conspiracy' and distributing material calling on the sailors to organise and 'join hands in a movement to bring about a mutiny'.[28] Whether or not this was a fair version of events is largely immaterial. A printed pamphlet was sent to the Minister of Defence which stated that if the sailors' demands were not met, 'armed force might be used'. On the pamphlet's cover was a depiction of bluejackets with rifles and bayonets with a caption suggesting mutiny. There were telephone calls to newspaper offices warning that the Squadron would not sail at all. A newspaper editorial argued that the trouble had come about due to the actions of 'subversive elements having no association with the Navy' who were 'dangerous enemies of society'.[29]

Admiral Hyde was invited to make a speech at a welcoming dinner hosted by the Lord Mayor of Melbourne at the Town Hall. He was cheered when he declared that the assembly on Prince's Pier had never happened at all. He made a 'vigorous defence of the loyalty' of the sailors and stated that the rumours of dissatisfaction had only come about when the men had 'been flooded with seditious literature from Communist Headquarters'.[30] In the 1930s, Communism was a bogey to the Navy, which kept an official list of sailors who had 'Communist tendencies'. The promotion prospects of those on the list were reduced while those who attempted to re-enlist were refused employment.[31]

On 10 November the Squadron sailed from Melbourne without incident and with 'customary naval alertness'. There was 'not the least sign of disaffection'.[32] According to Admiral Hyde, of the 2000 men posted to the four ships only one did not report for duty.

What actually happened on Prince's Pier? There *was* a meeting of sailors and they *were* disaffected, despite the claims of their Admiral and politicians. There was

> evident discontent . . . due to the delay in dealing with properly presented complaints and to a suspicion that both sympathy and understanding were lacking at headquarters [because naval] 'administration . . . [was] woodenly unresponsive and exasperatingly slow'.[33]

One report claimed the number of sailors at the meeting may have reached 200. Other accounts mentioned a 'small portion of the personnel'. The meeting was held to discuss common problems, with Communist subversion playing no great part although the preparation of a printed pamphlet suggests some premeditation.

It is unclear whether the men in the gathering were on duty and, therefore, actively refusing duty, or proceeding on leave and threatening to refuse duty on their return. The first possibility clearly constituted a mutiny. In the latter case, their action was still an offence under the *Naval Discipline Act* as a mutiny had been proposed. What is certain is that as the ships sailed, there remained considerable unrest despite there being 'not the least sign of disaffection'. A crisis may have been averted by the mere discussion of grievances branded as mutiny by self-interested officials, but the underlying problems remained.

With the popular press interested in the Navy's problems, the actions of outsiders in encouraging mutiny, an offence under the *Crimes Act*, was tested in the courts as an outcome of two odd affairs in 1932 that came about after the agitation at Prince's Pier. *Smith's Weekly* ran a number of articles in the latter part of 1932 that incurred the displeasure of the Naval Board, and the Board considered legal action against the paper.[34] This did not eventuate. In November, at the time the fleet was in Melbourne, the *Truth* newspaper ran an article that alleged there was widespread insubordination among ordinary sailors in the RAN. This was publicity the Navy did not need as it attempted to regain the confidence of the lower deck and the community. This time the Naval Board took decisive action. The publisher of *Truth* was charged with the crime of inciting mutiny and the case went to trial. Sir George Pearce, the Minister for Defence, announced that 'sensational and inaccurate reports of disaffection in the Australian Navy' which had been published in *Truth* were 'calculated to create insubordination'. He had the matter referred to the Commonwealth Attorney General for consideration as to whether there should be a prosecution. Sir George conceded that 'naturally the reductions in salary made recently by the government and formerly by the Scullin government were not popular' but in his view, it was 'a gross reflection of the personnel of the Australian Navy to suggest that insubordination arose from this'.

The *Canberra Times* carried an article on the matter on 10 November, the same day the ships left Melbourne without incident, which reported comments by the Minister enlarging upon his earlier announcement. He argued that there had been a movement 'obviously and cunningly directed to use the grievances of ratings as a means to seduce the men of the fleet, create disaffection and bring about an organised strike or mutiny'. He went on to note that it was a 'sinister purpose' based on 'lying statements'. The Government believed that 'knowledge should be spread of this dastardly plot to sow the seeds of mutiny'. The Attorney General had charges laid the following day. William Payne, *Truth*'s publisher, was charged with the offence 'that by means of an article headed "Navy Issues Strike Ultimatum", Payne knowingly attempted to invite the lower deck ratings of HMA Ships *Canberra, Australia, Albatross* and *Tattoo* and other ships of the RAN to commit an act of mutiny'. The penalty provided under the *Crimes Act* for this offence was imprisonment for life. Payne was taken into custody and his case was heard before Mr Justice Lowe in Melbourne on 23 November.

In his opening address the prosecutor, Leo Cussen, called the article in *Truth* 'an insidious attempt to incite mutiny in His Majesty's Navy' and argued that the attempt 'would have been mischievous if not for the fact the Navy remained loyal'. The essential issue in the charge, according to Cussen, was that 'any person who recklessly publishes matter of this description is guilty of an offence' whether the matter was true or not. Mr Gorman KC, acting for the defence, argued that the matter was one of news or comment on news and was, therefore, legitimate content. He based his case on whether in fact there had been an ultimatum delivered to the naval authorities concerning sailors' grievances. If there had been an ultimatum and it was delivered, the article was fair comment and the prosecution's case collapsed.

Sir George Pearce was called to give evidence. He denied there had been any ultimatum, before admitting that 'cabinet was concerned about the situation of lower deck ratings' and had 'taken steps to ameliorate their conditions'. He went on to deny all knowledge of any official reports relating to incidents at Prince's Pier. The Minister then denied knowledge of another matter that defence counsel raised. Gorman asked: 'As head of the Navy, you surely received a report of certain happenings on the *Australia* when she was coming down from the Solomons?'

The precise nature of the matters to which Gorman referred remain a mystery as the ship's formal 'Report of Proceedings' for the period does not mention anything of note. When Admiral Hyde entered the witness box, he was asked a similar question. He explained that he had not received an official report but had heard about 'allegations of certain happenings'. Later in the cross-examination, he denied knowing 'that the captain of *Australia* had addressed the crew about going on with their grievances sanely'. Mr George Macandie, Secretary to the Naval Board, also testified. He said that the Board had not considered any ultimatum but added that 'no inquiry was made whether such a document had come before the Board'.

Mr Justice Lowe summarised the case for the jury. He offered a thumbnail definition of mutiny. 'Mutiny', said the judge, was a decision by sailors 'not to man the ships, not to take them to sea or to refuse any lawful command by their officers'. In order for William Payne to be guilty of incitement to mutiny, the jury had to consider whether there was 'insidious suggestion' in the article. One other matter was raised by the judge. He asserted that incitement to mutiny had nothing to do with liberty of the press, as the Commonwealth Parliament had overruled that defence when it made incitement to mutiny an offence under the *Crimes Act*. After the judge's address, the jury retired at 11.17pm. They returned with a 'Not Guilty' verdict at 11.35pm. Payne was discharged.

Although the *Truth* case has been the only instance of a civilian being tried for incitement to mutiny, similar incidents have also resulted in legal proceedings. One example from the same period concerned one Ronald Gorman (no relation to Mr Gorman KC who defended the publisher of *Truth*), who was charged with 'having attempted to seduce Kenneth Seymour, serving in the King's forces, from his duty and allegiance'. Gorman's crime consisted of having handed out pacifist leaflets outside a drill hall in the Sydney suburb of Hurstville. In his case, the jury failed to agree on a verdict and Gorman was not retried.

DE ZEVEN PROVINCIEN, 1933

One of Australia's closest neighbours the Netherlands East Indies (now Indonesia) faced a naval mutiny early in 1933. Senior Dutch naval authorities attributed the mutiny to the influence and example of Australian sailors during 1932, and to clear public support for the Dutch mutineers within Australia. At the height of the mutiny, there were calls for the mutineers to be granted asylum in Australia. This outraged the Dutch government and put the Commonwealth in a difficult position. The crisis began in *De Zeven Provincien* (*Seven Provinces*), a very old battleship with a mixed complement of 450 Dutch and Javanese sailors. Built in 1909, it had long since become obsolete and been allocated to service in the Dutch colonies.

Throughout the Dutch naval squadron based in the Netherlands East Indies, there had been unrest over recent cost-cutting measures which paralleled the situation in Australia. A 10 per cent reduction in sailors' pay in 1932 was followed by a 14 per cent reduction from 1 February 1933, in place of a scheduled 17 per cent increase. Throughout the previous month there had been disturbances at Surabaya, the main Dutch naval base. Equipment was sabotaged and there were instances of individuals refusing duty. An unofficial navy trade union, the '*Marine-bonden*', was formed by a group of disaffected sailors. The formation of the quasi-union and the nature of the protests indicates clearly that the disaffection was caused by the pay disputes and was not an orchestrated rejection of naval authority. The flashpoint was an incident in the cruiser *Java* on 30 January 1933 when a number of men (described as 'corporals', the equivalent of petty officers) refused to attend their place of duty at 6.30am. The ship was boarded by marines and 40 European and 24 Indonesian sailors were arrested and charged with mutiny. (The official records of the time refer to the Indonesians as 'native' sailors. They were mainly Javanese. The word 'Indonesian' is used here in preference to 'native'.) Sailors in the destroyer *Piet Hein* also refused duty and several were arrested. One of those charged was later acquitted of mutiny through a technicality that could also have been applied to other mutinies. The man's lawyer argued successfully that a whistle or bosun's call being sounded did not constitute an order in the usual sense of the term.

News of these events reached *De Zeven Provincien* when it was off Nias Island, Sumatra. From later official accounts, the men had also heard of and discussed the mutinous incidents which had just taken place in the RAN. The captain of the battleship was warned that the men were considering a mutiny. Foolishly he dismissed the warnings and took no special precautions when he went ashore to socialise on Saturday, 4 February. Dissidents in the battleship, mainly Javanese sailors, apparently led by a quartermaster named Paradja, decided to take action while the captain was absent. They passed out the ship's small arms and surrounded nine junior officers on the bridge. Some other officers wanted to attack the mutineers but the sailors warned that they would kill their captive officers if there was any violence towards them. The first lieutenant escaped on a raft and informed the captain ashore that he was no longer in control of his vessel.

The mutineers decided to head for Surabaya and demand restoration of their pay. They sent a message to the authorities that their actions were in response to 'unjust reductions' in pay and the imprisonment of a number of ratings who had protested over the reduction. The captain commandeered a small steamer and set off in pursuit. For four days the battleship and the steamer cruised south-east along the coast of Sumatra. The mutinous warship maintained a speed of around eight knots, its economical cruising speed, and made no attempt to outrun the pursuing steamer. As *De Zeven Provincien* had a range of over 5000 miles (8300 kilometres) at this speed, there remains the possibility that the mutineers intended steaming to Australia.

The mutiny was well-reported in Australian newspapers (for example the *Sydney Morning Herald*, from 7 February to 11 February 1933). It was the topic of heated debate in Sydney's Domain on Sunday, 5 February, when *De Zeven Provincien* was still in the mutineers' control. The crowd in the Domain 'passed' a resolution calling on the Dutch government not to use force and imploring the Australian government to give the mutineers asylum. The League Against Imperialism (Sydney District Committee) wrote to the Australian Prime Minister calling for asylum to be offered to the mutineers and for 'the right for Australian workers in the Australian Navy to freely fraternise with the Dutch navy strikers'. Their call was echoed by the Anti-Imperialist League of South Australia.

The small steamer shadowing the battleship made continual broadcasts of its position. On 7 February, the cruiser *Java* and the destroyers *Piet Hein* and *Evertsen* made contact and fell in behind *De Zeven Provincien*, well beyond range of its eleven-inch guns. The cruiser and its consorts made no attempt to attack the battleship. This may have been because senior officers were uncertain of the temper of their own men, given that so many had recently mutinied. It may also have been a tactical decision. *De Zeven Provincien* had a main armament of eleven-inch guns and a secondary armament of 5.9-inch guns (the same as *Java*). However, the battleship was not fitted with anti-aircraft guns and in pursuing a course along the coast eventually sailed within range of Dornier flying boats based at Batavia.

On 8 February, *De Zeven Provincien* sighted a squadron of eight Dorniers. The mutineers received a radio message demanding their immediate surrender. They signalled that they did not intend violence but simply sought a hearing for their grievances, and refused to surrender. The aircraft attacked with 50-kiloram bombs, striking the battleship forward of the bridge with at least one bomb. This may have been the first time that a battleship at sea was attacked and crippled by aircraft (the earlier incident involving aircraft attacking the mutinous Chilean battleship *Almirante Latorre* occurred when that ship was at anchor). Eighteen of the mutineers were killed, including Quartermaster Paradja. Three of the dead were European sailors, fifteen Indonesian. One hundred and eighty-four sailors (35 Europeans and 149 Indonesians) were arrested and charged with mutiny. At their subsequent courts martial, all were found guilty. The prosecution asked for jail sentences up to fourteen years. The court applied heavier penalties, with most of the mutineers receiving sentences of between six and eighteen years.

There was a further court martial of the nine junior officers who had been captured on the bridge. They were jailed for up to six months for the 'shameful neglect of their duty'. The captain was adjudged fortunate to have escaped court martial but was humiliated by the affair. One colonial official was overheard asking a colleague whether the captain had 'shot himself yet'. There was no doubt that the Dutch colonial administration in the Netherlands East Indies was shaken by this affair, and by the other instances of indiscipline. *De Zeven Provincien* was never repaired and was later scrapped. *Java* was sunk in action with the Japanese at the Battle of the Java Sea on 27 February 1942.

The British Consul in Surabaya, Mr J. D. Hogg, attended the trials. He reported to the British Government and to the Australian Prime Minister, Joseph Lyons, that the Dutch fleet commander attributed the 'present trouble to similar incidents in the British and Australian navies'. The Dutch colonial authorities issued a press release which blamed the incident on Australians because 'the minds of many of the sailors have been poisoned by the example given in the . . . Australian [Navy]'.

Conditions within the RAN did not improve after the troubles of 1932, however. In the latter part of that year there was a fruitless submission to the Naval Board from naval officers concerning their pay and conditions. There was no review of lower deck conditions. Indeed, in 1933, the system of welfare committees was terminated by the Naval Board on the grounds that they created dissent and were antithetical to discipline and good order. Hyslop remarks:

> This twenty-one year exercise in joint consultation was not wholly successful, in some respects its effect was not beneficial, but it was an instructive attempt to resolve conflicts in the fixing of rewards and conditions for a work force subject to the peculiar demands of naval life. It was probably too far ahead of its time in Australia to be successful; there was little in the way of joint consultation in the community generally. Controlling officers had the rough and ready understanding to deal with the revealed intricacies of human nature in the ordinary course of naval business. But this was quite inadequate in the situation created by the institution of joint machinery with its complex of novel quasi trade union relationships.[35]

Ordinary sailors were again left with limited avenues in which to express their grievances.

This void was keenly felt in the heavy cruiser HMAS *Canberra* which was not, by many accounts, a particularly happy ship. The punishment returns recorded an increasing number of penalties for minor infractions. Some charges, such as 'Did Sleep in Improper Place, namely a Mess Table', reflected a natural reaction to the poor living conditions.[36] Other charges recorded in the punishment log seemed to be either over-reaction or the result of a crackdown against increasing disaffection, particularly against the stewards. For example, Steward Solomons was charged with: 'Did not immediately obey the order . . . to serve drinks in an officer's cabin, namely Instructor Commander S—, MA, RN'. The Steward received seven days stoppage of leave. This appears to be an excessive punishment for being slow to serve one of the schoolmasters.[37] Had the officer been a watchkeeper, the failure to display some sense of urgency might have been justifiable.

The problems continued. On 25 August 1933, *Canberra* entered Jervis Bay on the New South Wales south coast and prepared to anchor for the night. Shortly before the officers' evening meal, normally served at 5.40pm, a group of stewards decided not to attend the officers' mess. It appears to have been an act of frustration rather than a plan of protest. The leading stewards simply 'walked off the job'. As it was a joint action and clearly refusal of duty, they could have been charged with mutiny. But such a charge would obviously have been an over-reaction to minor matters, such as not bringing the officers their drinks and meals. Instead of citing the men for mutiny, five leading stewards were charged with being absent from their place of duty at the order 'Clear Lower Deck'. They each received five days' stoppage of leave.[38]

The refusal of duty as a form of protest threatened to spread. Early the next morning a group of able seamen refused to leave their hammocks when piped to duty, but responded to direct orders from the petty officers. Seventeen sailors were charged with being: 'Slack in turning out of his hammock at 0530'. They each received two days stoppage of leave. At 9.30am, when the ship's company were required to report to their various divisions, six men—two leading seaman, three able seamen and an ordinary seaman—absented themselves and met in the lower conning tower, a secluded part of the ship. Shortly after the meeting began, they were discovered by the Master-at-Arms, possibly through an informant. The six denied having met in the lower conning tower for any reason. There was an absence of any further evidence to support possible charges of conspiracy to mutiny, which would, of course, have meant courts martial. Instead, the six men were charged with three offences that were dealt with at 'Captain's Defaulters'—namely, that each 'Was in an improper place', 'Did skulk from divisions', and 'Was out of the dress of the day'. For these unusual charges, each man was punished by five days' stoppage of leave.

These brief acts of protest and coordinated absences from duty all fell within the technical definition of mutiny. As each was dealt with promptly, within the ship's own disciplinary procedures and without harsh retribution, the potential of each incident to spread into a more general disturbance was squashed. The *Canberra* incidents and genuine mutinies in *Penguin* and *Moresby*, led to a review of naval discipline in late 1934.

There needed to be some way for sailors to protest unfair treatment which did not lead to a charge of mutiny. If resorting to 'strike action' was a particularly Australian propensity, it needed to be reflected in an Australian naval disciplinary code. Until such a code was passed into law, commanding officers struggled bravely and sometimes vainly to avoid their command being tainted by mutiny. Most of the problems resided in the definition of mutiny. This was a challenge the very anglophile Naval Board was unlikely to pursue with much vigour.

10

The tumultuous thirties

The problems faced by the Naval Board did not disappear with the economic recovery of the 1930s. Some of the Navy's older ships continued to cause problems. The Surveying Service seemed continually burdened with ill-suited vessels. As outlined in Chapter 6, the old sloop *Fantome* had been decommissioned shortly after the Naval Board recognised that it was unsuitable for extended periods of survey work. It was clear, however, that *Geranium* alone was insufficient for the urgent surveying duties that were required as a result of defence strategy reviews. The Naval Board sought another ship from the Admiralty and HMS *Silvio* was offered as a replacement for *Fantome*.

Silvio had been built in 1918 as a fleet minesweeping vessel (also rated as a 'sloop') and part of a group of ships referred to officially as the 24 Class. They were not large. The ships displaced 1320 tons and were 267 feet long with a standard ship's company of 82. As constructed, they were coal-burners. In comparison with *Fantome*, *Silvio* was more roomy and comparatively new, although much slower. Being coal-fired, like the older vessel, meant that there would be hot and heavy work for stokers and engine-room men in the tropics. *Silvio* also had the disadvantage of being 'war-built', which meant for many ships that construction had been rushed and corners cut. The result was often a damp and uncomfortable vessel. *Jane's Fighting Ships* offers an unflattering comment on the class: 'Are said to be indifferent sea-boats and roll a lot; not as successful as the [Flower Class]'.[1] *Silvio* and the other ships of the Class were nonetheless considered to be well suited for survey duties due to their superior boat davits and ability to embark minesweeping gear. Most were converted for survey work in 1923. *Silvio* was acquired by the RAN in 1925 and recommissioned in June of that year as HMAS *Moresby*, named in honour of John Moresby who discovered Port Moresby while on survey work in 1873. He died in the rank of admiral in 1922, aged 92.

Moresby sailed for Australia under Captain J. Edgell RN who later became Hydrographer of the Navy—the RN's senior surveyor. It carried out surveys in northern Australian waters and the Great Barrier Reef until December 1929, when it was laid up as an economy measure, among other cost-cutting decisions.

Once again, the easiest and most attractive method of cutting costs, as seen by administrators, was a reduction in wages. Under the *Financial Emergency Act* of 1932, the base rate of pay for an able sailor, £247 a year, was reduced by 7.5 per cent. Various allowances for active duty and deferred pay were also reduced. The charge for 'value of quarters' of sixpence per day levied on each sailor, remained unchanged, however.

On 27 April 1933, *Moresby* was recommissioned for a survey of areas of high strategic value around northern Australia. The captain, Lieutenant Commander H. E. Turner RN, had recently arrived in Australia from Britain to assume command of *Moresby*. By April of 1934, the ship was seriously undermanned and the captain was given permission to 'engage Aboriginals, up to six in number'. They were to be paid five shillings per week, with free rations and clothing, provided they were discharged from the ship before it left Darwin at the conclusion of its work.[2] From June to August 1934, the ship was engaged in surveying the eastern approaches to Darwin, Cape Hotham to Cape Don, with soundings in the Gulf of Carpentaria.[3] Initially, the survey work was successful and *Moresby* was assisted by aerial reconnaissance from an RAAF Moth aircraft. On 21 June, the work was derailed when the ship's capstan failed when weighing anchor in Kennedy Sound. *Moresby* was sent to Townsville for repairs on 29 June 1934.

The months leading up to the mishap had not been happy ones on board. The pay reductions of 1932 still rankled, and Lieutenant Commander Turner made representations to the Naval Board to review the pay of the officers, requesting 'hard-lying' money.[4] He had a greater chance of success on the matter of officers' pay than sailors' pay but the request was still refused. Funds were not available to cover this expenditure. The captain appealed, arguing that the extra money was justified 'in view of the particularly arduous nature of the work, involving abnormal exposure and discomfort', especially during the rainy season.[5] Meanwhile, the sailors who had to endure the hardest part of the 'arduous nature of the work' were manifesting their discontent through increasingly common acts of indiscipline. During June and July and into early August 1934, there were increasing numbers of men at Captain's Defaulters on a variety of charges including: 'Did speak improperly'; 'Failed to perform duty'; 'Absent from post'; 'Was slack in manning skiff when called away at 0645'; 'Absent over leave'; and 'Did return on board drunk'.[6] Some of the charges were the result of a natural reaction to the living conditions. This was certainly the case with Able Seaman Greaves, who was charged with 'Did sleep in an improper place, namely the stern-sheets of the motor-boat *Hearty*'. For this offence, Greaves drew seven days' extra duty and was told to sleep in the mess decks in future.

There were also more disquieting charges that evidenced a growing climate of ill-temper and violence. Able Seaman Neave was punished with fourteen days' extra duties for 'Behav[ing] with contempt to Petty Officer Langridge'. Able Seaman Fletcher went one further and was confined to the ship, subject to court martial in Darwin, on a charge of striking Petty Officer Langridge. Steward Cutler was perhaps a little hard done by when he was sentenced to 'Confinement under a canvas screen on board' for using threatening language to the Leading Steward and that he 'Did not immediately obey the order to wash glasses'. Lieutenant Commander Turner lamented to his superior, Captain Cuthbert Pope, Captain Superintendent at Darwin, on 30 June 1934, that 'there has been an increase of offences over a short period due, I consider, to the drafting of a large proportion of the sailors and the advent of new men at the last moment before sailing'. The Chief of Naval Staff, Admiral Francis Hyde, considered that Turner did not take strong enough action in punishing the defaulters and that 'weak action' by senior officers in previous incidents encouraged *Moresby*'s ship's company in their indiscipline.

In 1935 Admiral Hyde was to order an inquiry into discipline within the RAN but this had little to do with *Moresby*'s troubles in 1934. Hyde admitted candidly in his report on *Moresby* that the causes of unrest in the survey ship were:

    a. unsatisfactory pay conditions;
    b. unsatisfactory food;
    c. bad officers;
    d. subversive influence of persons whose direct objective is the causing of disaffection; and,
    e. to a lesser extent that section of the press which . . . magnifies the slightest incident and which seems to delight in publishing any matter which places . . . higher authority in a bad light.[7]

The Admiral was sensible enough to recognise the human problems on the ship. Living conditions were poor while the sailors endured 'bad officers'. He included 'subversive influence' because the Navy still feared the infiltration of Communist sympathies into the mess decks. He added the comments about 'the press' because they also were seen as being hostile to the RAN, particularly in the wake of reporting on the incident at Port Melbourne. (One sailor who was dismissed from *Moresby* offered his story to the *Truth* newspaper. This did not help the newspaper's reputation among senior officers after the 'incitement to mutiny' case.)

The inquiry into *Moresby*'s troubles found that some of the sailors were predisposed to insubordination and mutiny and some, according to Hyde, were a 'subversive influence'. They included Able Seaman Bell who, it was said, endeavoured 'to bring pressure to bear upon the Commanding Officer, HMAS *Moresby*, to waive the charge of striking against Able Seaman Fletcher'[8]; Able Seaman Ranier, who was a 'talker' and had a brother who had been discharged from the RAN because of his 'Communistic views'; Able Seaman Weston, who was apparently a 'sea-lawyer' with an excellent knowledge of the *King's Regulations*; Able Seaman Humphrey, who 'stated in evidence that he sympathised with Able Seaman Fletcher and that he himself might have struck the petty officer concerned or any other petty officer under the same circumstances'; Able Seaman Carr, whose 'general attitude was very unsatisfactory'; and Leading Seaman McDougall, a man adjudged to be a 'possible instigator of the trouble'.

The spark that finally ignited a mutiny in *Moresby* was the confinement of Able Seaman Fletcher on a charge of striking Petty Officer Reed after an incident on Sunday 19 August. At the early hour of 6.30am, Fletcher and Able Seaman Cadzow (later to be named as one of the principal mutineers) were taking stores from the upper deck to the various storerooms below under Reed's supervision.[9] Just before lowering a heavy case, Fletcher secured a rope around a stanchion to stop the case falling and was 'admonished' by Reed for getting the paintwork dirty. The sailors made no comment. They then lowered the case which slid out of the rope onto the deck. Reed then said, 'Cripes, are you people dumb, haven't you any brains?' Fletcher replied, 'I have brains', then pulled on the rope which Reed was also holding and said, 'Give us some slack'. Reed responded, 'I'm the petty officer here!' At that, Fletcher struck him on the jaw. When Reed looked up, the sailor hit him again. In the words of the charge sheet: 'Petty Officer Reed, to protect himself against further assault from Able

Seaman Fletcher, backed away from the forecastle hatch and ordered Able Seaman Fletcher to go aft to the Quarter Deck. Petty Officer Reed himself, went aft'. Fletcher remained on the forecastle where he was arrested by the master-at-arms. He did not resist. He admitted striking the petty officer, the essence of the charge brought against him to be determined by court martial at Darwin. Until the ship reached that port, the sailor was confined in irons. The incident incensed many of the sailors, who naturally took the side of Able Seaman Fletcher, and some made representations to the captain that were not well received.

Moresby headed back to Darwin. On 19 August the ship was still two days away from port. At breakfast in the mess decks, the men were discussing their situation when the option of refusing duty took hold, requiring very little instigation. At the later inquiry, evidence was given that Able Seaman Weston, a 30-year-old sailor from Bowral in New South Wales (who was reputed to have a thorough understanding of the *King's Regulations*), first encouraged the other sailors to refuse duty when they were called to divisions at 8.45am. Able Seaman Bell was also identified as 'a ringleader in the general mutiny'.[10] Able Seaman Raphael of Perth 'was one of the ratings who instigated the affair'. Able Seaman Ranier 'endeavoured to incite others'. Able Seaman Carr was 'considered by the Executive Officer and by the Master-at-Arms to be a ringleader'. However, the main force behind the mutiny was the fiery Scotsman, Leading Seaman McDougall. He advised his fellow sailors to 'do it properly' and went to each sailors' mess telling them 'Now's our chance'. When *Moresby*'s bosun piped the call for 'All watches of the hands fall in', 27 sailors did not respond. They were all able seamen. As *Moresby*'s complement included only 30 able seamen, this meant that 90 per cent of them did not report for duty. Leading Seaman McDougall, despite his incitement of the others, was one of the senior sailors who did report for duty when the call was piped.

The executive officer went below to the sailors' messes, flanked by the master-at-arms and his mate. There was little discussion. The sailors said simply that they were refusing duty 'as a protest' against conditions and discipline on board the ship. They did not have a list of demands or explanations. Their refusal of duty was virtually a spur-of-the-moment action that was set in train almost before they considered why they were doing it. It grew out of a general sense of frustration. The inquiry into the mutiny stated: 'There is evidence a number . . . of *Moresby*'s mutineers acted under the impression that they would "get away with it" and that no further punishment would follow their action'.[11] The executive officer and the first lieutenant (Lieutenant Commander W. Martin) reported to the captain that the men refused duty. Martin was ordered to return to the mess decks and inform the ship's company that any man who refused duty would be charged. He did so. The 27 men still refused to report for divisions. It was an impasse. The captain dismissed those of the men who were at Divisions. He then ordered the 'removal' of the sailors, who by now had gathered in one mess. It was a tense moment which could easily have become violent. The significant factor was that none of the more senior sailors, the leading seamen or the technicians, joined the able seamen.

The executive officer did not force the issue. He and the master-at-arms took the names of the mutineers, informed them that they would be charged by warrant (which meant that the captain would deal with the matter and there would be no court martial ashore) and withdrew. After further brief discussion among themselves, the would-be mutineers went to their various daily duties in ones and twos. They each came before the captain on the charge of being 'guilty of an act to the prejudice of good order and naval discipline in that he did fail to obey the pipe . . . at 8.45am'. Most were punished by the loss of badges and good conduct awards, although Able Seaman Neave was confined to cells on board the ship.

The Naval Board was alarmed by the captain's decision to punish the men by warrant and not by court martial. The Board was also surprised that he had brought the minimal change of committing an 'act prejudic[ial] of good order and naval discipline'. The Fleet Commander ordered an inquiry into the affair which reported that the 'incident was in fact a mutiny'.[12] The Board then ordered that six of the able seamen judged to be ringleaders of the mutiny, along with Leading Seaman McDougall, should be immediately discharged 'Services No Longer Required' with the forfeiture of deferred pay. At the same time there was a coincidental decision that perhaps amounted to a tacit acknowledgment that there was some cause for unrest among sailors: sea-going personnel were restored to full pay and allowances. The financial cutbacks prompted by the Depression were no longer necessary. There is, however, no further reference to pay rates for Aborigines employed for short periods in *Moresby* (and also HMAS *Geranium*) for five shillings a day. One wonders what the six Aborigines in *Moresby* thought of the events of August 1934.

In addition to the benefits conferred by Australia's economic growth, the RAN benefited materially during the 1930s from the growing belligerence of Japan in Asia and the Pacific, and the rising fears of militarism within Nazi Germany and its possible consequences for Europe and North Africa. These international developments prompted the Commonwealth Government to strengthen Australia's defences. In April 1934 the government approved a three-year development program which included the purchase of the Modified *Leander* Class light cruiser, HMS *Amphion*, which was still under construction at Swan, Hunter and Wigan Richardson's shipyard at Wallsend-on-Tyne. *Amphion* would become HMAS *Perth*. The Modified *Leander* Class cruisers were built to a basic late 1920s design which the Admiralty constantly altered and developed in the years before the war. The first five ships of the unmodified Class, *Leander*, *Neptune*, *Orion*, *Achilles* and *Ajax*, were launched between 1931 and 1934. The Modified Class consisted of three ships, *Amphion*, which was ordered first, *Apollo* and *Phaeton*. Although *Amphion* was ordered first, *Phaeton* was the first to be completed. It was purchased by Australia on completion and renamed *Sydney*. On commissioning, *Sydney* sailed for Australia on 14 July 1936. The arrival of the new cruiser in its home port was a major occasion for the city and the RAN. After a short maintenance period, *Sydney* joined the normal peacetime exercise programme which included longer cruises, such as to New Zealand for exercises with the Royal Navy's New Zealand Squadron, and shorter port visits. The Australian Government and the Naval Board were pleased with the performance of *Sydney*, and Prime Minister Lyons announced in March 1938 that a new three-year defence program would include the purchase of the other two Modified *Leander* Class light cruisers then nearing completion, to be renamed *Perth* and *Hobart*.

The commissioning and first voyages of these new cruisers were not without incident, however. On 7 August 1939, Melbourne's *Argus* newspaper 'unofficially revealed that a minor strike' had taken place in HMAS *Perth* on its arrival in New York to 'show the flag' at the World's Fair. The *New York Times* declared in a headline, 'Aussies Mutiny. British Officers Too British'. It could have been an embarrassing and public slur on Australia's naval reputation on the eve of a new war which fortunately was resolved by a face-saving compromise. *Perth* had been newly commissioned into the RAN in England with a ship's company sent from Australia, 500 men having sailed from Melbourne in SS *Autolycus* in May 1939 to man the warship. It was not a happy voyage for the sailors.[13] While the officers occupied passenger cabins, the sailors were accommodated in the ship's cargo holds, foul-smelling after being used to transport horses.

Perth's commanding officer, Captain Harold Farncomb, proved a hard taskmaster. While the newly commissioned cruiser was crossing the North Atlantic, in cold and foggy weather, Farncomb had the crew repainting the side of the vessel. They had to be swung over the side in canvas slings (known as bosun's chairs), swaying backwards and forwards over the grey sea while trying to apply the paint. In the words of one sailor: 'Captain Farncomb was a very autocratic man and his attitude towards the crew worked its way down through his officers'.[14]

One aspect of the ship's routine that particularly frustrated the sailors concerned junior officers' frequent visits to the forecastle where the sailors messed. It was the practice in the Navy that when officers passed, lower-deck ratings had to stand to attention. When the junior officers made a habit of visits to the sailors' messes, even ratings who had been on night watches and were trying to sleep had to be roused out of their hammocks to stand at attention as a sub-lieutenant or lieutenant passed by. If the men did not pay the officers the appropriate respects, their names could be taken and the men placed on report. And 'if the transgressor looked a bit unhappy with proceedings, he took the risk of being charged with silent contempt. A charge that could not be refuted'.[15]

As *Perth* docked in New York, the already irritable ship's company were informed over the main broadcast that not only was weekend shore leave cancelled but that they would have to wear white uniform during day leave, and change to blue uniform at 6pm. This meant that shore leave would have to be interrupted as each man would be required to return to the ship to change into blue uniform at 6pm. It was a small issue and only a minor irritant in itself, but it was universally considered unreasonable and amounted to the last straw for many on board. They registered a formal complaint about the order. The sailors were then ordered to muster on the quarterdeck. Instead of obeying, over 60 men gathered on the forecastle, as the Royal Navy mutineers at Invergordon had done only a few years before. *Perth*'s officers were issued sidearms. They confronted the sailors on the forecastle and ordered them below decks. This was the first time that the officers of an Australian warship had been armed to face sailors who resisted orders. In no earlier mutiny had the officers considered it necessary to be issued with sidearms.

On that tense day in New York, not one sailor moved. Such a failure to obey orders clearly constituted a mutiny. Farncomb himself approached the offenders and, in a statement that sits oddly with naval regulations, threatened that he would 'declare their strike a mutiny' unless the men dispersed immediately. They still refused. There was a stalemate. The ship was alongside a wharf and the actions on deck were visible onshore—it was obvious that a number of locals were taking notice and becoming concerned by the unfolding conflict. Not only were the newspapers alerted but the civilian police were also called. One of the participants later wrote about what followed: 'New York police arrived armed to the teeth. They carried enough weapons to start a major war and nobody knew whose side they were on, [so] the fiasco was called off'.[16] The *Argus* did not report the threatened intervention of the New York Police Department, an intervention that, if it had taken place, would have reverberated throughout the RAN and the RN and caused acute diplomatic embarrassment to all. According to the *Argus*, Captain Farncomb then attempted to resolve the matter personally, stating that his order concerning uniforms stood but that any man who wished to wear a blue uniform ashore could apply to him personally for permission to do so. It was a face-saving gesture that maintained the facade of discipline yet defused the situation. The men dispersed; nearly every one applied personally for permission to wear blues and all who did apply were granted permission.

The rest of the stay in New York was uneventful. However, when *Perth* left the city there were a number of deserters.[17] There remained a degree of dissatisfaction among the ship's company which was reflected in the large numbers of absentees and deserters after various port visits. When *Perth* returned to Australia, there were no less than 70 absentees at the conclusion of shore leave in Sydney. Captain Farncomb reported that 'Steps were taken [which] . . . coupled with a certain amount of disciplinary action . . . reduced the number of absentees on the next occasion . . . to thirteen'.[18]

Stoker Norm King of *Perth*, in his memoirs, recorded one event which offers some insights into the character of the feared Captain Harold Farncomb. As a result of the incident in New York, many sailors took steps to obtain a copy of the regulations that governed all aspects of their shipboard life, the *King's Rules and Admiralty Instructions*. Stoker King thumbed through the regulations and discovered that attendance at religious services was not compulsory. Every Sunday, those on board *Perth* who were not on watch or on duty were summoned to the quarterdeck for a weekly religious service. Stoker King, who did not claim to be a devout churchgoer, made a request to be excused attendance. His request went through the proper channels, from the Regulating Chief Stoker to the master-at-arms to the Divisional Officer to the Commander to the Captain. Farncomb's response was: 'I go to church; you gentlemen [the officers] go to church; why should a stoker want to be excused? Case dismissed'.[19] Despite dismissing the request, Captain Farncomb evidently reviewed the matter, as Stoker Norm King was later excused having to attend the religious service—he was given extra duty in the boiler room instead.

Soon after leaving New York, *Perth* received the news that war had been declared in Europe. Over the main broadcast, the captain declared that the ship was on a war footing, with lookouts keeping watch around the clock. Norm King records in his memoirs that the captain added, 'Any lookout found asleep on watch would be shot'.[20] The comment, if it were actually made, could not be taken literally.

The evidence suggests that Captain Farncomb was an unnecessarily harsh disciplinarian. On the other hand, in his defence it may have been due to the firm discipline he instilled in a raw ship's company that *Perth* later achieved such a proud war record. Neither Captain Phillip Bowyer-Smyth RN, who succeeded Farncomb (and had been an advocate for Seaman Patterson at the HMAS *Australia* courts martial in 1919), nor *Perth*'s third and last commanding officer, Captain Hector L. Waller RAN, who would lose his life when the ship was sunk with heavy loss of life in February 1942, made any further reference in their reports concerning disciplinary problems or large-scale absences in HMAS *Perth*.

From the comments of sailors at the time, and the facts of the incident in New York, it seems that the character of *Perth's* captain was a contributing factor to the mutiny in 1939. What sort of person was Harold Farncomb? Indeed, what sort of commanding officer did the RAN train its men to be?

Harold Farncomb, who was to be involved directly and indirectly in three mutinies, was born in Sydney in 1899 and joined the Navy in 1913, a member of the first intake of the fledgling

Royal Australian Naval College.[21] The RAN that Farncomb joined as a fourteen-year-old boy was imbued with centuries of naval tradition, despite having been in existence for less than two years.

The boys who made up the first entry to the Naval College in 1913 were forced to endure hardships unknown to their successors.[22] After beginning their naval training at Osborne House on Corio Bay in Geelong, the temporary site of the Naval College, the 1913 intake was relocated with all of the college's books, equipment and stores to the permanent site at Captain's Point, Jervis Bay, in 1915.[23] By this time, a number of the essential buildings at the site had been completed.[24] At the end of 1916, the first 'term' had completed their four-year course, which included courses in engineering, seamanship, gunnery, navigation, mathematics, physics, chemistry, English, French, history, geography, physical training and Bible study, and were preparing to graduate. When they joined the college in February 1913, their average age was thirteen years and seven months. Most were now seventeen-and-a-half years old and more than 20 centimetres (8inches) taller and 19 kilograms (43 pounds) heavier.

It remained important that Australian officers like Farncomb were trained with their British contemporaries. This was affirmed by Lord Jellicoe, latterly First Sea Lord at the Admiralty in London, who toured Australia in 1919 to advise the Commonwealth Government on the Dominion's naval defence requirements. He suggested that the Admiralty 'endeavour to give Dominion officers experience . . . in the British Navy by frequent interchange with officers of the Royal Navy'.[25] At his graduation in 1916, Farncomb was awarded the Grand Aggregate Prize and set his sights on reaching the top of his service and being the first in his term to be promoted to the ranks of commander and captain.[26] He completed his sea service as a midshipman in HMS *Royal Sovereign* and was promoted to lieutenant in October 1919 after achieving five First Class Certificates. Farncomb spent much of his early career as a staff officer specialising in operations and intelligence. He was promoted lieutenant commander in 1927 and served for the next two years in the battle cruiser HMS *Repulse*. Thus he was closely acquainted with the men, the ships and the commanders who were involved in the Royal Navy mutiny at Invergordon, and no doubt formed an opinion on where to attribute blame for the crisis. Farncomb completed the Imperial Defence College course in 1930 and was promoted to commander in June 1932. He then returned to sea as executive officer of the heavy cruiser HMAS *Australia*, which escorted the

Richard Parker, who was involuntary 'president of the floating republic' which the mutineers at The Nore attempted to establish in 1797; an ex-schoolmaster whose seditious activities brought him to the gallows. (from the *London Illustrated News*, 20 July 1935)

Left A crucial moment in the mutiny at The Nore: Richard Parker, handing the men's demands to Admiral Buckner, addresses the Admiral without removing his hat.
Right The end of the misguided 'president of the floating republic': the execution of Richard Parker.
(Both from the *London Illustrated News*, 20 July 1935)

Admiral Horatio Nelson's flagship, HMS *Victory*, now berthed at its permanent home in Portsmouth. (Official photograph, Royal Navy)

The Queensland Navy's gunboat *Gayundah*, one of the ugliest ships ever to sail in Australian waters. Critics likened it variously to a gargoyle and to a floating steam iron.

HMAS *Psyche, Pelorus* class light cruiser, at Hong Kong. A British warship lent to the RAN, it saw patrol duty in Indian and Malayan waters in 1915 to 1917; it was old and worn out, and conditions on board—especially in the tropics—were very trying.

HMAS *Encounter*, light cruiser, was part of the Australian Naval & Military Expeditionary Force dispatched from Australia in August 1914 to occupy German territory in New Guinea.

The battle cruiser HMAS *Australia*, RAN Flagship, passing through the Suez Canal at Kantara on her return home in 1919 from active duty with the British Fleet. It was not a happy ship; *Australia*'s ship's company was involved in several mutinous occurrences on return from service, notably the 'Fremantle incident'. (Royal Australian Navy official photograph)

HMAS *Australia* being scuttled off Sydney Heads in 1924—a sad end to a troubled career.

HMAS *Canberra*, County Class heavy cruiser, seen here in Sydney Harbour before World War II, was involved in the infamous 'Prince's Pier incident' in Melbourne in 1932, along with HMA Ships *Australia*, *Albatross* and *Tattoo*.

HMAS *Voyager*, V Class destroyer, involved in numerous actions in the Mediterranean during World War II, saw a 'sit-down' strike in July 1940 which was quickly defused by commonsense action on the part of its captain.

Above The second HMAS *Australia*, County Class heavy cruiser, commissioned in 1927, was the site of a Board of Inquiry into the mutiny in HMAS *Pirie* during 1943.

Below Wartime divisions at HMAS *Cerberus* (Flinders Naval Depot): this training establishment was the venue for most RAN wartime basic training before personnel were sent to sea. (Royal Australian Navy official photograph)

HMAS *Nestor*, N Class destroyer, sister ship to HMA Ships *Napier*, *Nizam*, *Norman* and *Nepal*. The men of *Nestor* refused to put to sea under drunken officers in early 1941 when the ship was being commissioned at Scapa Flow. (Royal Australian Navy official photograph)

Sailors in HMAS *Nizam*, 3 November 1944—probably not the men involved in locking themselves in the mess decks in 1941 to protest against what they saw as unreasonable conditions of service.

During World War II, HMAS *Pirie*, *Bathurst* Class corvette, saw the most serious and protracted mutiny—directly attributable to incompetent and insensitive leadership—ever suffered by the RAN. (Courtesy Dr G. Davis)

Junior sailors from HMAS *Pirie*, caught in a cheerful moment in the tropics. (Courtesy Dr G. Davis)

Above A gun crew in HMAS *Pirie*. In action against Japanese dive-bombers off Oro Bay, New Guinea, in April 1943, *Pirie* suffered seven dead and four seriously wounded.
Below Ship's bell, HMAS *Pirie*. The plaque below the bell was presented to the ship by an American chaplain who was on board at the time of the action at Oro Bay. (Both courtesy Dr G. Davis)

Above New Zealand 'mutineers' gathered at the Devonport Reserve at 8am on Wednesday, 2 April 1947, while the RNZN general mutiny was in progress. (Courtesy I. Smith)
Below Garden Island as it looked at the time of unrest over naval pay in the late 1960s; several RAN vessels can be seen tied up alongside.

Above HMAS *Supply*, Tide Class fleet tanker, was involved in the Whitlam Labor Government's symbolic protest against French nuclear testing at Muroroa Atoll in July 1973. (Royal Australian Navy official photograph)
Below The frigate HMNZS *Otago* played a major part in the combined Australia–New Zealand protest activities at Muroroa Atoll.

Above The *Leander* Class frigate HMNZS *Canterbury* replaced HMNZS *Otago* at Muroroa when *Otago* returned to Auckland. *Below* HMAS *Adelaide*, US *Oliver Hazard Perry* Class frigate, bound for duty in the 1991 Gulf War. One sailor went absent without leave before the ship sailed. He was court-martialled and dismissed from the Navy. (Both Royal Australian Navy official photographs)

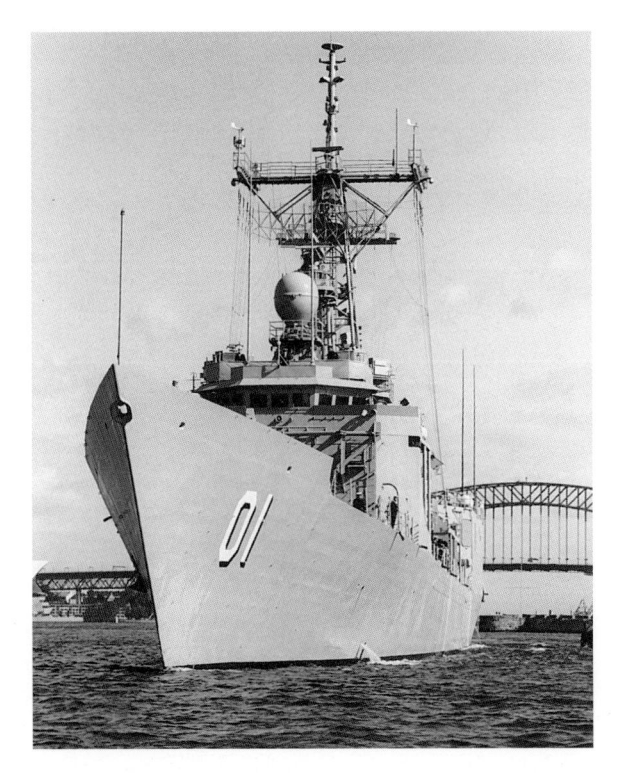

Duke of Gloucester back to England in 1935, and for which duty he was made a member of the Royal Victorian Order (MVO). Farncomb remained in Britain to take up a posting to the Americas desk of the Admiralty Naval Intelligence Division. He was promoted captain on 30 June 1937, six months before his classmate John Collins. To compensate for his perceived lack of command experience, Farncomb was immediately given command of the newly commissioned sloop HMAS *Yarra*, in 1937–38. He returned to Britain to complete the Senior Officers' Course and Tactical Course in the first half of 1939 after which he was appointed commissioning captain of HMAS *Perth*.

After his short tenure in *Perth*, Farncomb was to serve the entire war at sea in command positions. In June 1940 he took command of the heavy cruiser HMAS *Canberra* in which he remained until he assumed command of the sister-ship *Australia* in December 1941. Farncomb was an extremely gifted sailor. He was technically proficient and possessed the ideal temperament for wartime operations, an aggressive and resolute man who trusted his own judgment, occasionally against the advice of others, and made no secret of his professional ambitions. Farncomb was not an easy man to know and was respected rather than liked by those serving under him. In contrast to the other Australian cruiser commanders of his generation, such as Captains John Collins and Joseph Burnett, Farncomb, a strict disciplinarian, was often harsh, abrasive and intolerant of any lapse among those under his command.

He preferred force to persuasion and relied on law rather than goodwill. In several instances, his unbending attitude to routine and order produced a degree of resentment and hostility which drove some of his men to defy his authority, even to the extent of initiating a mutiny. As noted in Chapter 11, there was a brief episode of collective insubordination in *Australia* which was quashed by Farncomb's prompt and stern response.

While some might have praised Farncomb for strong and resolute leadership, he was a poor manager of men and a deeply flawed human being. His greatest weakness, and it became better known as the war progressed, was his liking for alcohol. While he never drank at sea, his drinking ashore made some senior officers feel that his reliability in all circumstances was suspect. Regrettably for those who suffered under his totalitarianism, the Naval Board was not especially concerned about the absence in Farncomb of humanity, compassion or justice. Farncomb retired as a rear-admiral and subsequently qualified as a solicitor.

With the outbreak of war in September 1939, RAN ships were deployed across the globe in defence of Imperial interests and Australia's seaborne imports and exports. The number of RAN ships increased rapidly, to reach a peak of 337 by the end of the war. Many of these vessels had to be manned by Reserve personnel. While the 'Hostilities Only' reservists were new to naval life and naval discipline, for the greatest part they accepted the Navy as they found it and were prepared to endure hardship and deprivations 'for the sake of the nation'. This was true only to a point, however. When the familiar spectres of poor living conditions and flawed leadership intruded on the mess deck, the reaction of the men was unpredictable. Notwithstanding the imperatives of war, Australian sailors refused to be abused and exploited, as the following chapter illustrates.

11

World War II

The war years saw a number of incidents that could have been described as mutinies. That they were not recorded as such was due to most commanders treating their men with compassion and common sense. Instead of arresting would-be mutineers and instituting courts martial, the officers involved either considered their grievances or took some form of summary action short of formally laying charges. Most of these incidents were resolved as they occurred, by discussion and prompt action. Any one of them could have resulted in indictments for mutiny if a strict (and over-scrupulous) legalism was applied. Small ships, probably because of their crowded and uncomfortable conditions, were the most likely to experience unrest. Only two major incidents resulted in charges of mutiny and subsequent imprisonment.

HMAS *VOYAGER*, JUNE 1940

When hostilities with Italy commenced after midnight on 10 June 1940, the ships of Australia's so-called 'Scrap Iron Flotilla' were in Alexandria Harbour. Known officially as the 10th Destroyer Flotilla, consisting of the V & W Class destroyers *Stuart*, *Vendetta*, *Vampire*, *Voyager* and *Waterhen*, the ships saw frequent action in the Mediterranean during 1940. The ship's log of *Voyager* for early July recorded numerous engagements with the enemy. Some were bombing and strafing attacks; others were encounters with submarines.

From 10–15 July, the veteran warship was engaged on convoy duty between Malta and Alexandria. On 10 July, shortly after leaving Malta, *Voyager* was machine-gunned from the air but there were no Australian casualties. On 11 July, the ship withstood one aircraft attack in the morning and four in the afternoon. The following day brought one more attack. When the ship arrived safely at Alexandria on 15 July, there was a sense of relief among the ship's company, even though they were not beyond the reach of bomber aircraft and there were occasional air raids on the port. After brief periods of shore leave, *Voyager* proceeded to sea on 19 and 20 July but saw no enemy activity on either day and returned to Alexandria. In five days, it was scheduled to sail once more on convoy escort duties.

On 23 July, there was a brief mutiny, referred to by the ship's company as a 'sit-down strike'.[1] The matter did not become official but it is clear that there was a collective refusal to obey orders. On this occasion, there was nothing wrong with the morale of the ship's company or the operation of ship, elderly though *Voyager* was. The Fleet Commander, Admiral Andrew Cunningham, had characterised the Australian destroyer men as 'the most lively and undefeated fellows I have ever had to do with', an attitude which came through despite the very poor living conditions for sailors on board all V & W Class destroyers. The Australians were prepared to endure much where the exigencies of wartime service made spartan standards inevitable, but sometimes they felt they were asked to endure too much.

Two versions of what occurred on 23 July and the specific reasons for the mutiny have been recorded.[2] One version suggests that a group of older sailors refused to allow normal work or permit the ship to sail until more adequate anti-aircraft guns were installed. *Voyager*'s main guns, of 1914–18 vintage, were designed for defence against torpedo-boat attacks and did not have the elevation required to engage modern aircraft. In order to direct fire at attacking aircraft, the ship had to make an abrupt turn and heel over so that the guns would be raised sufficiently by the angle of the decks to allow them to bear and fire on the planes. The other version contended that the 'strike' was prompted by an order from the first lieutenant, directing that the ship be repainted in camouflage colours, a task that would mean the ship's company had to work all day and into the night with no opportunity for shore leave.

Both versions concur that around twelve men sat down outside the mess deck and refused to move until the situation was resolved. The first lieutenant gave orders that the men muster on the main upper deck but they refused to comply a second time. The first lieutenant sensibly did not take hasty action, and the captain was summoned. The substance of their discussions is unclear as the captain did not set down any details for the official record. Whatever they discussed, the stand-off was defused. The painting of the ship was re-scheduled so the ship's company would still be able to enjoy some shore leave that night. There was also a suggestion that a captured Italian anti-aircraft gun be mounted on the ship to augment its armament. The 'strike' quickly resolved itself. On 25 July, *Voyager* left Alexandria with a convoy of five ships bound for Port Said. There were no repercussions from the incident. Good sense had prevailed.

HMAS *NAPIER*, FEBRUARY 1941

There were several incidents involving the ship's companies of the N Class destroyers *Nestor, Napier, Nizam, Norman* and *Nepal*. These ships constituted the 7th Destroyer Flotilla and were manned and maintained by the Australian Government although remaining entirely under Admiralty control. They were large destroyers, displacing 1760 tons (1795 tonnes) and measuring 356 feet (108.5 metres) in length. They had good endurance and could reach a maximum speed of 33 knots. Men who served in the N Class vessels did not record complaints about the conditions on board, even after they became very crowded with the extra personnel required to operate additional equipment. (Their original complement was 226, but by 1943, most of these ships had to accommodate a ship's company of 300.) However, a number of the sailors were disparaging in their descriptions of the N Class's sea-keeping qualities. Complaints of sea-sickness due to the ships' excessive movement were common. In 1945, a sailor recorded that HMAS *Nizam* rolled 82 degrees in the Great Australian Bight. Ten men were lost overboard and later recovered.[3] The same source described conditions in January 1944 as being very bad, with 'lots of sea-sick sailors'.[4]

The mutinous incidents in the N Class destroyers typically occurred when the ships were no longer in the thick of action but when the ships were relegated to supporting tasks. Some were driven to refusing duty when particular grievances developed against the backdrop of discomfort caused by the ships' poor sea-keeping characteristics. In the first weeks after the ships were commissioned, there was a brief but minor incident in *Napier*, the flotilla leader, when a group of sailors staged a 'strike' and refused to leave the mess decks when ordered. The matter was reported to the first lieutenant who responded with a message warning the sailors that if they did not report for duty, he would 'flog 'em out of the mess decks with ropes' ends!'. This intentionally humorous response defused the situation and encouraged the men to return to duty although their grievances remained. The ship continued its preparations for combat in bitterly cold and snowy weather. On 8 February 1941, when the ship sailed from Greenock in Scotland (all the N class were built in Glasgow), 24 men failed to report for duty at the conclusion of their shore leave.[5]

HMAS *NIZAM*, APRIL 1941

There was a similarly brief incident in *Nizam*, another of the N Class destroyers, when the ship was completing its post-commissioning work-up. The captain instituted changes to the 'settled conditions of service', such as watchkeeping and messing arrangements, that normally applied during wartime on board a destroyer.[6] The sailors made complaints through the 'usual channels' which involved discussing grievances with their divisional officer before they were conveyed to the first lieutenant and then to the captain. The grievances were dismissed.

When both watches (all of the ship's company who normally stood watch) were called to muster, the men refused to leave their mess decks. Indeed, they closed the bulkhead doors and clipped them shut from the inside. The captain and first lieutenant were understandably angry, as there was little they could do short of having the doors cut open. Maintaining their dignity, the officers remained in the wardroom while a mediator carried proposals from the mess decks to the officers, who responded with counter proposals. The situation was resolved when the captain agreed to restore the accepted 'settled conditions of service' and drop the changes that had been made. The men readily returned to duty. What could have been a serious incident leading to charges of mutiny was resolved with restraint and patience on both sides. The sailors had a reasonable grievance and the captain made a measured response that defused the situation. Of course, it was a shrewd move on the sailors' part to clip shut the bulkhead doors, as this made it hard to prove a charge of mutiny against any individual. With the doors closed it was difficult to identify anyone positively while it would be just as difficult to demonstrate that anyone actually refused a direct order. It would be arduous addressing a particular sailor with an order directed through a closed steel door and then proving he had heard the order!

HMAS *NESTOR*, 14/15 MAY 1941

When the new destroyer *Nestor* was undergoing trials and training at Scapa Flow in northern Scotland in early 1941, it undertook a number of missions to the north of the British Isles. The weather was cold and stormy—not unusual in those latitudes in winter. A member of the ship's company recorded something of their experience:

> 29/2/41: . . . very rough. Most of the boys very sick.
> 26/3/41: . . . seas very rough. Got bollicking . . . icy cold . . . bully beef for dinner . . . [tinned fish] for tea.
> 30/3/41: . . . damn boat is nearly rolling over half the time. . . . no supper . . . nearly everyone sick.[7]

At the same time as the ship was working-up, it became evident to the ship's company that the captain, first lieutenant and engineer officer were engaging in heavy drinking sessions.[8] One morning when the ship was scheduled to proceed to sea for further trials, the ship's company refused to leave their messes and prevailed upon the ship's doctor to go by boat to inform the Admiral that *Nestor*'s men would not put to sea under drunken officers. The Admiral sent marines to arrest the three officers before he appointed another officer in command. No charges were laid against the sailors involved.

The incident was recorded in the personal papers of both a senior sailor and an officer. The petty officer noted:

> 14/5/41: Weather very good. Supposed to go to sea 2100 but had a little trouble on boards [sic]. The Captain and the Jimmy [Executive Officer] were too drunk and totally unfit to take the ship to sea so all the hands went for and refused to sail until a sober and responsible officer came on board. At 0200 in the morning, the Captain of the supply ship *Tyne* came over and our own Captain and Jimmy were placed under arrest. Still being paralytic. It was bound to happen sooner or later as they were heavy boozers.[9]

The view of Lieutenant Tregurtha was more sympathetic:

> *Nestor* did not commission as scheduled. Her Commanding Officer, disgracefully egged on by a junior officer, had become an alcoholic and was undergoing a court martial. He was dismissed

his ship and by exercising self-discipline to overcome his problem, later on served with distinction.[10]

The issue of drunkenness on board ships, particularly among officers, was an issue that caused deep resentment among sailors. When one of their number returned on board drunk he was often charged with varying offences. When an officer was intoxicated, he was escorted to his cabin and there the matter usually ended. It was not just hypocrisy that infuriated the lower deck. Officers who lacked self-control were rarely accorded much respect. And without respect, the exercise of leadership was problematic. As one able seaman observed of his officers in an N Class destroyer:

> The officers put up a disgusting show, by still being drunk from the night before, and this was at a time when the ship was being navigated through a British minefield. There was a lot of bad feeling over this drunkenness.[11]

HMAS *NAPIER*, 27 MAY 1942

Another incident involving *Napier* took place at Mombasa in Kenya on 27 May 1942. The ship had experienced limited action but had witnessed the horrors of naval combat firsthand. On 2 April 1942, *Napier* refuelled from the heavy cruiser *Dorsetshire* which was reported sunk by Japanese aircraft just two days later. Later, *Napier* embarked survivors from the carrier *Hermes* which was also sunk by Japanese planes. The destroyer then crossed the Indian Ocean to participate in the unpopular campaign against the French on Madagascar while the ship's company heard of more stirring events closer to Australia as the Battle of the Coral Sea was being fought. A sailor in *Napier* spoke for many when he remarked that the 'crew is down in the dumps. No action at all, just plodding along with this decrepit fleet, bloody awful situation, need to drop a few patterns [of explosives] to wake them up'.[12]

At the end of May, *Napier* was at Mombasa on the east coast of Africa. It was hot and there was heavy rain which made the area uncomfortably humid. To make matters worse, there were no recreational facilities in the port. The men were bored and fed up. But the issue that drove them to breaking point was a lack of pay. Pay-day came and went without the men receiving their wages. On 27 May, there was a mutiny which followed the familiar pattern. In the words of one sailor: '[We] sat down on the mess deck. We gained our point'.[13] It was not so much a challenge to authority as a simple protest. The men had a justifiable grievance they believed was being overlooked. Like those in the other N Class ships and in *Voyager*, they simply sat down until their point was taken seriously. There was absolutely no intention of committing the crime of mutiny in wartime. The lower deck had no desire to reduce the fighting capability of the ship or even to usurp the legitimate authority of the command structure.

In each of these cases, Australian sailors had simply felt strongly enough about an issue that they had to take a stand. That was all. When their officers reacted and addressed their grievance or even when they acknowledged some justifiable cause for complaint, that was sufficient for the men to return to duty. It was only when officers responded in an authoritative fashion and resorted to the letter of the law, which technically defined these actions as mutiny, that these sorts of incidents became more serious. One such occasion, the first of two incidents in World War II that resulted in charges of mutiny being formally laid, occurred at the very outbreak of hostilities with Japan.

HMAS *WESTRALIA*, 26 DECEMBER 1941

Westralia had been built for Huddart Parker Pty Ltd as a large oil-burning passenger liner for service on the routes around Australia's coasts. The ship entered service in 1929. In November 1939, *Westralia* was requisitioned by the RAN for use as an armed merchant cruiser (AMC). Such ships were given an armament of four-inch or six-inch guns, and sometimes the equipment necessary to handle a reconnaissance floatplane, before being deployed for patrol duties to protect Australia's trade routes from German and Italian raiders. *Westralia* was armed with seven six-inch guns for surface action and two three-inch anti-aircraft guns. By the time Japan entered the war, the threat of attack to merchant ships by commerce raiders had diminished. There was now a need for troop transports. As a large ex-passenger liner already in naval service, *Westralia* was converted for use as a troopship, together with two sister ships, *Kanimbla* and *Manoora*. The three vessels were then designated 'landing ship infantry'. It was in this role that *Westralia* served for the rest of the war.

In late 1941, however, *Westralia* was carrying out various patrol and escort duties around northern Australia. In November, the ship had arrived in Darwin, having escorted a floating dock from Brisbane to the northern base. From then until early December, *Westralia* patrolled the Arafura Sea, and also towed targets for naval and air force gunnery exercises. The work was mundane with little excitement or variation in the heat of summer. Some men actually enjoyed serving on converted liners because their size and accommodation made them an incredible improvement on most purpose-built warships. However, conditions in *Westralia* were not all that some might have desired. The stokers' mess was extremely hot—'always over 100 degrees [Fahrenheit]'[14]—because it was placed over machinery rooms used for the evaporating plant. There were only two showers for every 60 men. The tropical heat, limited ablution facilities and cramped living conditions meant that the men suffered a variety of skin problems such as rash, ringworms, boils, scabies and tinea.[15]

The food served by the galley was another source of complaint. The men's regular diet consisted of powdered eggs, dehydrated potatoes, boiled salt mutton and prunes, with the concession of a daily cup of lime water to counter scurvy. There were maggots in the eggs (it was a 'lucky dip to find a good egg'[16]), rats in the prunes and cockroaches in the meat and potatoes. Diarrhoea seemed to alternate with constipation for most serving in *Westralia*. Not for the first time, naval administrators had difficulty providing fresh provisions for ships operating for extended periods in Australia's tropical north. There were also shortcomings in the disciplinary regime. Stoker J. Searle noted that men lodging a complaint through the normal channels at divisions had to justify the complaint to avoid retribution. If it was judged that the complaint could not be justified, the complainant was punished for making trouble.[17] It is easy to imagine tensions building on the lower deck.

On 8 December 1941, *Westralia* and *Zealandia* (which was subsequently sunk during air raids on Darwin) embarked 'Sparrow Force', an amalgam of units gathered to defend the island of Timor, and sailed with 445 troops on board. The trip was uneventful and the ships returned to Darwin on 16 December. *Westralia* and *Zealandia* sailed again for Cairns. Problems with the coal-burner *Zealandia* made it a very slow passage. The two ships anchored off Goode Island when *Zealandia* signalled that it was unable to proceed as 'her firemen were unfit for duty'.[18] Heat exhaustion among engine room staff was a primary cause of slow voyages in tropical heat. (The energy-sapping heat reached temperatures of 120 to 140 degrees Fahrenheit in *Zealandia*.)[19] *Westralia* continued to Cairns independently with the captain noting in his report that the ship's floatplane was flown off on 24 December to take the commander of the troops and the ship's paymaster to Cairns to arrange disembarkation and the 'purchase of fresh provisions'.[20]

The urgency evident in flying off the ship's paymaster to arrange for fresh provisions hinted that a serious problem had arisen on board the AMC. Quite simply, the ship was running short of edible foodstuffs. Patrolling in the Arafura Sea, followed by direction (at very short notice) to transport troops to Timor, had left little time for the paymaster to arrange provisions for the ship's company and the 445 embarked troops. Moreover, the provisioning of troops sent to Timor and other areas in the Netherlands East Indies (Indonesia) had practically emptied the stores and commissaries around Darwin. Consequently, *Westralia* had very limited supplies when it was directed to return to Cairns with an additional 117 personnel on board. The situation was exacerbated by *Zealandia*'s slow progress. There was no alternative but to place the ship's company on short rations. One sailor noted privately that *Westralia*'s ship's company had only rice and prunes to eat for nearly three weeks.

There were other causes for dissatisfaction. The ship arrived in Cairns at noon on Christmas Day. Instead of a Christmas dinner or barbecue, the men were again fed rice and prunes as a main meal. The troops were landed by the lifeboats, in itself an onerous job, which was 'considerably hampered' by strong southeast trade winds.[21] The ship's company worked all afternoon. The ship's boats returned alongside and were secured by 5.45pm, with re-provisioning and loading completed by 8pm. At 8.15pm, *Westralia* was ready to sail but its departure was delayed when the floatplane could not be re-embarked. *Westralia*'s departure was cancelled, as it appeared that the floatplane would not be re-embarked until the next day. Captain Hudson, a British officer, refused to allow any shore leave as he anticipated an early start the next morning. The ship remained at anchor with the entertainments of Cairns tantalisingly near. After the hard day's work, long weeks with limited shore leave, exceptional heat and short rations of poor food, the men believed they were entitled to at least a few hours of shore leave to celebrate Christmas Day—which had almost ended anyway.

160 MUTINY!

At midnight on 25–26 December, a fresh watch was called out to relieve the men on duty. *Westralia* was to proceed a short distance offshore in preparation for recovering the floatplane at first light. No-one responded and the captain was advised. At 1.50am, the deck officer observed over 100 men standing on the deck, surrounding the winches in a formation that would prevent the anchor from being raised. The captain sent the master-at-arms to convey his order that the men were to disperse immediately and return to their mess. They refused to obey the order and were in a state of open defiance of lawful authority. Without discussion, the captain issued two further orders. First, he ordered the machine guns mounted on the bridge wings to be manned and the guns 'were trained forward as a precaution'.[22] Captain Hudson then ordered 'Action Stations' sounded at 1.55am. The names of those who mustered for duty were recorded while the absentees were also noted. The master-at-arms was then ordered to place all the men on the forecastle under close arrest. There were 104 of them. It remains the largest number of men involved in a mutiny in the RAN.

Because of the large number who participated, the handful considered to be the ringleaders were kept under arrest and confined to cells pending their courts martial for mutiny. *Westralia* weighed anchor at 3.30am and anchored again off the Low Islands to recover its floatplane. In the course of the next morning, the executive officer questioned the men involved in the incident before they all agreed to resume their normal duties. On that basis, the ship proceeded back to Darwin in accordance with its orders and arrived without further incident on 30 December. *Westralia* was then ordered to Garden Island in Sydney. Following the ship's arrival on 9 January, *Westralia* was placed under the authority of the Senior Naval Officer who was directed to undertake an inquiry into the unrest and subsequent mutiny, and to impose legal proceedings where appropriate. The fate of those charged with mutiny is unknown as none of the files dealing with the incident can be located.

HMAS *AUSTRALIA*, 1942

In 1942 there was an incident in the heavy cruiser HMAS *Australia*, the ship commanded by Captain Harold Farncomb, who had already faced a mutiny in *Perth*. A number of the ship's company staged a 'strike' over working conditions and limited recreation time and gathered in their mess decks. When the matter was reported, Farncomb went down to the accommodation spaces himself. As the captain stalked the decks, men were selected at random and arrested by the master-at-arms at Farncomb's instruction. The arrested men were marched to the quarterdeck and sentenced to various terms of detention on board. The remainder of the 'strikers' returned to duty. There was no further action.

HMA CORVETTES *LITHGOW, TOOWOOMBA* AND *GERALDTON*

Despite the imperatives of war and the need to avoid assisting the enemy in any way, there were several instances of sailors refusing duty during operations in the corvettes *Lithgow, Toowoomba* and *Geraldton*, all short-lived incidents that did not result in formal charges. The incident in *Toowoomba* even had a farcical aspect. Most of the sailors had been working all day loading stores while their ship was alongside in Sydney. After supper, the lower deck was ordered to muster on the quarterdeck. Feeling they had worked hard enough that day, the men refused to leave their mess. This was clearly an act of mutiny. Ironically, what the men did not know was that the captain had recognised their hard work and had drinks prepared on the quarterdeck to express his appreciation for their efforts. After a short period, during which all was explained, the men emerged from their mess somewhat abashed but grateful for their captain's thoughtfulness.

WARTIME MUTINIES IN ALLIED NAVIES

The Royal Canadian Navy (RCN) suffered a serious mutiny in July 1943 when a 'large section of the ship's company'[23] in the Tribal Class destroyer *Iroquois* refused duty and locked themselves inside the forward lower mess, a strategy which frequently proved very effective in lower-deck mutinies. In *Iroquois*, the officers had no alternative but to plead with their men to end the mutiny. Eventually the sailors emerged and their grievances were heard and recorded at the subsequent inquiry conducted by British naval officers.

Notwithstanding its long and painful experience in dealing with insubordination and unrest, the Royal Navy was not without its share of mutinies in World War II. A significant incident with characteristics similar to the *Westralia* mutiny took place on board the landing ship, HMS *Lothian*. In early 1944, the British Prime Minister, Winston Churchill, wanted to send a squadron of British ships into the Pacific Theatre to operate alongside the Americans in the naval war against the Japanese. Australian and New Zealand ships had already participated in the joint operations as part of Allied taskforces. The US Chief of Naval Operations, Admiral Ernest J. King, was reluctant to accept any British contribution but shortly after D-Day (6 June 1944), he bowed to pressure and requested the contribution of six landing ships to help train American forces in the conduct of amphibious landings. The landing ships were actually converted freighters with HMS *Lothian* acting as the flagship. The squadron was designated Force X and placed under the command of Rear Admiral Arthur Talbot. The ships sailed on 3 August 1944.[24] The freighters, although converted into warships with the addition of guns and naval crews, were slow and overcrowded. *Lothian* had a ship's company of 550, including the Admiral's staff, in addition to army and air force liaison personnel. The conditions on board were poor and made worse by the breakdown of the ship's freshwater system as the vessels neared the Panama Canal. Admiral Talbot earlier had cause to advise and warn the Admiralty about poor morale in *Lothian*.

The strenuous voyage across the Atlantic was prolonged by port visits and hurricane alerts. On 1 September 1944, Force X reached Balboa in Panama, having been delayed in the Canal Zone for a week, at anchor in the tropical heat while the flagship was tied up to a wharf. On the main mess deck in *Lothian*, about a hundred men held a meeting to discuss their shared grievances. The mood of the meeting rapidly became tense. *Lothian*'s executive officer sent the ship's master-at-arms to order the sailors to muster on deck but they were in no mind to be upbraided. The master-at-arms became the focus of anger and abuse while the men still refused to move. The ship's Marine detachment was called out and armed. The executive officer went below to the mess decks in an effort to persuade the ship's company to follow orders, advising the men that a refusal to muster would be considered mutiny. His words heightened rather than lessened the tension. When the Captain of the Royal Marines confronted the defiant men, there was a brief scuffle. The officers withdrew and the hatches leading below deck were closed and locked. Guards were posted.

The imprisoned men started pounding on the hatches and it soon became evident that they might give way. The hatches were opened and the sailors emerged, gathering on the foredeck where they blocked the anchors and winches. The situation was complicated by the embarrassing presence of American visitors on *Lothian*'s bridge. The captain addressed the men and warned them that they were engaged in a mutiny. He had the Royal Marines assemble with bayonets fixed and threatened to disperse the mutineers with force unless they returned below peaceably. When the captain added that as far as he was concerned the mutineers could get off his ship, the crisis took a curious and unexpected turn, his words starting a rush for the gangways. Under the astonished eyes of the American visitors, the ship's officers hesitated in ordering the Marines to attack the mutinous sailors. The Marines were shouldered out of the way and a number of men rushed off the ship and milled about on the quay. A small group of Marines under a sergeant were sent after them and ordered a return. They were ignored. One of the ship's officers started reading the *Articles of War*, reminding the men of the legal consequences of their actions. A number of men returned to the ship but seventeen resisted. A party of Marines was directed to return the men to *Lothian* with whatever force was necessary. There was another brief scuffle before the mutineers were subdued and returned to the ship, where they were placed under armed guard.

Force X sailed on but never saw action in the Pacific War. The men and the ships were kept occupied with drills and support roles in rearguard areas for more than a year. The seventeen mutinous sailors were court-martialled and received sentences of imprisonment ranging from 90 days to one year. Those punished with the longest prison terms were the men who had assaulted the Marines and seized their weapons. The remainder of the mutinous group was dealt with by the captain with institution of extra drills and training. The executive officer was also court-martialled for 'not having exerted his utmost endeavours' to put down the mutiny. He was dismissed from his ship.

The *Lothian* mutiny, the worst experienced by the Royal Navy during World War II, involved a ship unsuitable for the operations in which it was embarked and living conditions which became intolerable. By way of contrast, the RAN's most serious mutiny in World War II, on board HMAS *Pirie*, was the result of many more factors conspiring against the maintenance of good order and discipline.

12

Vanity and mutiny

The most serious and protracted mutiny ever suffered by the RAN occurred in the corvette HMAS *Pirie* during World War II. The event and the lessons to be learned deserve detailed treatment in a separate chapter. The *Pirie* mutiny epitomised the typical Australian sailor's response to poor treatment: 'Let's just stop work and see what happens'.[1] The mutiny also highlighted a repeat of the kind of poor leadership which had characterised several earlier incidents of insurrection. Another compelling factor in the *Pirie* mutiny was the poor habitability of this class of ship.

Sixty corvette-minesweepers of the *Bathurst* or Town Class were built by Australia to a British design during World War II. Fifty-six were commissioned into the RAN between 1940 and 1944, with a further four built for the Royal Indian Navy. HMAS *Pirie* was built by BHP at Whyalla in South Australia and was launched in December 1941. The corvettes were intended for minesweeping, escort and general wartime duties. They were equipped with a range of weapons, from a four-inch gun or twelve-pounder mounted forward of the bridge down to depth charges and machine guns, but they were slow and under-powered. The *Bathurst* Class were propelled by a triple expansion engine, fabricated in railway worskshops, with twin screws that provided a nominal maximum speed of 15.5 knots in calm water.[2] This was half the top speed achieved by an average cruiser or destroyer. Under the pressure of wind and storm-driven seas, a corvette might manage just half its designed performance and during the war there were many reported instances of surfaced submarines drawing ahead of pursuing corvettes.[3]

Much has been written about living conditions in corvettes. For neither officers nor sailors were there many comforts, the vessels being overcrowded and particularly uncomfortable in tropical weather and in heavy seas.[4] Nicholas Monsarrat, author of *The Cruel Sea* and a wartime corvette commanding officer, remarked that 'a corvette will roll on wet grass'.[5] His first impression of these vessels was: 'This is going to be damned crowded'. After serving in a corvette for several months, a stoker concluded: 'It had the worst movement of any vessel I sailed on—it didn't just roll and pitch like larger ships. It lifted its stern in a sort of screwing motion then dropped and smacked into the water. It was like no other ship I've experienced'.[6] In anything but a balmy summer's day, the scuttles (portholes) had to be closed. Below deck in the ship's company's living quarters there were seldom daylight or fresh air while the ship was at sea.

A corvette ship's company was not large. The usual complement of a ship like *Pirie* allowed for six officers, 12 or 13 chief petty officers and petty officers and around 50 sailors. These men had to live and work for long periods in a space just 62 metres long and 11 metres wide. While one might expect a greater degree of camaraderie in a corvette than in a much larger ship, there was a distinct gulf between officers and sailors. Officers slept in bunks, not hammocks. They had slightly more living space and privacy. The wardroom mess possessed a bar staffed by stewards to serve the officers both drinks and meals. The officers were also entitled to the usual marks of respect from the lower deck. The sailors did not have any of these comforts, although they might have known and socialised with their officers during their previous civilian life.[7]

Pirie's stokers messed forward in the lower deck of the ship at the waterline. In this class of corvette, there were normally ten men to a messdeck the size of a small room.[8] The forecastle area was an ill-lit space and perpetually damp from the condensation of sweat and seawater. Men rose from their rest with hammocks soaking wet. While the obvious action would be to suspend the bedding and allow it to dry, naval regulations directed that bedding had to be carefully and tightly rolled and stowed. If this was not done there was scarcely room in the mess for the meals to be served and eaten. When the men returned to their hammocks they returned to damp bedding. The incidence of sickness was high. Pneumonia was common and frequently turned into tuberculosis (TB) which in such crowded quarters, could spread quickly. The wartime navy had a high rate of TB infection.

The officer appointed in command of *Pirie* on its commissioning was Lieutenant Commander Charles Ferry Mills. He was born at Roma in Queensland in 1903 and joined the RAN College as a Cadet Midshipman in 1917 when aged thirteen years. Exactly four years later he was advanced to the rank of midshipman. Mills was promoted to sub-lieutenant in 1924 and two years later passed his examinations for the rank of lieutenant. In 1930 he was among the officers retrenched by the Naval Board as a cost-saving measure. Those who left the service involuntarily at that time were found employment in the Commonwealth Public Service as third division clerks. Mills passed nine years as a public service clerk in the Taxation Department until the outbreak of war gave him the opportunity to rejoin the navy. He was appointed Security Officer (Intelligence) at HMAS *Lonsdale*, an administration and reserve training establishment at Melbourne. Two years later he was promoted to lieutenant commander and transferred to HMAS *Penguin*, another training establishment, in Sydney.

The closest Mills had come to enemy action in this period was when a Japanese reconnaissance aircraft from the submarine *I21* flew over Sydney on 30 May 1942 to observe Allied warships in the harbour. He was among the many defence personnel who witnessed the aircraft. No special precautions were undertaken after this incident, with the result that on the night of 31 May–1 June, three Japanese midget submarines were able to penetrate Sydney Harbour and sink the ferry-cum-barrack ship *Kuttabul*. In October 1942, at the age of 39, Mills' opportunity for command came at last. He was appointed Captain of *Pirie*. To date his career had been undistinguished. His appearance was unremarkable—indeed, he was overweight. Members of the ship's company described him as being flabby and ruddy-faced. At sea in the tropics he wore a khaki shirt and shorts. During his earlier stint in the navy he had been nicknamed 'Beryl' after Beryl Mills, a famous actress of the time, but when he joined *Pirie* it was not long before he was given other, more disrespectful, nicknames. Men using the water cooler on the deck below the captain's cabin would call up the companionway 'Offal Guts', 'Fender Belly', and similar epithets when the cabin door was open. It appears that Mills did not initially realise the insults might be directed at him.

Mills spent much of his time enforcing a strict disciplinary regime among his new ship's company. Where other corvette captains allowed their men to go ashore in a variety of uniforms, Mills insisted that his men wear their best dress uniforms, known as 'Number 1s'. He rigorously enforced the division between officers and men and maintained a lofty isolation as the captain of one of His Majesty's warships. A respected leader might have got away with such egotistical behaviour, it perhaps being considered a personal foible. But the men arriving for service in *Pirie*, almost all of them 'Hostilities Only' sailors on their first sea-going posting, soon came to regard Mills as a bully and had little respect for him. One sailor commented: 'He couldn't give a simple order. It had to be close to abuse, with overtones of contempt and a sense of his own superiority'. The captain was also rude to his officers, particularly to the first lieutenant, Lieutenant Robert A. Lorains RANR(S), so rude in fact that the ship's company eventually developed some sympathy for their officers.

The other officers in *Pirie* were either reserve or volunteer reserve rather than permanent navy like Mills, even though he had only been recalled to service on the outbreak of war. Because they were only 'Wavy Navy' (a reference to the shape of the stripes on their rank insignia), Mills considered himself additionally special. Lieutenant Lorains had been an officer in the merchant navy service before the war. A native of Newcastle-on-Tyne, he was competent at his job without being exceptional. Whenever possible he avoided the use of navy terminology, to the frustration of his captain. For example, during an air raid alert at Milne Bay one evening (admittedly, on this occasion Mills was ashore), Lorains did not use the approved phrase 'Gun loaded; half-cocked'. Instead he asked: 'Got any bullets up the barrel?'

If the captain did not at first understand how his men saw him, he was soon disabused of any illusion. Tensions began to mount even while most of the ship's company were in shore quarters at Whyalla. A young sailor named Bob Gillam wrote a letter to a RAAF friend which was intercepted by a censor and referred back to Mills. The captain summoned the sailor and in front of Sub-Lieutenant Young, Gillam's Divisional Officer and a man well regarded by the ship's company, insisted he read out some words where the handwriting was unclear. Gillam had to articulate his references to the captain as 'porcine' and 'repugnant' and 'not the sort of person one would want anything to do with'. He also stated in his letter that the ship's company referred to their captain as 'Offal Guts' and 'Shit Belly'. For his impertinence, Gillam found himself confined to the ship without leave.

After commissioning and completing a standard fleet work-up, *Pirie* was deployed in escort work in the South-West Pacific where the strategic situation was beginning to favour the Allies. After being rebuffed at New Guinea and Gaudalcanal in early 1943, the Japanese commander (and mastermind of the Pearl Harbor strike), Admiral Isoroku Yamamoto, planned an air offensive to re-establish command of the sea, gathering together over 400 aircraft at Rabaul and in the Solomon Islands. After a strike against the Americans at Guadalcanal, Yamamoto ordered a raid on the Australian forces in New Guinea. The operation was planned for 11 April 1943 with its primary focus the ships and transports in Oro Bay. At that time *Pirie* was escorting the freighter SS *Hanyang* from Milne Bay to Oro Bay with supplies for an advanced unit of Australian troops. It was a dangerous run as *Pirie* would be well within range of the Japanese-held airfields. The two ships were about 19 kilometres from their destination when they came under Japanese air attack.[9]

Warships without air cover were extremely vulnerable. The battleship *Prince of Wales*, together with the battle cruiser *Repulse*, had succumbed to Japanese air attack off Malaya despite having the benefit of the most modern anti-aircraft batteries, experienced ship's companies and the freedom to steam at speed in open water. *Pirie* had only its twelve-pounder and assorted light weapons to defend itself and *Hanyang*. The gunnery officer and the seven men of the twelve-pounder gun crew stood at their posts as the Japanese approached. The first aircraft to attack dropped a bomb which hit *Hanyang* and damaged its steering gear. A second aircraft attacked *Pirie* and, despite the ship's defensive gunfire, dropped a number of bombs which straddled the corvette's bow and stern. However, accurate fire from *Pirie* struck a Japanese dive-bomber which crashed into the sea. There was another attack by dive-bombers that caused further damage to *Hanyang* before another aircraft dived at *Pirie* from the starboard quarter. An eyewitness, Jim Downes, described the result:

> The plane that got us was a single engine Zero divebomber. It came in at about 10–15 degrees off our starboard quarter at about 11.00 o'clock high. As it commenced to dive Keith Chenery asked me to help reload his starboard oerlikon (his loading number . . . was in the wing of the bridge, injured). We got it loaded in time for Keith to pour plenty of bullets and tracers into it as it released its bomb. It was strafing all the way down—I would say the foredeck and the gun's crew were the recipients. I was expecting the ship to turn to starboard, off the line of the falling bomb, but it turned to port!—Directly in line with it. My last thought as I hit the deck alongside the flag-locker was that the bomb would go straight down the funnel. When the smoke and glass and stuff cleared it was obvious we were hit down near the geometrical centre of the bridgehead . . .

One bomb had narrowly missed the port bow but the second struck the bridge, killing the gunnery officer and penetrating plating on the foredeck, where it exploded and killed all but one of the main gun's crew. The explosion also set fire to the sailors' kit lockers in the mess decks. More aircraft attacked with cannon fire. *Pirie* was strafed three times, with the steel decks penetrated by a succession of rounds. The Japanese attackers were eventually driven off by Allied fighters. The ship's casualty list was seven dead with four seriously wounded. A number of other men suffered minor wounds. There was no address or comment to the ship's company from their commanding officer after the engagement. However, in his Report of Proceedings, Mills recorded his 'pride and satisfaction in the bearing of my officers and ship's company throughout the action'.[10] After the corvette reached Oro Bay, an American chaplain who had been on board with two army officers volunteered for the task of burying the seven dead at sea with full honours. Bravery awards were recommended by the chaplain.

After the battle in Oro Bay, *Whyalla* escorted *Pirie* to Milne Bay for temporary repairs. The first lieutenant organised the repair teams that restored a degree of order to the ship. A close examination of the damage revealed how fortunate *Pirie* had been. If the bomb had impacted with the deck without hitting the bridge first, it would certainly have penetrated the ship's magazine. *Pirie* would have exploded and sunk. The Japanese had identified *Pirie* as a destroyer and claimed the ship had been sunk. Propaganda could so easily have been fact.

The ship's company naturally swapped stories of the action. Some men had gone by the bridge and seen the body of the dead gunnery officer covered by a piece of canvas. It seemed to some that it was the coxswain who was directing activity on the bridge rather than the captain. It was the coxswain who conned the ship through the engagement and steered the random zig-zag course that had almost saved *Pirie*. During the action, as the air raid alarms went off, the captain had thrown himself to the deck (as had some other sailors who had never been under fire before). A couple of hardened sailors noticed Mills' action. The next time the dive-bombers attacked and the captain fell to the deck, two men fell boots first on his back. Mills took no action. Others felt he should have asserted his authority and upbraided the sailors, but he seemed too distracted.

One incident that aroused anger was the treatment of a young sailor who had joined the ship just a month earlier. He had been in the crow's nest on the mainmast and was badly wounded in the action, his hand shot off and a bullet through his shoulder. The sick berth attendant (SBA) wanted to administer morphine to ease the pain. The only morphine was kept in a safe inside the captain's office and the SBA needed both the captain's permission to administer it and the combination of the office safe. In the stress following the action, the captain could not remember the combination.[11] There were other stories as well. Many decided that the captain had not given any direction from the bridge during the engagement and that each man had acted as he thought best. If any men deserved commendations after the action, they would have included the coxswain, the SBA, and Able Seamen Chenery and Downes, the men who shot down the Japanese plane.

After the action in Oro Bay, the daily work routine in *Pirie* was left in the hands of the first lieutenant. The captain was hardly seen. The bomb and cannon holes in the forward mess deck were covered by tarpaulins. Nevertheless, water poured in with every tropical squall. The decks had been hosed down but the ship's company were still conscious of an odour of fuel. Hosing down seemed to spread the smell into all quarters of the ship. The ship's drinking water had been contaminated by fuel and owing to the fumes cooking was impossible. In any event, many on board were unable to eat while they remained shocked by the violence of the action and the loss of their shipmates. As *Pirie* and its ship's company recovered from their ordeal, there were continuing air raids by Japanese planes, mainly against ground installations around Port Moresby. In the third phase of the operation against Port Moresby, several ships were sunk or damaged during an attack by 100 aircraft.

On 14 April, *Pirie* left Milne Bay escorted by HMAS *Swan* and headed south, arriving at Townsville on 16 April. The captain did not endear himself to the ship's company by his behaviour during the passage to Australia. He put his arm in a sling even though he showed no sign of having been injured. His wearing a sling had another effect—because of the bandages, he did not wear a shirt. Several sailors spoke of his physically repulsive appearance with his naked belly covered with black hair bulging over his shorts.

On *Pirie*'s arrival in Maryborough three days later, the ship's company expected shore leave, pay and the delivery of mail. They were disappointed, however. While there was a small amount of mail their pay had not been arranged. At least there was good food. The men were fed eggs, bacon and milk. A case of brandy appeared in the junior sailor's mess. As soon as the ship arrived in port, however, dockyard workers came on board and started to remove the damaged decks and superstructure with acetylene torches and pneumatic hammers. *Pirie* became a bedlam of noise and smell. Only a limited number of men were granted leave in the afternoon but several others slipped down the gangway anyway. They paid a visit to the Commercial Hotel and savoured bottles of XXXX beer for two shillings a bottle. On their return they were spotted by the captain, who immediately paraded and chastised them. A voice elsewhere in the ship called out to the captain, 'Why don't you close your eyes?'

The Naval Officer in Charge at Brisbane approved leave for *Pirie*'s men, a maximum of ten days including travelling time. This restriction meant that sailors from South Australia, Western Australia and Tasmania would have little time at home before returning on the crowded railways. Moreover, there was still no sign of any wages and most had little money in their pockets. A rumour spread that pay was being withheld because officers of the permanent navy despised Mills as being 'nothing more than a taxation clerk' and were getting their revenge by making things difficult for his ship's company. Meanwhile, in Vic Cassell's words:

> ... the Skipper, with an amazing lack of sensitivity, lived ashore in the relative comfort of a hotel with his wife. Only someone who has done so can appreciate what it is like to live aboard a ship in the tropics when she is stationary and without air-conditioning.[12]

The captain's wife had come to Maryborough despite the difficulties of travel. Compounding his insensitivity, the captain visited the ship daily, accompanied by selected local dignitaries and notables whom he took on a tour of the corvette to inspect the damage while he regaled them with stories of the action. The captain's wife did not endear herself to the ship's company either, as she insisted on being saluted when they passed her in the streets of Maryborough. One sailor dodged the issue by exclaiming, 'Are you really Mrs Mills? You're a different Mrs Mills to the one that was with the Captain at Cairns'.

While the repairs were being completed, the men who had not been granted leave lived in misery. The entire forecastle deck had been removed and covered by tarpaulins which leaked with the overnight rain. The men had to endure several centimetres of foul-smelling water on the mess decks, where they had to eat and sleep. They made a complaint to the coxswain, who passed it on to the captain, asking Mills to inspect the mess deck in the hope of some compassion. The captain's only comment was: 'Clean it up before you go ashore'. He denied that there was any need for the ship's company to be accommodated ashore. Despite the hard lying on board *Pirie*, the greatest aggravation, in the opinion of some among the ship's company, was the sheer boredom of waiting for the repairs to be completed. The unpleasantness of life in *Pirie* was emphasised when HMAS *Rockhampton* arrived on 23 April for refitting and tied up alongside. *Rockhampton*'s captain was not a martinet and allowed his men to go ashore in long trousers and tropical shirts. As *Rockhampton*'s men had to cross *Pirie* to reach the wharf there was much banter between the two groups, which occasionally degenerated into worse behaviour.

The repairs took four weeks. When they were completed on 18 May, *Pirie* sailed to Townsville while awaiting orders to rejoin the Allied naval forces in the Pacific. The temper of the sailors did not improve. They had expected that when the ship was ready for action there would be a short period of leave ashore before they resumed long watches and arduous duty in warmer areas. However, there was still no word about leave as *Pirie* swung at anchor in Townsville waiting for orders. When they finally arrived, the corvette was assigned to convoy escort duties on the Australian east coast. Mills responded to the orders with bravado: 'The *Pirie* is too much a fighting ship to accept your offer of a milk-run'.

The telegraphist who sent the message reported its content to the mess decks, where the men were disgusted with such a response after Mills' actions in Oro Bay. Some of the ship's company, writing later of their experiences, considered this message to be the final straw. From that point on there was increasing talk of the captain's shortcomings, and escalating contempt. There was no concerted discussion of mutiny but the mood on the lower deck was conducive to some sort of protest action. Despite Mills' deprecation of 'mere' convoy escort work, it was no sinecure: just a few days earlier, on 14 May, the hospital ship *Centaur* had been torpedoed off Morton Island and *Ormiston* torpedoed off Coffs Harbour on 12 May. The Japanese were obviously still a threat to coastal shipping. *Pirie* escorted two ships to Sydney then joined a larger convoy of fourteen merchantmen and five other corvettes for the return to Townsville.

The mess-deck mood remained tense and the probability of defiance escalated with each new day. Leading Stoker 'Dixie' Dean had left the ship at Brisbane on compassionate leave after the death of his mother in Melbourne. When he arrived in Townsville to rejoin *Pirie*, someone on board called down from the bridge:

'We're having a mutiny tomorrow!' The aggrieved sailors met in the forward mess decks on 8 June and resolved that they would press their complaints on the captain the next day. In their words, it was a 'bitch session'. There was a list of demands. They wanted a short period of leave, which should have caused no problem as the ship was idle anyway. They wanted their mail, which was weeks overdue. They wanted their pay, which still had not been delivered in full. There was a collective decision that gradually coalesced into a simple plan: 'We'll sit here and see what happens'.

In order to emphasise their dissatisfaction, the meeting resolved that the able seamen and ordinary seamen, around 25 men, together with about the same number of stokers, would not leave their mess decks the following morning. The leading seamen and those of similar rank would go about their usual duties in order that the ship's routine was not disrupted unduly and that *Pirie* could still sail immediately if urgently required to do so. It was also decided that since the more senior sailors were men with family responsibilities, who hoped to make a career in the Navy, they would not be drawn into the affair, the younger men accepting the senior men would be better off without 'black marks' on their records if the men were punished for their planned action.

The next day (9 June), when the order 'Clear Lower Decks' was piped, the ordinary seamen and stokers, around 45 men, did not respond. The matter was reported to the captain. He ordered the first lieutenant to direct the sailors to parade on the quarterdeck. They refused, instead asking for the opportunity to discuss their grievances with the captain. The first lieutenant and the acting coxswain came through the mess decks and gave a direct order to each man remaining on the forward mess deck to fall-in on the quarterdeck. When men refused the orders they were deemed to be in a state of mutiny. In actual fact, they sat around in the mess decks not knowing what to do next—it seems no-one had planned any action that would follow the refusal of duty. It was a case of sitting and waiting to see what would happen next. There were no demands. There was no statement of protest. The men's action had been merely a gesture. In what now appears to be an absurd over-reaction, a detachment of sailors carrying rifles and fixed bayonets appeared on the wharf. For the third time within four years, sailors in an Australian warship were confronted by armed men and the whole ship was placed under armed guard. The firing mechanism of the ship's main gun was removed.

The crisis was described by one of the mutineers in the following account.

Early in the evening a sailor told me that there was going to be a 'sit-down' strike by the ship's company the following morning. After supper I called the three telegraphists into the wireless office, which was adjacent to the mess-decks, and asked them what they knew about it. They said that they had heard that it was 'on' but had not been in on any discussions about it. It was not necessary for me to ask them why the sailors intended to strike. I knew the enmity towards 'Beryl', particularly by the sailors, had been growing since he first appeared on the scene.

As we did not know any of the details, or who was taking part, and to ask someone was thought to involve a certain amount of risk, I warned the others to keep out of it. I told them to come to the office (which was almost soundproof) immediately after breakfast and we would remain there until it was all over.

During the course of the evening there were discussions amongst the various crew members in Nos 1, 2, 3 and 4 messes, which were on the forecastle mess deck. They agreed that neither Leading Hands nor Petty Officers would be asked or allowed to take part. It was considered that a 'sit-down strike' was an event of little seriousness and that things would be over and settled quickly. It was further agreed that everyone would tell the same story 'that they had no objection to going north. But not with "Beryl" in command!'

Bob Shipp, a stoker, was in his hammock but still awake when some of the libertymen returned on board slightly 'under the weather', on the night before the mutiny. They insisted on telling him, rather noisily, what was going to happen in the morning. Bob [Shipp] was watchkeeping (four hours on, four hours off) . . . in the engineroom [with Stoker Cig Branch]. They were looking forward to 24 hours liberty on completion of their 24 hours on, after the morning watch. The refusal of the rest of the ship's company to 'stand to' did not worry them because it would not affect them. So they thought. In the subsequent inquiry two out of the three 'Taswegian' stokers on board copped punishment. The third, Alan Reeves, had only rejoined the ship that day after being wounded at Oro Bay.

On the morning of 9 June the sailors were called, as usual, at 6am. At 6.30am, they were employed washing down the upper deck until 7.15am when 'hands to breakfast' was piped. At 8.15am the quartermaster piped 'hands fall in' but it was not obeyed. The sailors congregated in their mess deck and were joined by the other lower deck junior ratings. The Leading Seaman of the fore and aft parts reported the matter to the [First Lieutenant] who was waiting to delegate the work for the forenoon. Together they went to the mess deck where the men were all sitting around the mess tables talking.

The First Lieutenant asked them if they had heard the pipe. There was no response. Although this was considered by the ship's company to be no more than a 'sit-down strike' it was, technically, a mutiny. After ordering one sailor to fall in, without any response, the First Lieutenant and the acting Coxswain went to the captain's cabin, and reported the matter to him. After discussion, the captain ordered that the pipe 'hands fall in' be repeated immediately. Again there was no response from the men. The captain questioned the two Leading Seaman and acting Coxswain at length and they were emphatic that they had had no indication of the intention of the ship's company not to turn to.

The captain then ordered the acting Coxswain to proceed to the mess deck and find out what grievances were alleged by the men. When he entered the mess deck, the men were in a very high spirited mood. On asking them to nominate their grievances there was an unrestrained response from all sections of the mess deck. The men were virtually leaderless. Some of those that took a prominent part in the earlier discussions stepped back. Some had already left the ship.

While the 'sit-down strike' had apparently been discussed within the ship's company over a long period of time it appears no provision had been made for any subsequent developments. The younger men, who were in the majority, did not realise the gravity of the situation and treated the matter as a joke. Consequently, with youthful exuberance, they nominated grievances that were purely on impulse and had little bearing on their original reason for the 'strike'. The acting Coxswain listed the grievances and submitted them to the captain.

After receiving the list, the captain gave them consideration and then ordered 'clear lower deck—everybody aft' to be piped. The quartermaster walked through the mess-decks making this pipe. The pipe was obeyed by leading hands, Petty Officers and Engine Room Artificers. One cook and one coder were the only junior ratings who answered the pipe. After addressing those present, mainly senior ratings, the captain asked them for their co-operation in finding out the cause of the trouble. He then went ashore and reported to the Naval Officer in Charge, who immediately advised the Naval Board of the incident.

The immediate aims of the men had been achieved but being without a leader no one took the initiative to get the men back to work. They anticipated some sort of reaction from the Naval Board and most, if not all, would have been happy to return to work once the matter had been brought to the attention of a more senior authority. No opportunity was taken during the six hours (from 7.15am–1.15pm) to have an officer address the men and explain the possible consequences of their actions.

On board *Pirie* the ship's company went to dinner at 12pm but did not fall in to the pipe at 1.15pm. An armed guard was placed on the wharf abreast the ship at 5.20pm and the Naval Officer in Charge came on board. 'Clear lower deck—everybody aft' was piped and this time, the men fell in on the quarterdeck. The Naval Officer in Charge read articles ten and eleven of the *Articles of War* and called on any men who were unwilling to sail the ship to stand aside. Nobody responded. He warned them that the ship would sail at 8.30pm.

The corvette sailed for Cid Harbour as scheduled. Two sailors who had been on 24 hours leave and had no knowledge of the mutiny returned to their ship at 6pm to be confronted by the armed guard on the wharf. They had not expected to find a ship under siege.

To ensure his version of events was the first to circulate, Lieutenant Commander Mills hastily prepared a report on the mutiny:

> At a few minutes after 0815 my Executive Officer, Lieutenant R. A. Lorains RANR(S) reported to me that the sailors had not obeyed the order of the pipe of 'hands fall in' at 0815. At this time we were secured on the West side of Concrete Pier at Townsville having arrived there at approximately 2100 on Monday 7 June as escort for convoy BV 65. On receiving the First Lieutenant's report, I asked him if he knew what the trouble was. He replied that he knew of nothing which might have caused the incident. I then sent for the Coxswain and asked him if he knew of anything to cause the ship's company to refuse to answer the pipe. The Coxswain replied that it was a complete surprise to him. He had been in his office at the time of the pipe and did not realise it had not been obeyed until he came up through the mess deck. I then ordered (at about 0825) that the pipe 'hands fall in' should be repeated and this was done without any result. I then sent for the Coxswain again and told him to endeavour to find out what was the trouble on the mess deck and let me know. He came back about ten minutes or a quarter of an hour later with a list of alleged grievances. These were as follows:
>
> > Unfair treatment.
> > Working afternoons while in tropics.
> > Dress of the Day.
> > Routine too severe.

Should be entitled to a bottle of beer per man per day in tropics.
General routine as compared with other corvettes.
No consideration for ship's company during refit re leave and living conditions.
No confidence in First Lieutenant or Captain.
Volunteering for northern waters without considering the ship's company.

On receiving this list and having studied it briefly, I sent for my Engineer Officer, Engineer Lieutenant F. G. Hoffman RANR (S) who carries out the duty of the ship's censor and I asked him whether, in the course of his duty recently, he had noted any matters which may have indicated discontent. He informed me definitely that he had noted no such matters. At approximately 0900 I sent for the Coxswain and told him to have 'clear lower deck—everybody aft' piped. This was done and the pipe was responded to only by the ERAs and Leading Rates in the ship and one Cook named Harris. I did not muster those that actually fell in but having looked them over, I believe all Leading Rates and above in the ship were present. I spoke briefly to the men fallen in and said that the incident of the morning had been a complete surprise to me and that I was disappointed to think that a ship's company that had done as well as I consider we have done recently, should suddenly turn round and take action similar to that of wharf labourers. I told the ratings fallen in that it was their duty to endeavour to assist the First Lieutenant and myself in finding out the cause of the trouble and that I desired their co-operation in that connection. I then dismissed them and as they were going forward I called the Leading Telegraphist and sent a message through him to the Leading Signalman that I wanted him.

... The Leading Signalman had obeyed the pipe but it was not until some of the hands were well forward that I decided that I wanted the Leading Signalman. He came aft at once with pad and pencil and I made a signal to the Naval Officer in Charge requesting transport to report to him.

Before leaving the ship I informed the First Lieutenant where I was going and told him to report to me by telephone any developments, but to take no further action as regards the men. I then proceeded to the Office of the Naval Officer in Charge, reaching there between 0945 and 1000 and reported the details as above to him.

On reading this report one cannot help but be struck by Mills' ineffectual response. His first reaction on receiving the list of grievances was to have the ship's censor advise him on whether the men had made similar comments in their letters. One can only assume his aim was to depict the mutiny as a spontaneous challenge to his authority rather than a protest about his consistently poor leadership. It is curious that Mills then addressed the men who had not mutinied to tell them how disappointed he was in the actions of the ship's company.

The tragedy of the *Pirie* mutiny originated in the many things the captain did not do. *If only* the captain had gone down to the mess decks to confront the men who had disobeyed the pipe. *If only* he had discussed the grievances directly with them, instead of inquiring whether anyone had written a word or two in their private letters. *If only* he had talked to the men with a hint of compassion. These considerations would have cost nothing but clearly Mills' insecure personality precluded him from adopting a more generous attitude. Even if he had gone to the mess decks and explained to the men the seriousness of their actions, he probably would have met with a more positive response. The men themselves said later: 'If he had come down and said anything to us, we would have gone back to work'. Perhaps the key lesson learned from this and other similar incidents during the war, such as the 'sit-down strike' in *Voyager*, was that where officers were prepared to face their own men in a crisis, the sailors were satisfied with an opportunity to merely air their grievances. In almost every instance, the men wanted an avenue for venting their frustration with the war and the shortcomings of naval administration.

Mills was also guilty of escalating the mutiny. There was never any hint or threat of violence in mutinies occurring within the RAN. Even the *Perth* mutiny only reached the stage of insubordinate gestures. Mills should have realised that he was not in any physical danger from his men. Yet he did not grasp what he was losing (and lost) by seeking the support of the Naval Officer in Charge rather than facing his men. If Mills had resolved the matter quickly, he could have remained in command with his record unsullied. He may even have been decorated for the battle in Oro Bay. (In similar circumstances an award was given to another captain in recognition of the gallantry displayed by his entire ship's company.) Mills may also have been promoted again before peacetime retirement enhanced by a distinguished war record. As Shakespeare wisely counselled: 'There is a tide in the affairs of man that if taken at the flood leads on to fortune'. It was Lieutenant Commander Mills' fate that he missed a moment that could have kept him on the crest of a wave despite his own complete unworthiness.

Pirie arrived at Cid Harbour in the Whitsunday Islands off Queensland without further incident the morning after the mutiny. Mills was informed that a Board of Inquiry would be convened at 11am that day. Cid Harbour was the base of Task Force 74 which comprised the cruisers *Australia* and *Hobart* with six Australian and American destroyers. The role of the task force was regular patrolling of the area between Australia's north-east coast and the Solomon Islands. Rear Admiral Sir Victor Crutchley VC commanded the squadron as Rear Admiral Commanding HMA Squadron. The officer given responsibility for inquiring into the *Pirie* affair, as the President of a Board of Inquiry, was the commanding officer of HMAS *Australia*, then anchored at Cid Harbour. For better or worse, the president was Captain Harold Farncomb, an officer with little known sympathy for mutiny, who would be assisted by two other officers. Farncomb had been involved with mutinies in HMA Ships *Perth* and *Australia* (see Chapters 10 and 11). It was said he 'held the *King's Regulations and Admiralty Instructions* as holy writ like a Southern Baptist Preacher brandishing the Bible and breathing damnation on those who broke its laws . . .'. The inquiry would be conducted under the Imperial *Naval Discipline Act*, as Prime Minister Robert Menzies had formally passed control of Australian ships and men to the Admiralty on 7 November 1939.

Selected men from *Pirie* were called one at a time to give evidence. To those who waited anxiously in the corvette, there seemed no logical reason why one man was chosen to testify and not another. The official record of the inquiry has been criticised by some of the sailors involved. Some evidence which they thought was relevant was not recorded. (This may not have been deliberate because the two shorthand writers recording the proceedings had to appeal to speakers to slow down).

The 24 men who appeared before Captain Farncomb and the two other officers were without formal representation, despite the seriousness of the proceedings, and this certainly constituted a denial of natural justice. They were in a traumatic situation, now realising how serious their actions had been, and conscious that the inquiry had all the characteristics of a trial. For young sailors anxious to clear themselves but eager not to 'dob in' their mates, confronted by senior officers and a president who had a fearsome reputation for discipline, the inquiry was a severe ordeal. They were pressed to disclose the names of the ringleaders. They were asked for the reasons behind the mutiny. They were invited to express their grievances—but they well knew that if they were too forthright in their opinion of Mills they would draw from Farncomb the fires of wrath upon their heads. On the overnight journey to Cid Harbour, there is no doubt that someone on the mess deck had told them that refusing an order was mutiny, and that mutiny in wartime carried the death penalty.

When asked for their opinions about Mills and his performance, what could they say? They could not express their real feelings about his ineptitude or offer a candid assessment of his leadership. The Navy's rigidly hierarchical system of authority did not encourage or welcome criticism of seniors by juniors, let alone junior sailors criticising a ship's captain. The young men on the mess decks of *Pirie* had very few proper channels available to them for the expression of complaints. They were not allowed to make written complaints. If they brought charges against an officer and those charges were found to be unwarranted, they could face summary proceedings. Their only avenue of redress was to make verbal representations to their captain. It is likely that many of the men did not even know that. Whatever the extent of their procedural knowledge, verbal appeals to Mills had been fruitless.

On 13 June, Rear Admiral Crutchley summoned Mills and informed him that as the Board had been unable to identify the ringleaders of the mutiny, the matter would be passed back to him as *Pirie*'s commanding officer. He was directed to initiate summary action against the offenders. *Pirie* sailed for Palm Island and anchored there. At 8.05am on 15 June, the ship's company were assembled and punishment warrants were read out. Some of those interviewed by the inquiry panel were punished, others were not. Others who were neither questioned nor given the chance to defend their actions were also punished. There seemed to be no logic in the selection. The charge for all but two of the men was 'did join a mutinous assembly'; two others were charged because they 'did wilfully disobey to persuade others to resume duty'. Ten men received gaol sentences ranging from 21 to 60 days, four others received lesser punishments. Overall, one in four of those involved in the mutiny was singled out for punishment. None of the men was given an opportunity to speak in his own defence, claim mitigation or request clemency during the punishment parade. While the *Articles of War* deemed mutiny a most serious offence, the *Articles* also provided that no man could be convicted of mutiny without the opportunity of a court martial. This right included due process and the entitlement of the accused to have the support of a 'friend'.

Some sailors pointed out later that many of those punished

had been in a position to observe the incompetence of the captain during the action in Oro Bay. The sick berth attendant was among those gaoled although he had been in the sickbay during the mutiny attending to his normal duties. He had distinguished himself by his conduct during the battle but had also confronted the captain over the issue of the morphine. Another commented that the men punished were the articulate ones, the ones who could speak for themselves. After the warrants were read out, Mills launched into a bitter tirade against Lieutenant Lorains.

In stark contrast to Mills' handling of the matter, *Pirie* had been visited by Rear Admiral Crutchley before it left anchorage. The Admiral had inspected the ship's company before conducting rounds of the ship itself. He said to the assembled ship's company: 'Mutineer! Mutineer! What a terrible word. We will call it a "strike".'

Of course, there was no such word as 'strike' in the naval lexicon and the incident in *Pirie* was clearly a 'mutiny'. Rear Admiral Crutchley's remark to the men, and even the advice from the Board of Inquiry that the captain of *Pirie* should handle the matter, was reminiscent of the handling of the Bridging Train mutiny in 1916 (see Chapter 6). In both cases an admiral had wanted to put the affair into perspective, the seriousness of mutiny as an offence not seeming to match the character of the mens' actions. In 1916, the Bridging Train had had an experienced leader in Lieutenant Commander Bracegirdle who, by force of character (and with some latitude from Vice Admiral Wemyss), managed to resolve the 'mutiny' without further incident or injury to naval discipline. In 1943, Lieutenant Commander Mills was incapable of resolving the crisis despite the unlikely assistance of Farncomb and the magnanimity of Crutchley. This was almost entirely because he was the principal cause of the unrest. It was a shortcoming of rigid naval procedures and traditions that no distinction could be made between a good leader and a poor one in the administration of justice or the preservation of human dignity.

The men who received prison sentences were taken from the ship and transported to Stuart's Creek Gaol at Townsville. The gaol's governor was sympathetic to the sailors and was reluctant to place young servicemen with hardened criminals serving long sentences. He gave the *Pirie* men duties in the hospital, the library and the gardens, and afforded them some limited freedoms. The men found that gaol life was not unlike naval service, with its regular duties, plain food and cramped but adequate living quarters. Some said later that they were treated with more consideration in gaol than they been in their ship and, of course, they did not have to endure the capricious authority of their former captain. On release, the men were redrafted to various ships and shore estabish- ments as they tried to put the events of June 1943 behind them.

Most of those involved in the *Pirie* mutiny insist there were no ringleaders. It was an action that emerged from a consensus born of shared frustration. For that reason there were no plans or lists of well-considered grievances. On the other hand, some mention a particular leading seaman, the most senior sailor on the ship after the Coxswain, as the instigator. The man had been a petty officer several times but had been reduced in rank for various reasons. He was older than the rest of the sailors and he knew the *King's Regulations* through persistent transgression. When the day of the mutiny came, he gave advice to those considering action. But as a leading seaman he had taken no part in the defiant actions on the mess decks, instead obeying the pipe to fall in on the quarterdeck. Yet, it is unlikely that he or anyone else was a Machiavellian figure behind the scenes. All that was needed was someone who was wanting to wound but unwilling to strike.

Lieutenant Commander Mills was as much a victim of the mutiny as his ship's company. On 19 July 1943, he was informed by the Secretary of the Naval Board that:

> In connection with a Board of Inquiry held on board HMAS *Australia* to investigate the circumstances attending the refusal of duty of ratings on board HMAS *Pirie* on Wednesday 9 June 1943, I am directed to inform you that from the evidence available, the Naval Board is of the opinion that you failed in your duty in that you did not personally take immediate and resolute steps to terminate the mass refusal of duty. I am therefore to acquaint you that you have incurred the severe displeasure of the Naval Board.

When the captain received this message he said to another officer: 'This means the bowler hat for me'. He was posted back to the training and administration establishment HMAS *Cerberus* in November 1943, the delay designed to prevent any suggestion that he was being punished as a result of his unsatisfactory performance.

During Mills' last months in command, he struggled to assert his authority. In September alone, he charged four men by warrant for being 'absent without leave three hours and thirty minutes', and two men were gaoled for having stolen property (several bottles of liquor from the Clubhouse Hotel in Townsville). The captain recorded that the extra offences were due to 'new hands being drafted to the ship who failed to realise that discipline and obedience to orders is essential'. In October, he was listing offences such as 'an act prejudicial to good order and discipline in that [the named sailor] did . . . fail to lash his hammock'. For this, nine men received extra duties. On 15 October, two men were charged with 'did wash clothes in an improper place'. It was clear that even the heavy-handed official response to the mutiny in Townsville could not impose discipline upon sailors who had lost confidence in their commanding officer. It was a human tragedy that went on far too long.

Mills was succeeded in command of *Pirie* by Lieutenant Commander D. L. Thomson. A review of the punishment returns from *Pirie* reveal that under Thompson the ship's discipline did improve. In the five quarters that Mills exercised command in the corvette, instances of punishment had increased. In the quarter ending December 1942, there were six punishments awarded (usually stoppages of leave or extra duties); in the quarter ending March 1943, there were twelve men punished; in the quarter to June 1943 (including the mutiny) there were 23 punishments; in the quarter to September 1943, the number of punishments went up to 26, and in the next quarter, to December 1943, there were 30 punishments.[13] In the quarter to March 1944, when Lieutenant Commander Thomson had taken command, there was just one offence in five weeks, and Thomson could note in the punishment returns 'the general conduct of the ship's company has been very good'.

One can only speculate on the drama that could have been averted if Lieutenant Commander Mills had faced his men on the mess decks of the *Pirie* that morning. The letter from the Secretary of the Naval Board to Mills clearly concluded that there had been a failure of leadership at that critical moment, yet twelve young sailors were punished as a result of their captain's shortcomings. Moreover, their punishment was a public one inasmuch as they were convicted and gaoled, an experience that remained with them the rest of their lives. Lieutenant Commander Mills was not publicly punished. It appeared the Navy had to protect the image of its authority. Charles Mills died on 11 March 1947 and two days later was buried at Flinders Naval Depot.

The final judgment on *Pirie*'s captain ought to come from one of the men subjected to his deeply flawed leadership.

The 'mutiny' . . . was a reaction against a person who did not know how to use the power granted to him temporarily but who regarded it as an inherent right. To the 'mutineers', a continued acceptance of the abuse of power was, in effect, a denial of their view of 'the Navy' as the kind of organisation they had been proud to join. As a member of the permanent navy—with the straight rings which exemplified the best of its traditions—the commanding officer represented the Navy. And because, in practice, he showed none of those naval virtues, we felt betrayed. Combine such a feeling with certain unattractive personal characteristics which some of us found repellent and eventual trouble was inevitable. In later life, one can view the episode as truly tragic, for, in the failings of his character, the commanding officer held the seeds of his own destruction and it was his fate that the Navy, which probably was the core of his self-esteem, was the instrument for his downfall. On a personal note, I never had any bitter feelings about 'Beryl'. Although there was nothing about him I wish to emulate. I always thought him rather comical—a kind of music-hall Captain Queeg, if such can be imagined.

The corvette resumed convoy escort work between Australia and New Guinea in late 1943, and received a full refit in Sydney in December. To mid 1944 *Pirie* operated out of Darwin, and in the later part of the year undertook dangerous minesweeping work around the Great Barrier Reef, in November becoming part of the Minesweeping Flotilla of the British Pacific Fleet. At the end of July 1945, the ship was on convoy duty off Okinawa and Iwo Jima. On the Japanese surrender, *Pirie* led the RAN ships into Tokyo Bay.[14] The corvette returned to Sydney in February 1946 and paid off in April, in May leaving Australian waters for the last time, eventually to be transferred to the Turkish Navy. *Pirie's* Australian service had been barely 30 months.

13

Mutiny in New Zealand

The Royal New Zealand Navy (RNZN) was established by Royal Warrant in September 1941. In 1991, the RNZN's fiftieth anniversary was celebrated nationwide, along with the production of an official history. This commemorative publication described most facets of the RNZN's first 50 years but made no mention of one of the most significant events to overtake it in peacetime—the 1947 general mutiny. Some may say that the incident of April 1947 was unimportant; that it was a strike rather than a mutiny; that it involved few men; and, that it was brief and confined to Auckland. In fact, it was described at the time as a 'serious mutiny' by naval officers, parliamentarians, officials of the defence ministry, editorial writers and commentators; it swept throughout the fleet and involved hundreds of men; it continued for nearly a month; and its legacy caused difficulties for the RNZN for more than a decade.

The trouble began in the North Island city of Auckland. The main RNZN shore base was HMNZS *Philomel* at Devonport in Auckland. The name *Philomel* has a history much longer than the RNZN. When King George VI sanctioned use of the title 'Royal New Zealand Navy' in September 1941, HMS *Philomel* was a training ship tied up near the Calliope Dock in Auckland (the bulk of the trainees were accommodated in shore barracks). The history of *Philomel* encapsulates much of the history of naval activity in New Zealand. Naval forces in the South Pacific were initially under the jurisdiction of the Commander-in-Chief, India (see Chapter 4). New Zealand waters were relatively quiet until Royal Navy ships based in Australia were heavily involved in combat during the wars with Maori tribes in 1843–47 and later in 1860–64. (On 28 March 1860 Leading Seaman William Odgers in HMS *Niger* won the first Victoria Cross awarded in the Southern

Hemisphere during an assault on a Maori fortification at Omata.) In 1859, the British naval presence in the South Pacific was reorganised. A new command was formed and from then until the formation of the RAN in 1911, RN ships in New Zealand waters were part of an Australasian squadron.

The New Zealand colonial administration became the first to establish a local naval force when in 1863 it fitted out several small ships for duties on the Waikato River during hostilities against tribes supporting the 'Maori King' movement. One of these vessels, *Pioneer*, was designed and built in Sydney by the Australian Steam Navigation Company. It was fitted out as a river gunboat armed with two iron turrets that housed twelve-pounder guns. In the same year heavy loss of life occurred when the steam corvette HMS *Orpheus* was wrecked off Manukau Harbour at Auckland. With the end of the Maori wars there were no further hostilities in New Zealand waters until 1917, when the German raider *Wolf* sank a number of vessels by gunfire and mines.

In 1877, British naval squadrons in the South Pacific area were again reorganised. New Zealand agreed to contribute financially towards the maintenance of a joint naval force based in Sydney, the Australia Station. Part of that force was an Auxiliary Squadron of warships dedicated to local service. HMS *Philomel*, built at Devonport Dockyard in England in 1890, was one of a class of five small cruisers sent out in 1891 to form part of the Auxiliary Squadron. The Calliope Dock built at Devonport on the north shore of Auckland's harbour and completed in February 1888, was intended to serve as a refitting base for warships of the Australia Station although it was under the control of the Auckland Harbour Board. The dock's namesake, HMS *Calliope*, was the first ship eased onto the blocks. Local citizens donated six casks of beer for the ship's company to celebrate. Late in the festivities, a fight broke out between the blue jackets and the local police, only quelled when *Calliope*'s commanding officer sent the ship's Royal Marine detachment ashore. The precincts of the Calliope Dock at Devonport were thus no strangers to conflicts involving sailors.[1]

At the end of the nineteenth century, naval contingents from Australasia were despatched to both the Boer War in South Africa and the Boxer Rebellion in China. HMS *Philomel* sailed to South Africa and landed a unit consisting of Royal Marines and parts of the ship's company which became part of a relieving force marching on the besieged town of Ladysmith. It could be said that at least some of its guns fired in anger: two of the cruiser's

4.7-inch guns were mounted on field-gun carriages and sent inland accompanied by the guns' crew. In the early twentieth century, a naval armaments race between Britain and Germany and the growing naval power of Japan, demonstrated at the Battle of Tsu-Shima by the defeat of the Russian Fleet, prompted the Admiralty to propose an expansion of Fleet Units in the Pacific with each Dominion supporting a unit. Australia would finance and man a new dreadnought as the flagship of the Australian Fleet Unit while New Zealand would finance a dreadnought as the flagship of a Fleet Unit based in China. On this basis the battle cruisers HMS *New Zealand* and *Australia* were ordered. *New Zealand* was completed in 1912 at a cost of £1,698,224. The taxpayers of New Zealand would still be paying for the ship after it was scrapped following World War I.[2]

On the formation of the RAN, New Zealand's contribution to local naval forces had to be reorganised. The British government agreed to turn *Philomel* over to the New Zealand government in 1913 to be permanently stationed in New Zealand for the training of sailors enlisted in the Dominion. On 15 July 1914, *Philomel* commissioned at Wellington. The ship's company was augmented by Reservists and re-commissioned into the Royal Navy. *Philomel* escorted convoys to the former German colony of Samoa before sailing into the Indian Ocean and the Persian Gulf for general patrol duties. In May 1917 the cruiser was sent back to Wellington for decommissioning.

Lord Jellicoe (later Governor-General of New Zealand) conducted a review of naval defences throughout the Empire, including New Zealand, after World War I on behalf of the Admiralty. Following the publication of the 'Jellicoe Report', an Order-in-Council dated 20 June 1920 created the New Zealand Division of the Royal Navy. It was to comprise a small sea-going component, of two Royal Navy cruisers under the control of the New Zealand Government, and a training base at Auckland. In 1921, *Philomel* made its second-last voyage from Wellington to Auckland. (Its last voyage was as a stripped hulk, towed out to sea and scuttled in 1949.) From 1921 to 1946, *Philomel* served as the training centre at Auckland. Extra holes were cut in the ship's sides for ventilation. Huts and cabins were erected on the upper decks. The guns were removed and a single mast retained for drilling trainees. With the outbreak of war imminent during 1939, the training facilities were greatly extended by the building of shore barracks.

In 1939 the Royal Navy despatched a pair of light cruisers, *Leander* and *Achilles*, to serve with the New Zealand Division as its two main units. When the war began the New Zealand Government decided to retain *Leander* in New Zealand, while *Achilles* was sent into the Atlantic where it reinforced a cruiser group that later tracked down and neutralised the German raider *Graf Spee* in the Battle of the River Plate. Four New Zealanders were killed in that action. This first engagement of a warship from the New Zealand Station helped bring about an awareness of the contribution the country could make in its own right, which contributed to a movement calling for the establishment of an independent New Zealand navy.

Leander saw action shortly afterward. It destroyed the Italian raider *Ramb I* on 27 February 1942 off the Maldive Islands in the northern Indian Ocean, and then transferred to the Pacific where it joined United States forces in operations against the Japanese Navy in the Solomons. On the night of 12–13 July 1943, *Leander* engaged a Japanese cruiser-destroyer force with two American cruisers and destroyers. All three Allied cruisers were badly damaged by torpedoes although heavy losses were inflicted on the Japanese. Twenty-eight New Zealanders died. *Leander* limped to the United States where arrangements had been made to carry out repairs. American dockyards gave a low priority to repairing the New Zealand cruiser, however. As a British-built ship, it was not believed to be compatible with American naval operations, and was not completely repaired until the end of February 1944. The ship was by then considered unfit for further war service, and returned to Britain for decommissioning. The Colony Class cruiser *Gambia* was lent to New Zealand as a replacement and saw service with the British Pacific Fleet.

Achilles returned to New Zealand in 1945, literally crowded to the gunwales with returning servicemen. Over 2000 were embarked on the passage from Sydney to Auckland. Shortly after the war, both *Gambia* and *Achilles* were returned to the Royal Navy. *Achilles* was transferred to the Royal Indian Navy and later, as *Delhi*, saw active service during hostilities with Pakistan. The two ships of the *Dido* Class allocated by the Admiralty for the New Zealand Station in 1946 were not as suitable as the vessels they replaced. *Achilles* and *Leander* displaced 7000 tons, were 544 feet long and had a complement of 640. The new ships, the small anti-aircraft cruisers *Black Prince* and *Bellona*, displaced 5700 tons and had complements of around 480 men. Smaller fuel tanks reduced their cruising range. Built hurriedly toward the end of the war to meet a belatedly recognised requirement for escort vessels, mainly in the Atlantic and the Arctic, the ships of the

Dido Class were heated but not cooled. Extra guns and equipment were mounted until their margin of stability became minimal. The additional men needed for the extra guns had to be crammed everywhere. By the end of the war the complement had risen to 550. The ships had also been driven hard and borne the brunt of heavy fighting. Five of the sixteen ships of the class were lost during the war.

Technical publications were not kind to the *Dido* Class. One description stated that 'to man the armament accommodation would be at a premium, added to which the additional turrets and their supports severely encroached upon living spaces'.[3] And after the war, 'little or no structural alterations were implemented, especially with regard to habitability'. This was at a time when new warships were being designed to provide accommodation in bunks to remedy the health problems caused by cramped, damp hammocks. A final judgment held that 'the class was the least adaptable to modern requirements'. But given the low priority of the New Zealand Station to the Admiralty, these ships were the best available and the most that could be offered.

In addition to the two cruisers, the peacetime RNZN would also comprise escort craft, in anticipation of New Zealand having its share of occupation duties in the post-war Pacific. Two corvettes were lent to the RNZN. *Arabis* and *Arbutus*, built in 1943 and 1944, were Flower Class corvettes, not too dissimilar to the RAN *Bathurst* Class. The Flower Class were built quickly and in large numbers for wartime convoy escort duty. They were not intended to carry out extensive patrol duties in the broad reaches of the Pacific. They displaced around 1000 tons. By 1947, only *Arbutus* remained manned and in commission.

Much soul-searching found no place in the new navy for *Philomel*. In January 1946 the ship was declared redundant and sold for £750. At its paying off, the New Zealand Naval Board sent a signal acknowledging its contribution: 'When HMNZS *Philomel*'s colours are hauled down at sunset this evening, the tradition which she has established during her long career will live on in the depot to which she has given her name'. The bow anchors of the old cruiser were mounted close to the entrance of the shore base bearing the same name.

While a new navy was being planned, some old problems needed attention. There had been concerns raised over pay and conditions even when the RNZN was formed in 1941. Due to war these matters could not be properly addressed. By the end of hostilities, it was obvious something had to be done, as naval pay rates had slipped far behind those of comparable civilian occupations and of the air force and the army. Many sailors were forced to accept low wages because they had enlisted for a set period of service, some as long as twelve years, and could not resign. In 1945, Commander Davis-Goff, assisted by a welfare committee, was tasked with reviewing a wide range of issues relating to pay and conditions. Discussions took place, leading to an understanding that pay increases would be offered in early 1946. The announcement of a pay review was important for many wartime sailors who were thinking of the Navy as a post-war career. In the first post-war election, the leader of the New Zealand Labour party, Peter Fraser, made a commitment to grant pay rises from 1 April 1946. He was duly elected and took office as Prime Minister. The RNZN looked forward to the pay review.

In March 1947 *Black Prince* was tied up at *Philomel* shore base at Auckland. The ship was manned by only half its complement, which included 80 New Zealand sailors. *Philomel* was also under-staffed. The corvette *Arbutus*, fully manned, was secured alongside *Black Prince*. The minesweeper HMNZS *Hautapu* was stationed at Timaru. The acting RNZN flagship, *Bellona*, was to return to New Zealand after exercises with the Australian Fleet. On the surface there seemed no reason for a general mutiny to begin, but the pressures which would eventually erupt into open insurrection had started building two months earlier, during a cruise in *Arbutus*. During late 1946 and early 1947, *Arbutus* had been engaged in mine-clearance duties in the Hauraki Gulf. This was difficult and dangerous work. The minefields which had been laid to protect Auckland's shipping lanes had now to be cleared so the approaches to the harbour were safe for general shipping. The work consisted of retrieving the mines, using the detailed charts that had been drawn up at the time of mine-laying, and then destroying the mines with small attached explosives. There was no room for error. *Arbutus* would be lost if the charts were not perfectly accurate and the ship struck a misplaced mine. (Despite this, a few mines were overlooked, one being discovered and destroyed in the 1990s.) The sailors were recompensed for the arduous and dangerous nature of the work by an extra payment of one shilling and sixpence a day. *Arbutus* was then despatched on a 'show-the-flag' cruise, visiting a number of small Pacific islands in the course of a two-month voyage.

The living conditions in *Arbutus* were no better or worse than in the Australian *Bathurst* Class corvettes, but there were few portents of the trials to come as it steamed towards the islands.

The ship's upper decks were repainted to make a good impression among the local people. At the beginning of March, *Arbutus* was alongside at Papeete, the main town of Tahiti. Once the ship was refuelled, it was a time to relax. Some of the officers were entertained by the leading citizens of the French colony, and most of the ship's company had leave ashore. In normal circumstances, a ship establishes a shore patrol to keep watch for men on unauthorised leave. The shore patrol from *Arbutus* met a group of French sailors and unfortunately succumbed to extravagant Gallic hospitality. By early afternoon the shore patrol was drunk and most of the ship's company were absent from the vessel. There were curious parallels with the experience of the *Bounty* 150 years earlier—the charms of Tahiti proved irresistible to sailors who had spent long periods at sea living with hardships.

Aboard *Arbutus* there remained a minimum ship's company, consisting of the officer of the watch and a sailor on 'anchor watch'. There was also a gangway guard, as regulations demanded, a lone sailor equipped with an unloaded rifle and full regulation kit, which included webbing with a bayonet in its scabbard. The Tahitians were friendly and enticing as they gathered on the quay in a crowd numbering more than 200. The guard was offered a quaff of local beer. He resisted the invitation only briefly; it was a hot day. The officer of the watch suddenly became aware that the gangway guard was slumped and insensible on the wharf. Over his body, Tahitians were pouring up the gangway into the ship, intending to souvenir whatever could be carried away. The officer tried to stem the tide but eager locals forced past him even as he tried to block the gangway. Driven to desperation, and aware that civilians were emerging from below decks with kit and gear, the officer dashed down the gangway, retrieved the rifle from where it had fallen across the gently snoring body of the guard, unlimbered the bayonet from its scabbard and fastened it to the weapon. Then with fixed bayonet and, in the words of a sailor who witnessed the event, a 'blood-curdling cry', the one man charged the crowd and soon cleared the ship. With the locals at least temporarily at bay, the officer patrolled the wharf with rifle and bayonet across his shoulder until other members of the ship's company returned. It took time to recruit a new shore patrol and round up the remnants of the first. It took even longer for all the ship's company to return from the Tahitian entertainments. By the time *Arbutus* was ready to sail, it was well behind schedule. The ship cleared harbour and headed south with the engine-room staff under orders to drive their machinery at its best speed to make up time.

The weather turned for the worse during the night. Then another problem emerged. The oil fuel taken on board at Tahiti was contaminated with water and the hard-driven machinery broke down. As *Arbutus* was slowed to a limp, the worst of the storm enveloped the little ship. Although the Flower Class corvettes were built for the North Atlantic and its testing seas, the days and weeks of bad weather that *Arbutus* experienced in March 1947 tested its weatherly qualities to the limit. For days the ship took 'green waves' over its bows, until even the doors on the bridge and wheelhouse, the highest parts of the ship, were stove in by the weight of water. The helmsman had first to be tied to the wheel. Then, for days on end, the ship had to be steered by hand from the emergency steering position right in the stern of the vessel where the rudder could be turned directly by struggling sailors. In the engine room, working day and night to nurse the engine and repair the frequent breakdowns caused by the contaminated fuel, the stokers and engineers suffered the agonies of seasickness as well. 'We worked with buckets between our knees, so that we could be sick in the buckets without having to leave our post'. The ship's cat had been born while *Arbutus* was serving with the Atlantic convoys. Even it was seasick for the first and only time while the corvette laboured home from the islands.

There was another significant hardship although it seemed trivial in itself. There had been an altercation in the galley while *Arbutus* was docked in Tahiti, one senior sailor fighting another in the petty officers' mess. One man had suffered a broken arm. Later, in a fit of pique, all the mess crockery was thrown overboard. For the petty officers at least, this meant that meals were limited to what could be eaten cold and in the fingers. The entire ship's company were sick and weary when at last the ship limped into base at Devonport at the end of March. They arrived to the news that the ship would be in port only long enough to take on provisions, sailing immediately to the Cook Islands to deliver aviation fuel and vital stores. This news did not go down well.

At the same time there was mounting dissatisfaction in *Black Prince*, arising from a number of incidents but particularly the cruiser's refit program. One of the constraints of the refit was the closure of all toilets on board; this meant that the sailors had to use the toilets ashore, and for this they needed the permission of a supervising officer, each and every time. Unfortunately, this limitation coincided with a bout of dysentery affecting many sailors. One older sailor, driven to desperation by his need and unable to find his supervising officer, left the ship without permission. He was subsequently charged with leaving *Black Prince* without permission and received seven days punishment. The incident caused considerable comment on the mess decks in both ships and throughout the base.

There were thus pockets of dissatisfaction to build on when the news reached all the sailors at Auckland at the end of March that the government had broken its promise to review pay rates and to make them retrospective. That night, the petty officers and leading seamen in *Arbutus* calculated that their services, and their tolerance of conditions that would stretch anyone to the limit of endurance, were worth much more than ten shillings a day. And the government did not even value them enough to consider itself bound by the promises that they had accepted in good faith. When the majority of sailors returned to duty on the morning of Monday 31 March, dissension grew rapidly. The details of the new pay rates were generally known even though the Prime Minister was not due to announce them officially until Tuesday night. The men were incensed. Whereas army privates and aircraftmen would receive ten shillings and sixpence per day, sailors would only receive four to six shillings per day. Warrant officers would receive 23 to 25 shillings a day whereas leading seamen would receive around 17 shillings a day. In addition the new tax scales would absorb most of the increase for single men. Other disadvantages were a reduction in canteen benefits and the end of free travel for men in uniform (although soldiers would be issued with free travel vouchers).

A further cause for anger was the reputed decision not to make the pay increases retrospective to April 1946, when the pay review was first proposed. Other conditions caused rancour; the insensitivity of some even now seems amazing. Sailors were paid sixpence per day uniform clothing allowance and then charged three times the pre-war cost of similar items of clothing. Another broken promise concerned welfare committees. After agitation to obtain a formal channel for grievances, the Admiralty rather than the New Zealand authorities, had finally approved the formation of lower-deck committees. However, they specifically excluded any consideration of, or action on, matters of pay, shipboard routine or conditions of service. Sailors were to remain without a means of expressing grievances on the very matters of greatest import to them. This included the new pay rates.

There had already been months of dissatisfaction while the Fleet waited for the results of the pay review. When its conclusions were made known, the months of delay and disappointment made the men's feelings of anger and frustration even deeper. During the course of that last Monday in March, the refitting of *Black Prince* came to a halt and groups of sailors gathered almost spontaneously. When the loading of aviation fuel for the Cook Islands into *Arbutus* ceased, the officers refused to allow any more of the ship's company to leave the vessel. The senior officer at *Philomel* was Commander Peter Phipps, a New Zealander who was later to have a long and distinguished naval career, achieving the rank of vice-admiral and the bestowal of a knighthood. During the course of the afternoon he received indications that the dissatisfaction was more widespread than anticipated.

The first day of April, ironically April Fool's Day, dawned cool and cloudy. The clouds in the west looked grey and heavy and rain seemed likely. By 8am, however, the clouds were clearing and there were patches of sunlight speckling Devonport Base, Calliope Dock and the grey warships tied up alongside the wharves. At mid morning a cold wind had developed and was rattling windows in gusts. Several petty officers and leading seamen from *Arbutus* had been in discussion with personnel from *Black Prince* and *Philomel*, the *Arbutus* men expressing their determination not to accept their situation but to make a protest, to take whatever steps were necessary short of violence to remedy their position.

When Commander Phipps arrived at the base he was informed by his subordinate, Lieutenant Commander Harding, that leading seamen and other ranks planned a meeting in the base canteen during the lunch hour to discuss their concerns. The commander informed his superiors of the situation and received a reply that the Prime Minister had promised that 'the pay will be announced in the papers tonight'.[4]

The first acts of disobedience came when *Philomel* personnel were required on morning parade. The commanding officer was informed that the men would refuse duty as a protest against the failure of the Government to make the new rates of pay, still not officially announced, retrospective to 1 April 1946. This group of sailors, numbering about 100, then left the parade ground area and word was spread that there would be a meeting of all sailors, including those posted to the ships, in the base canteen at noon. Commander Phipps then ordered all sailors of the base to assemble in the gymnasium where he intended to pass on the Prime Minister's message. Years later, Phipps commented:

> Peter Fraser had been responsible for the delay. He wanted to be sure everyone got a fair deal . . . I had 'clear lower deck' piped for noon, with all hands to muster in the gymnasium. The chief petty officers and petty officers turned up, but the leading rates and below gathered at the canteen, as they had planned.[5]

After addressing the men in the gymnasium, the commander walked over to the canteen. He commented later that he approached the group of sailors from the rear of the room so he could see who was there. The 'leaders were already known'. Phipps addressed the meeting, pleading for a return to duty and giving details of the pay scales about to be announced by the Prime Minister. He also pointed out that they were already guilty of an 'act of indiscipline and . . . would have to take the consequences'. Such was their frustration that the men were unimpressed.

There was continuing discussion before the meeting decided to present a petition to the Naval Board detailing their three principal concerns. First, there was a demand that the new pay rates be made retrospective to 1 April 1946 as the government had promised. Second, the men demanded that the sailors' welfare committees be made effective and empowered to address issues relating to pay and service conditions. Third, the men included a demand that there be no punishment for their actions. This final demand, similar to those made by the mutineers at Spithead in 1797 and at Invergordon in 1931 (and agreed to by the authorities in resolving those mutinies), was evidence that the sailors were aware of the seriousness of their actions in refusing to return to duty. Commander Phipps was a long-serving, correct and loyal officer, who had a distinguished record of service during the war, particularly in command of the corvette *Tui* when it sank a Japanese submarine. He saw the mood of the meeting and, after noting details of the petition to be conveyed to the Naval Board, agreed to convey the sailors' concerns to higher authorities. He then left to communicate urgently with the Naval Board in Wellington.

An additional complication on that day was a scheduled visit of the Governor-General. The senior officers of the base had that visit in mind when the day began and were determined to have *Philomel* and the ships alongside as presentable as possible. The bosun's pipe sounded the signal for the return to work at 1pm. The *Philomel* men, now joined by sailors from the minimum-manned

Black Prince, resolved instead that they would 'go on strike as a protest against the government's failure to carry out a formal promise . . . that the higher rates would be made retrospective'.[6] The mood was very tense. Discipline on the base was in the hands of the master-at-arms and his 'boat's crew', but they were vastly outnumbered by the mutineers, who now numbered about 170. Older sailors, many with one or two rows of medal ribbons from the Pacific and Mediterranean campaigns, spoke to the men at the meeting which continued in the canteen. It was these sailors who defused much of the tension, by emphasising that the men's action was against the Government and not the Navy—although it is doubtful whether this distinction affected the legal status of their actions. This was a genuine mutiny inasmuch as the sailors had defied a direct order from their superior officers. Nevertheless, it was noted that the sailors who walked off *Black Prince* were punctilious in saluting the white ensign as they disembarked.

Observers commented that the sailors were very calm and controlled at all times. One man who had had a glass of rum was prevented by his comrades from taking part in the mutiny so that no-one could accuse the mutineers of being affected by alcohol. The remainder of *Arbutus*'s ship's company were still unable to leave the ship, even though work was at a standstill. At 2pm, however, some of the sailors from *Philomel* and *Black Prince* 'moved in an orderly procession to the jetty alongside the corvette'. There was discussion backward and forward between the corvette's officers and the mutineers, with the result that the remainder of the corvette ship's company decided to join the mutiny, leaving only the officers and petty officers in the ship. The group of mutinous sailors, now numbering over 200, waited in the canteen area for a reply from the Naval Board.

By 4pm, 'afternoon liberty time', the Naval Board replied to the petition. However, the meaning of the response was unclear, particularly regarding the retrospectivity of the pay rise. The backdating was a crucial issue for many of those who had recently married or were planning marriage and looking to a lump sum of backdated pay to start their married life. The uncertainty over retrospectivity led to the mutinous sailors resolving to leave the base, although a few expressed anxieties about whether the master-at-arms would have orders to prevent their departure. It was, then, a tense group of men who began to move towards the main gates of the base. One of the participants described the scene and his feelings as he walked away:

The wind started to gust and blew in our faces as we walked. There was dust in the wind and it stung my cheeks. I wondered whether anyone would try and stop us by force. Although we were such a large group, I sensed the tenseness and nervousness. We had had years of strict discipline ingrained in us every waking hour of the day, and now we were setting that aside, defying everything that had been drummed into us over the years. As if in subconscious reaction, the rank of men I was marching with moved closer together, until our shoulders were almost touching. There was a feeling that as long as we stuck together we would come out of it alright. The gates were up ahead. I saw a small knot of petty officers and other men who I recognised as the Master-at-Arms' mates. They were uncertain and talking quickly amongst themselves. What would we do if they formed a cordon to try and stop us?

Then there was a buzz in our own ranks, a low sort of humming that was hardly words. The detail guarding the gate looked up at us. Then I realised they were more nervous than we were. We were a tight-knit bunch of two hundred men stamping grimly and determinedly towards the gates.

I heard a voice from someone in our group that said, 'Step back, Nobby'. Then the gate detail all took a step backwards together and the way was clear for us. I felt light-headed as we marched past. It really was like a march past because all of us turned our eyes right to watch the gate guards as we passed through and they in their turn kept their eyes fixed on us.

We were through the gates! I had a sense of drifting along. Where to next? There seemed to be a common feeling that we had come a long way in just a few paces, but now we didn't know where to go. Who had thought that far? There had just been the common feeling, 'Right—we're walking out'. Having done that, we milled around for a few moments then followed a small group of former Pommy sailors who headed for Devonport Reserve and the Band Rotunda. 'Who's for some music?' someone said. I thought in my heart that we'd certainly be facing the music, and no mistake!

As the sailors prepared to march out of the base for a nearby open space Commander Phipps attempted to intercept them, again pleading with the men as he walked along beside them. Another participant later stated that their commander was agitated and argued desperately for the sailors to return to their duties, at least for the duration of the Governor-General's visit. An ex-stoker recalled:

He was anxious and worried what it would look like if the Governor-General arrived late in the afternoon and the base was deserted. One or two men told him politely that it was a bit late to think about that. Most were silent, and looked straight ahead. From force of habit, we fell into step. So we marched in good order off the base, for what was the last time for most of us.

Phipps put the blame for the walkout squarely on the government: 'Primarily, it was Mr Fraser's mistake in not insisting that the pay be made retrospective'.[7] As the sailors set foot outside the base it was obvious to any observer that the men were in a state of open defiance and mutiny.

The visit by the Governor-General was cancelled at the last moment. Preparations for the occasion had a strange consequence, however. Many of the sailors had been nominated for an honour guard and had been preparing for a parade in full uniform, including webbing and ceremonial arms. Some of the master-at-arms' detachment, and other petty officers, also wore bayonets in scabbards as part of their ceremonial dress. Journalists who heard of the unrest and soon gathered at Devonport Reserve noticed the men wearing scabbards. A rumour then spread that naval authorities had armed loyal servicemen with a view to returning the mutineers to duty at bayonet point. The rumour persisted, although the mutiny was entirely non-violent.

The sailors gathered on the football field in Devonport Reserve, a park near the base, and lingered there indecisively. A group of leading seamen drafted a message for the press, reiterating that the protest was 'solely a protest against the government in its failure to live up to the stated promise of the Prime Minister'. When it was obvious that no reply to their demands would be received that day from the Government, the sailors dispersed. The only sailors still left at *Philomel* were eighteen British seamen and the sick berth staff in the naval hospital. There was a Cabinet meeting at Wellington that evening. At 8pm, the Prime Minister announced that the pay rates would be made retrospective to 1 April 1946. But as so often happens, the government had moved too late. The frustration of the sailors was too deep and legitimate orders had been defied. Legally and in fact, the sailors had mutinied. Their actions could not be ignored or overlooked.

The sailors met next day on the Devonport Reserve at 8am. The Prime Minister's announcement was considered. Some men complained that the finer details of the pay package were incomprehensible. Some of the married sailors commented that under the amended tax scales they were actually worse off with the new rates and conditions. The meeting lasted barely ten minutes, ending in a unanimous resolution that contained two demands. First, there should be no 'victimisation' of the mutineers. Second, the lower deck welfare committees should be genuinely representative and able to consider a range of shipboard issues. Observers noted that the men then moved off in an orderly procession to present these demands to Commander Phipps. Many sailors wore good conduct badges representing eight years continuous service. They were anything but agitators or malcontents.

The master-at-arms stopped the procession at the entrance to the base. A few moments later, Commander Phipps came to the gates where, in the words of a witness, 'he was given a most attentive hearing'. However, his words offered the men nothing other than a call to resume duty and accept whatever punishment was determined. The sailors' response was to present their demands. They pointed out that in the course of recent meetings of sailors' committees under the guidelines of the relevant *Admiralty Order*, 219 recommendations had been offered by their committees, only six of those had been approved by higher authority and of that six only one had been implemented. Hence their repeated calls for effective committees to consider issues of shipboard conditions.

The local member of parliament, Dr Finlay, then promised the men that the Government would give 'every consideration to their requests'.[8] On this note, the mutineers moved away quietly to the band rotunda in the reserve, taking with them Dr Finlay's assurance that the Prime Minister would respond within two hours. While waiting, the sailors took up a collection for seventeen of their number who were penniless—each received nine shillings from the proceeds (or about one day's pay). By 11am, there was still no reply and the men began to disperse, with the intention of meeting again the next day. Just before noon, Prime Minister Fraser's reply arrived, received by only a handful of men still on the reserve. The Prime Minister told the sailors he felt they would have been better advised to contact the government 'through proper authorities' if they wanted an explanation of any points of the new pay package that were unclear. In the meantime, the Prime Minister would 'discuss the matter with the Chief of Naval Staff, Commodore G. H. Faulkner'. He went on to call for them 'to resume normal duties and to trust to the good sense and decency of the authorities . . .'.[9] The advice was too late and it was unheeded.

Coincidentally, there was serious industrial discontent aboard civilian ships at this time as well. The Merchant Service Guild presented the mass resignation of 250 masters and deck officers of vessels listed on the New Zealand Shipping Register to the representatives of shipping companies as a protest against the new awards of pay and conditions. It seems there was general unrest on the Auckland waterfront in reaction to the privations of wartime conditions being continued.

Overnight consideration did not incline the government towards concession or sympathy for the sailors. When the striking sailors returned to the dockyard gates at 10am on Thursday, they were offered a blunt alternative: return to duty immediately or face immediate discharge. The Naval Board had decided that personnel must 'accept such disciplinary measures as might be enforced, or be discharged from the RNZN—services no longer required'. The Government agreed. The gates were closed and guarded by a squad of petty officers reinforced by a contingent of police constables. This response came despite the absence of violence at Auckland and the repeated protestations of loyalty by the mutineers. New Zealand was not under threat of war, these men were not raw recruits and their main demand was simply for a responsible and effective committee to hear their grievances. Representatives of the New Zealand Ex-Navalmen's Association were present as well. They offered legal assistance and a willingness to mediate with the government but only if the men withdrew their demands and returned to duty. Obviously the Association did not like the men's actions either. Commander Phipps was also at the gates and did not mince words. He challenged the notion that the men were on strike! 'I . . . give a message to all men who have taken part in this mutinous action . . . those who are prepared to accept naval punishment are to return on board by 10am this morning'.[10] Those who did not return on board would be summarily dismissed. The government recognised that the manning of the Navy would be set back 'for five or seven years' and would accept the repercussions of its decision.

The sailors returned once more to Devonport Reserve to consider their situation. Dr Finlay was present and advised that men who had joined prior to 1940—the longest-serving and most experienced men, as well as those who had made the greatest sacrifice for their country—would likely forfeit all benefits if they were summarily discharged. His warning, and the events at the dockyard gates, seemed to have the opposite effect from the one desired. Instead of weakening, the sailors' resolve stiffened.

A leading seaman spoke to his mates and finished with the question: 'Do you want to be civvies?' His question was 'answered with a thunderous "Yes!"'. Just 23 men slipped away from the group and reported for duty. They were charged with taking 'part in a technical mutiny without violence'.[11]

An event then took place which, even 50 years afterwards, loses none of its poignancy. Long-serving sailors, 187 men who previously had emphasised their loyalty to New Zealand, a loyalty that was already well-proven, stripped off their category badges, insignia of rank and good conduct awards, and medal ribbons. They returned to the dockyard gates for the last time to convey their decision and to collect their personal gear. Insult was added to injury. The master-at-arms would only allow the men onto the base singly, under escort, to collect personal belongings. And this was made conditional on the men returning all items of service clothing and equipment before departure. The men literally could not go away with the clothes they wore, even though they had paid for their uniforms through pay deductions over the years. There was an indication that the naval authorities were concerned at the loss of experienced men. They called a meeting of chief petty officers and petty officers to gain an assurance that they would not join the mutineers. These men, 20- and 30-year veterans, expressed their sympathy with the mutiny and disagreed with the harsh treatment meted out but, at a reconvened meeting, agreed to remain on duty. On the near-empty base, these senior sailors had to undertake all duties from sweeping to cooking in the messes.

That afternoon *Arbutus*, manned by the few sailors who returned to duty and the British personnel who had not joined the strike, proceeded to sea immediately, bound for the Cook Islands. Perhaps it was thought that the handful of loyal sailors should be quarantined from further infections of mutiny. There was a further irony in that *Arbutus*, the small ship whose arduous cruise had provided a spark for the mutiny among some senior sailors, was not properly provisioned for its passage to Raratonga. It was despatched so hurriedly that virtually all of its provisions were canned pilchards. 'We had them cold and we had them hot,' said a sailor. 'In fact, you name any way to prepare tinned pilchards and we had it, plus a few more most people hadn't thought of'. When *Arbutus* reached Samoa, they came across some American sailors who invited them to their own base in Pago Pago for meals of fresh fruit and fresh vegetables. What was the source of such good fresh food? New Zealand!

Prime Minister Fraser spoke again in the evening. He did not express any remorse over the events at Auckland. Rather, there was the first hint of a campaign that would soon be waged against the now-dismissed sailors. 'The serious acts of indiscipline of a number of ratings . . . were very much to be regretted', he said, and went on to explain that on dismissal from the RNZN, the men had forfeited 10 per cent of their deferred pay and all of their accrued leave, and had lost any retrospective benefits and increases of pay dating back to April 1946. The decision to apply this harsh 'sentence' was made without giving the men the benefit of a hearing or a court martial. There was no going back on the Government's part. When a number of younger sailors, some accompanied by their parents, went back to the dockyard gates seeking to reverse the dismissal decision they were ignored. The gates remained steadfastly closed even after one parent and at least one junior sailor pleaded for entry in a tearful state. If the offences committed by these young sailors had gone to court martial there would have been a period of time for the accused to assess their situation and take advice.

The small number of sailors who did return to duty were charged with mutiny under the regulations and received various punishments. One leading writer who had twelve years service was reduced in rank, lost good conduct badges and received the equivalent of 28 days' imprisonment. Others received stoppage of leave and stoppage of pay.

The consequences of the Government's action on the RNZN were soon apparent. *Black Prince* was to be fully manned in June but after the events of early April, there were insufficient numbers of trained personnel available and a decision was made to lay up the cruiser indefinitely. If the government hoped that this would be the only postscript to the strike, they were wrong. In Lyttleton, the minesweeper HMNZS *Hautapu* docked. On the morning of that day (8 April), seven sailors at the Lyttleton naval base, HMNZS *Tasman*, had refused duty and demanded to be discharged like the men at *Philomel*. The captain of *Hautapu* was then given a letter signed by a number of the ship's company expressing their dissatisfaction with the Government's attitude towards welfare committees. They also wanted an undertaking that no disciplinary action would be taken against the 'strikers' and that they themselves would be discharged. Notwithstanding the harsh example made by the Government of the Auckland men, the *Hautapu* sailors also refused duty. Once again, there was a strong reaction. The sailors were warned of the consequences of their action but when little effort was expended in negotiating their genuine grievances, most of the ship's company mutinied. They walked off their ship keenly aware of the consequences of their actions. Once again, retaliatory action was swift. Commander Davis-Goff was sent to discuss the situation with the men at *Tasman* and in *Hautapu*. The seven men who refused duty at *Tasman* returned to their work but were charged with mutiny and sentenced to 60 days detention (later commuted to 14 days). The police were called in and warrants for the arrest of the sailors were issued. The charges were 'wilfully disobeying orders and improperly leaving their ship', a clear description of mutiny. The *Hautapu* men were arrested by police and charged with mutiny. They were convicted and sentenced to 60 days detention (reduced to 24 days). There was some local sympathy. The Ashburton Branch of the Returned Services Association passed a resolution which 'deplored the fact that the men were treated as mutineers when they had no quarrel with their officers, the matter being purely a domestic one'.[12]

Nearly 200 sailors were dismissed in the course of three days. Again the men suffered by the abrupt cessation of their careers with the added financial penalty of forfeiting their accumulated entitlements and benefits. In most cases this amounted to around £500 or the equivalent of two years' pay. Again the Navy suffered. Already there were too few sailors to man *Black Prince*. 'All except a few' from *Arbutus* had been discharged. A replacement ship's company had to be drawn from seconded sailors from *Black Prince* and *Philomel*. *Hautapu* was manned with a draft of trainees from a naval electrical school and sailed immediately for Auckland where the remnants of the ship's company was used to keep the base functioning. Only the RNZN flagship, the cruiser *Bellona*, was fully manned, but in Australian waters. The officers reported sanguinely that 'there was no evidence of disaffection'. A week after the event, a reporter stated that Devonport base 'retains its deserted appearance'. Petty officers remained responsible for carrying out all essential work. Tradition was under strain because 'officers and all classes of ratings are being fed from a general mess' as there was a lack of cooks.[13]

The accusation of Government vindictiveness is supported by evidence of official attitudes towards the dismissed men when they applied for new work. Senior officers in the Government stated 'that in view of the circumstances under which the men had left the Navy, the State would not employ them in another capacity'. A former sailor who had served five years as a torpedoman–electrician was offered employment with the Post &

Telegraph Department as a linesman. The appointment was vetoed at the last moment because 'ex-naval men . . . could not be employed' even though the Department was under a separate administration from the State Services.[14] When a legal opinion was obtained on the Government's attitude, it appeared that such bans were only enforceable in the case of men dishonourably discharged and could not be applied in the case of 'dismissal—services no longer required'. The opinion did not sway the decision-makers, however. Not only did civil servants acquiesce in the unlawful decision of Government but they did so despite legal advice that the decision was unlawful. There was only one alternative employer for men trained as naval telegraphists—the Post & Telegraph Department. A ban on the ex-naval men effectively removed their livelihood.

There were other areas of blatant injustice. A former torpedoman applied to a firm of electricians for employment as an adult trainee. Wartime ex-servicemen were entitled to a training subsidy, but this application was placed in abeyance. Other rehabilitation benefits available to ex-servicemen, such as housing assistance and furniture loans, were denied to the dismissed sailors in the short term. Mr Clarence Farthington Skinner, Minister for Rehabilitation, expressed the Government's policy in bleak terms: 'Rehabilitation privileges are deferred until the period for which [a rating] had contracted to serve has elapsed'.[15] The Government said that there was, of course, no suggestion of victimisation. Its policy was adopted 'in fairness to those many other naval men who decided to remain in the service for their full contracted periods'. The dismissed sailors also missed out on naval 'prize money'. This was a sum of money calculated on the value of enemy ships and property captured during the war which was shared out among the men of all the Imperial navies.

Adding insult to injury, when some of the sailors returned to the base seeking personal effects some time after the mutiny, they found their personal lockers had been smashed open and their effects stored in one large heap in a storeroom. The men were given only a short period of time to rummage through the heap and find valuables, which ranged from tools to photographs. It was a near-impossible task.

There was only muted support for the men in the wider community. A meeting was called in Auckland of various ex-servicemen's associations, including the RSA, the Naval Men's Association, the Air Force Association, the 2nd NZEF Association and the Home Servicemen's Association. The meeting 'deplored the reported victimisation in civilian employment' but the 'organisations would not contemplate any move which might undermine the discipline of the armed forces'. In other words, the mutineers, despite their service to their country in war, had forfeited their rights as citizens because they refused orders for two days over broken promises regarding pay and conditions. At least the Services' Commercial Contract Centre could report that a former Lieutenant Commander had approached the Centre offering to employ some of the dismissed men.

While it appeared that dissatisfaction had died down after the mutiny, there was another act to come. The cruiser *Bellona* had been diverted to Lyttelton and Wellington before returning to the Devonport base in late April after its stint in Australian waters. The men had no cause for dissatisfaction over pay because the demand made at the first Devonport protest for retrospectivity had been met. The saga of the mutineers' dismissal, their forfeited benefits and the injustice they were meeting in civilian employment was by then well known. In case the lesson was still not obvious, the *New Zealand Herald* offered its own rather patronising warning: 'The men should pause and remind themselves that patience and adherence to duty . . . bear good fruit . . . Precipitate action will yield nothing but shame for them and for the land they profess to love and serve'.[16]

There was discontent on board *Bellona*, however. The sailors were given leave, a large number of them relaxing in Auckland pubs over Anzac Day. During the afternoon, a group of about a hundred met in Quay Street and despite the cautionary example of the dismissed personnel, decided not to return to the ship. They formulated three main demands: that naval rates of pay should be made equivalent with those in other services; that a welfare committee should be formed to discuss problems, and that men who wished to join the public service (after the earlier strike) should not be dismissed and victimised. Another 40 sailors due to return to the cruiser from leave assembled on the dock. After being addressed by the leaders of the larger group, several sailors turned around and walked away from the ship through the gates of the Naval Base, ignoring the master-at-arms' order to halt. The response of *Bellona*'s commanding officer, Captain Laing, was to send most of the remaining ship's company, about another 200 men, on leave immediately. A letter detailing the men's grievances was presented to the captain on 28 April for submission to the Naval Board.

By the time the first men who had taken leave were due back

on duty there had been no direct response to their letter from the Naval Board. The sailors were disappointed when the only reaction was a published statement from the Minister of Defence stating that those who did not return to *Bellona* would be treated as being absent without leave. Once again, the only response from those in authority had been unsympathetic and unyielding. The authorities also questioned whether warrants should be issued for the arrest of the sailors (as had happened with *Hautapu*'s men). There was also a proposal that *Bellona*'s own loyal personnel should be used to apprehend the dissenters (about 80 of *Bellona*'s men were RN sailors or Royal Marines). Fortunately, the captain dismissed this suggestion.

By the evening of 28 April, only 54 men had not returned to the ship. Two of these appeared next morning. After a formal default parade, the 52 missing men were marked as 'deserters'. Under naval regulations, a sailor who remained absent without leave for seven days had his paybook marked permanently 'run' with all pay and allowances forfeited. The recording of the 52 absentees as 'deserters' was contrary to regulations as they had not been absent seven days.

The actions of the 52 *Bellona* men amounted to mutiny and they, like the men involved in the earlier incident, should have been charged and given the right to a court martial. The Minister of Defence, queried about the promise to respond to the sailors' grievances, responded by reiterating that only those grievances received through 'proper service channels' would be considered.[17] A number of sailors returned to the ship while it remained in port for a lengthy period. On 23 June, the cruiser left Auckland for the Bay of Islands with twenty men still absent.

The men who returned to *Bellona* were charged with a number of offences, ranging from 'negligently performing their duties' and 'wilfully disobeying a legal command' to 'joining in a mutiny not accompanied by violence'. Some of the twenty absent men were apprehended by the civil police and also charged. The sentences meted out to all those charged ranged from fourteen to 92 days.

14

Postwar disappointment

In the years immediately following World War II there were several instances of mutiny in navies around the world—including those of India, Cananda, Thailand and Australia. Their causes resembled many of those which followed the 1914–18 war.

In February 1946 there were what V. P. Menon called 'very ugly' events when Indian naval ratings at Talwar Signal Station and at Bombay took control of their barracks and ships in Bombay harbour.[1] While these events were motivated partly by the slow rate of demobilisation after the 1939–45 war, subsequent inquiries also allocated blame to the growing tensions between British officers and Indian ratings. A Strike Committee was formed at Bombay, and the guns of the frigates *Jumna* and *Dhanush* were trained on the Taj Mahal Hotel and the Royal Yacht Club. The British Admiralty ordered the cruiser HMS *Glasgow* to Bombay with orders to take all actions necessary to protect the local expatriate population. Riots broke out in the city, fuelled by nationalism and inter-communal hatreds, and sparked by the example of insurrection in the Navy. Two hundred and seventeen people were killed before order was restored. Fearing that civil violence could get out of hand, nationalist leader Jawaharlal Nehru called on the sailors to 'surrender unconditionally'. Although a small group defied this call, most of the ratings responded and returned to discipline on 23 February 1946.

There were several inquiries into these events, an Admiralty Board of Inquiry putting the insurrection down to 'a lower deck indiscretion'.[2] While 476 sailors were dismissed or released 'services no longer required', this was the extent of the punishments. Following the granting of independence to India in 1947, all these sailors were granted government pensions.

In 1947, some months after the New Zealand mutinies considered in the previous chapter, the Royal Canadian Navy (RCN) suffered a mutiny in the cruiser HMCS *Ontario*. In February 1949 general unrest led to a widespread mutiny in HMC Ships *Magnificent*, *Athabascan* and *Crescent*.

Ontario, built as the RN cruiser *Minotaur* in 1943, had been in Canadian service for just over two years. It was a modified Colony Class ship with a wartime complement of 950; its establishment for peacetime duties numbered 730. In the RCN, as in other navies in the postwar period, sailors who had served without complaint during wartime appeared less willing to suffer grievances during peacetime service. Over time the ship's company of *Ontario* had built up a list of grievances, first among them being the heavy-handed discipline of the ship's executive officer. Their grievances were not addressed, so when called to muster one afternoon, a large part of the crew refused to answer the pipe and remained in their mess decks. Several sailors who had been part of the mutiny in *Iroquois* during 1943 (see Chapter 13) were then serving on the *Ontario* and may have encouraged their shipmates in this course of action.

Perhaps to the men's surprise, the Flag Officer Pacific Coast, Rear Admiral E. R. (Rollo) Mainguy, immediately agreed to transfer the executive officer, which defused the situation. Admiral Mainguy wrote later that this speedy transfer without investigation was 'neither completely wise nor completely fair'.[3] There was an aspect of the *Ontario* affair common to many other mutinies: a reluctance among those in authority to use the word 'mutiny'. This incident, and the later incidents of 1949, were referred to as 'insubordinate' activity,[4] although the refusal to report for duty was clearly mutiny. One other factor relating to the mutiny concerned some Canadian authorities—the men involved were not punished in any way. That sailors had refused duty over grievances, had demanded an officer's removal, and had their demands promptly acceded to, created dissatisfaction among officers and eroded discipline. The damage that had been done to disciplinary standards in the RCN became evident in the fresh outbreak of mutinies in 1949.

The mutinous episodes of late February and early March 1949 were officially attributed to poor conditions, poor food and limited periods of leave. Following the *Ontario* mutiny, naval headquarters circulated a directive that lower-deck welfare committees should be established on all ships to provide an outlet for the expression of grievances. Some commanders who resented this erosion of their authority did not establish the committees. A case could have been made that these senior officers may have themselves been guilty of mutiny in refusing to follow a clear order from their superiors. Certainly many sailors were aware of the directive and became embittered as time passed where welfare committees were either not established or were set up with tight restrictions on what could be discussed.

The first incident took place on 26 February 1949 in the destroyer HMCS *Athabascan* during a training cruise off the Pacific Coast of Mexico, near Manzanillo. There was a short, non-violent protest by about 90 sailors concerning the conditions on board. They returned to duty reluctantly after their captain promised their grievances would be considered. A few weeks later, on 15 March, hundreds of kilometres up the Yangtse River at Nanjing in China, 83 men on the destroyer HMCS *Crescent* staged a similar protest. They also returned to duty but only after demanding and receiving immunity from punishment.

On 20 March, the aircraft-carrier HMCS *Magnificent*, which had been in company with *Athabascan*, was also subject to a protest. This took the form of 32 men, mainly aircraft handlers refusing to carry out orders to clean the mess decks. Their grievances included having to clean up after officers' cocktail parties and having shore leave suspended. The immediate cause of the mutiny was the cancellation of the men's off-duty afternoon (their 'make and mend' time) in order to secure the private cars some officers had brought along in the carrier for their convenience when visiting Caribbean ports. These men also returned to duty, albeit reluctantly. *Magnificent*'s executive officer was one of those who had strongly opposed the concept of welfare committees for the lower deck. He 'did not believe in the desirability' of such committees despite the clear order that they be established.[5]

The official inquiry into the three incidents resulted in no disciplinary action being taken against any of the sailors involved. Their actions were described as mutinies but were caused, according to one officer, by 'poor bloody management'.

A few years later a serious mutiny reflecting political unrest occurred in the Royal Thai Navy (RTN) on 29–30 June 1951. It is known as the '*Manhattan* mutiny'.[6] On 29 June, a dredge called *Manhattan* was presented to Thailand by the United States as a foreign aid gift. During the presentation ceremony, a group of about 30 officers and sailors seized the Prime Minister of Thailand and imprisoned him aboard the coast defence ship *Sri Ayuthia*. *Sri Ayuthia* and its sister ship *Dhonburi* were armoured coastal defence ships equipped with eight-inch guns, built by the Japanese between 1936–38. They were damaged in an engagement with the French Indochina naval squadron on 17 January 1941, and later salvaged. Neither ship was fully seaworthy and in June 1951 were lying in the Chao Phya River near Bangkok where they served as training vessels. *Sri Ayuthia* was also Fleet Flagship.

The mutineers spent the night of 29 June negotiating a list of demands which revolved around liberalising pay and conditions in the RTN. They threatened to bombard Bangkok with the eight-inch guns of the *Sri Ayuthia* if their demands were not met. The leaders of the mutiny expected a meeting with representatives of the government on the morning of 30 June, but were nonplussed when they were suddenly attacked by Army and Air Force units. A bomb hit the *Sri Ayuthia*, passing through the cabin where the Prime Minister was being held without hitting him. The bomb exploded in the engine room several decks below and set the ship on fire. The mutinous crew were unable to fight the fire because they were under shore fire from Army artillery units, and the ship began to founder. The crew swam ashore (assisting the Prime Minister as well) and they were arrested as they landed. Casualties were minimal, and the mutinous officers served only short gaol terms.

Several of these incidents provide a context for yet another mutiny in the Australian survey ship *Moresby*, shortly after the cessation of hostilities in 1945. The Naval Board had decided to dispose of *Moresby*'s predecessor, the old surveying ship *Fantome*, in the 1920s when it recognised the vessel was unsuitable for extended periods of survey work, a decision undoubtedly hastened by the persistent disciplinary problems described in Chapter 6. Similar problems, caused by overcrowding and poor morale, were to plague its replacement for more than two decades, however.

HMAS *Moresby* carried out survey work in northern Australian waters until 1939 when pressed into service for occasional convoy escort duty. In 1944–45, *Moresby* returned to the monotonous but necessary duty of surveying. In September 1945, it had a moment of fame when the Japanese forces on the island of Timor signed the instrument of surrender on the ship's quarterdeck at Koepang. The ship's company then destroyed Japanese tanks and guns in the East Timorese town of Dili. The addition of the Javanese troops made conditions in the ship intolerable. This contributed indirectly to the mutiny which occurred soon afterwards. As in the cases of *Voyager*, *Pirie* and the corvette men, it is clear that Australian sailors will endure great privations in the course of action when they can see the necessity for hardship. *Moresby*'s sailors had worked seven days a week with only one afternoon in the week devoted to recreation for nearly three years. In peacetime, or in reserve areas, Australian sailors are not as ready to endure without complaint.

Originally designed for a complement of 82, by October 1945 *Moresby* had a ship's company of 130, extra men and additional equipment being required to carry out surveying duties. The ship also carried two small 8.5-metre motor launches used for inshore work (*Fantome* and *Endeavour*). The cramped conditions inevitably caused dissatisfaction and led not surprisingly to a succession of medical problems in the mess decks. It was a similar story to the causes of indiscipline in the sloop *Fantome* 25 years earlier.

During wartime, the men had accepted and endured conditions which were undoubtedly appalling. In December 1943, the Commanding Officer sent a report to the Naval Board describing conditions in his ship.[7] There was a high rate of sickness largely due to 'close confinement and high mess deck temperatures'. The main mess deck measured just 7.45 metres × 4.25 metres—the size of a combined lounge–dining room in an average project home. In this space, the 61 sailors of the Seaman Branch were meant to live and sleep. Accommodation for the 31 stokers was almost as crowded. The bathrooms for sailors and stokers had no running water; one bathroom, measuring 2.75 metres × 2.14 metres, the size of the bathroom in a typical suburban house, was shared by 70 men. There was one head (toilet) for every eighteen men. The captain reported that while the food was of generally acceptable quality, 'shortages are expected in the Tropics'.[8]

The Naval Board concluded that little could be done to ameliorate the living conditions in wartime, the rest of the ship being packed with survey gear and armaments. *Moresby* had to continue urgent surveying and charting work around northern Australia and the south-west Pacific Islands in cooperation with the United States Seventh Fleet.[9] The ship's company patiently endured. In October 1944, there were further reports from *Moresby*.[10] The conditions were 'very cramped, which [was] aggravated by the design of the ships not intended for tropical service and the large complement borne'. *Moresby* and its sisterships had been designed to operate over relatively short distances in the North Atlantic and hence had adequate heating but no cooling facility. They were also intended for a much smaller complement. The report added that there were no facilities for recreation or entertainment, an added hardship for a ship's company that spent long periods at sea on routine and monotonous duty.[11]

By war's end, the sailors in *Moresby* had had enough. They had taken no action while their country was still at war but conditions were too much to bear any longer, especially when the ship was pressed to accommodate extra passengers going to the surrender ceremonies at Koepang on 11 September. During that passage, many sailors slept on deck despite the discomfort of rain squalls. They washed in buckets of seawater drawn up to the deck. Most onerous of all, they were subject to what they believed was overzealous discipline; the senior petty officer in the ship was widely resented for his unpleasant personality and domineering manner. The man's actual billet onboard was Chief Boatswain's Mate. The ship had had a master-at-arms, the senior sailor normally in charge of enforcing discipline, but he had left the ship at the end of the war. His place was taken by the despised chief boatswain's mate, known as 'the Rat' (obviously in the Australian way of nicknaming a person after the opposite of a particular physical characteristic, in the way that redheads are called Bluey, and bald men Curly); this man was an ex-boxer of great physical strength, and was also a bully. Even 'the wardroom was exhausted and cowed' by the Rat, who had an excellent working knowledge of the minutiae of *King's Regulations*.[12] The sailors had made representations to their officers concerning him, but the officers had taken no action following their complaints.[13]

In the first weeks after the war, the ship resumed surveying duties.[14] The work did not go well. There was a haze from bushfires ashore that impeded sightings and the cyclonic weather of that time of year was unusually bad. The men spent most of the day working and in the evening, as frequent squalls approached, there would be repeated calls to hoist in boats, booms and ladders, to slope and frap awnings, and cover the guns. After each squall had passed the work had to be undone. These tasks were part of service life but in *Moresby* at that time the men were not granted any time off, or 'make and mend' as it is known in the Navy, to compensate for the extra duties. In addition, they were directed to undertake chipping, scraping and painting duties on well-rusted deck and ship-side plates. This was work which clearly would not last very long. The men even appealed to the chaplain to make representations on their behalf. This, too, was to no avail.

By 4 October the men were thoroughly fed up. The affair of the mutiny started almost casually. At breakfast on that day, one sailor gave as his opinion that it was time the crew had a whole day off. It had echoes of the actions of the sailors on *Pirie*'s mess decks: 'Why don't we just sit here and see what happens?' When the pipe 'All watches for exercise' was made, the sailors did not move from their mess deck. Instead, they joined in the chant: 'We want the captain'. Not all the men took part in the increasingly noisy protest, some taking the time to 'dog' down the watertight door to the mess deck and secure the dogs with hammock lashings. The order to report for exercises was repeated by the boatswain, then the first lieutenant. The captain also came to the door of the mess deck to repeat the order to report, not to negotiate with the mutinous crewmen. The captain then ordered that the door be undogged. The sailors responded immediately. As each sailor emerged from the mess deck, his name was taken. There the matter rested and the men resumed their duties while the ship returned to Darwin. Back in Darwin, the Senior Naval Officer convened an inquiry into the mutiny, the intent of which was to discover the identities of the ringleaders and the nature of the subversive plots they had discussed and proposed. As a consequence of both the nature and spontaneity of the mutiny, there were no real ringleaders to be discovered. The inquiry resulted in some embarrassment for the captain when he admitted that he did not know the reason for the mutiny because he had not asked why he had been called to the mess-deck door.

It was not possible to identify ringleaders with a degree of certainty that would survive court-martial proceedings, thus the inquiry decided to charge all the leading seamen who had failed to report for duty. On the captain's authority, these men were given ten days' imprisonment, then dismissed from the ship. They then returned to Sydney for re-posting elsewhere in the fleet. All the other men involved were given ten days' stoppage of leave, a punishment that was essentially meaningless as *Moresby* immediately departed Darwin on further survey work that exceeded ten days.[15] After carrying out an urgent survey of Yampi Sound in Western Australia, *Moresby* returned to Sydney in early December 1945. The ship was paid off three months later and sold for breaking-up.

The mutiny in *Moresby* was the last declared incident of its type in the RAN. Since that time, no Australian sailor has been charged with or convicted of mutiny in a sea-going vessel. However, a series of events at Garden Island Dockyard in Sydney during the late 1960s verged on mutiny and could have led to the kind of 'walk-out' that so damaged the RNZN in April 1947.

Although the key issue was again pay, taking action to redress the grievance could have set sailor against sailor rather than sailor against officer, as the following narrative reveals.

Garden Island in Sydney Harbour has been the Navy's fleet base since the mid nineteenth century. Referred to as 'the Garden Island' because the ship's company of HMS *Sirius* were allowed to use the island to grow their own vegetables in 1788, it was developed as a naval base and dockyard from 1856, with the whole island devoted to naval purposes after 1865.[16] With the construction of the Captain Cook Graving Dock between 1940–45, the island was connected to the harbour foreshore at Potts Point. Together with Cockatoo Island Dockyard (to the west of Garden Island and the Sydney Harbour Bridge) and Williamstown Naval Dockyard (on Melbourne's Port Phillip Bay), these shore facilities hosted the greatest concentration of Australian naval vessels and sea-going personnel until the 1980s when a second fleet base at Cockburn Sound near Fremantle was in greater use. The three dockyards had a long history of industrial unrest.

Strikes at Garden Island during 1916–17 were blamed on the International Workers of the World, also known as the 'Wobblies'. While Wobbly influence on Garden Island was minor, the movement was deemed an 'unlawful association', driven out of the dockyard and its members gaoled. After the Great Depression, the Garden Island Vigilance Committee was formed to organise and lead industrial action among the workers at the dockyard. By 1941, the Communist Party of Australia had control of the vigilance Committee while its members had a stranglehold over most of the workshop committees. The Committee tried a number of tactics to gain recognition as the principal workers' voice in matters of wage claims, demarcation disputes and conditions of employment, even agitating for a change in Dockyard General Manager. However, the split in the Labor movement in the 1950s, together with a growing distrust of shop committees by the Trades Hall Council in New South Wales, worked against the Vigilance Committee. After seeking the support of the Labor Council of New South Wales in its efforts to gain recognition, the Vigilance Committee agreed to abide by the 1961 ACTU charter on shop committees. This allowed some outside influence in Dockyard industrial relations and seemed to temper the sometimes outrageous claims and methods employed by the Vigilance Committee. When a new collective agreement for dockyard workers was negotiated in 1968, the establishment of a Joint Industrial Council as part of the dispute resolution machinery troubled the

Vigilance Committee. In April 1969, the Navy challenged the right of the Vigilance Committee to assume leadership in any dispute which arose at Garden Island. This prompted a number of strikes in which the Vigilance Committee sought to assert its dominance while securing its future status as the peak industrial organisation on the island.

While there was a clear distinction between the employment and conditions of service applying to uniformed personnel and to dockyard staff, RAN officers and sailors lived and worked within an industrial 'hothouse' whenever their ships were alongside at Garden Island. Naval personnel had seen first-hand the power of collective action and the role of strike action in the improvement of wages and conditions. This was the background against which unrest increased over the 'group pay' system introduced into the Navy during 1968–69. This new system attempted to maintain comparable wage rates between servicemen with trades and skills and civilian workers in equivalent occupations. Many sailors believed that every sailor in a particular rank ought to be paid the same amount to avoid creating first- and second-class sailors, and to them the justification for some employment categories receiving higher pay than others was not apparent. Even those who were beneficiaries of the new scheme felt it was unfair. Those feeling the greatest sense of injustice were marine and electrical engineering branch personnel—known colloquially as 'stokers' and 'greenies'. There were a number of isolated incidents in which sailors refused to light engine-room boilers and walked off their ships. This appears to have occurred largely in support and auxiliary vessels. There was no evidence of unrest in those ships preparing or returning from active service in waters off South Vietnam. There were also reports of cooks and stewards at the Naval Air Station, HMAS *Albatross*, leaving their places of duty and locking themselves in an aircraft hangar. However, none of these individual acts developed into collective action until August 1970.

Dissatisfaction over pay rates had been growing for months. A submission recommending pay rises for around 4000 personnel was sent to the Government in July of 1969. This followed a determination by the Commonwealth Arbitration Commission on a claim for increased industry allowances for merchant navy seamen. Maritime unions achieved an $8 per week wage rise in their awards. Engineer officers and shipwrights received the increase, and under the new system the increase should automatically have flowed on to naval engine-room staff, such as artificers, as it was a judgment based on work values. For months there was no response from government; more than a year passed. Disaffection among naval personnel was manifested by an increased rate of resignations. In contrast with 1932, when personnel enlisted for set periods with strictly limited options for free discharge, by 1970 sailors could resign at short notice. In the second week of August 1970, 24 engine-room artificers alone in the troop transport ship, the former aircraft-carrier HMAS *Sydney*, applied for free discharge.

In civilian life there was an increased mood of disputation generally. In that second week of August there were strikes in Victorian railways and electricity authorities, and in New South Wales council workers and employees of BHP (Australia's largest company) threatened stoppages. It was not surprising that sailors who had waited over a year for a supposedly automatic pay increase should have considered direct action in their turn. By mid August, most ships of the Australian Fleet were alongside at Garden Island. They included the aircraft carrier *Melbourne*, the converted troop carrier *Sydney*, the destroyers *Perth* and *Brisbane*, the frigates *Yarra*, *Anzac* and *Swan*, and the support vessels *Supply* and *Stalwart*.

On the morning of 17 August 1970, a message circulated by word of mouth among engine-room personnel in several ships. At 1pm, the usual hour for resuming work after lunch, the men would hold a 'stop-work' meeting to protest against the delays in granting a flow-on from the merchant marine industry allowance. At that hour, around 200 men gathered on the grassed 'triangle' of the Garden Island dockyard, still within the precincts of the establishment. There were representatives from five ships: *Sydney*, *Brisbane*, *Yarra*, *Anzac* and *Swan*. There were no men present from the carrier *Melbourne*, the destroyer *Perth* (which was preparing to sail to South Vietnam on 14 September) nor from the support ships *Supply* and *Stalwart*.

The Flag Officer Commanding the Australian Fleet was Rear Admiral H. David Stevenson. On being informed of the meeting, he went to where the men were gathered and listened to their grievance. He then addressed them outlining the situation on the pay submission and telling them that he would pass on their concerns to the Commonwealth Government. He also said that the dispute would be resolved within a week. On that note he asked those present to return to their ships. There was some scattered discussion but the mood of the meeting had changed after his address. The men agreed to return to work. Their 'stop-work' had lasted one and a quarter hours. It had no tangible affect on operations other than briefly delaying the sailing of HMAS *Swan*, which had been due to leave for a short passage to Jervis Bay.

There was a subsequent announcement from Fleet Headquarters that no disciplinary action would be taken against the men who had participated in what the newspapers referred to as the 'Navy walk-off'. However, in future the men would be expected to comply with formal Navy procedures for handling complaints. The announcement was a sensible one. In those years of civil protest over Australia's involvement in the Vietnam conflict, any strong action against the incipient mutineers would probably have drawn substantial support for them. This was in contrast with earlier mutinies (in Melbourne in 1932, for example, or in 1919 with the *Australia* mutiny) when public opinion was very strongly against sailors who resisted naval authority. Another difference in 1970 was the fact that dissatisfied sailors could more easily resign. A heavy-handed disciplinarian approach could have seen large numbers of skilled men leave the Navy, something it could ill afford. The measured reaction of Admiral Stevenson to the incident also contrasts with the aggressive mis-handling of the pay dispute at Auckland in April 1947. If the Garden Island 'mutiny' had been handled in a similar fashion, the Australian Navy could have suffered for years and the war effort in Vietnam been hampered.

The events of 17 August at Garden Island caused a flurry of Government activity in Canberra. The Prime Minister and former Navy Minister, John Gorton, was 'advised urgently' of the 'walk-off'. There were also discussions with the incumbent Minister for the Navy, James Killen, the Minister for Labour and National Service, Billy Snedden, and the Treasurer, Leslie Bury.[17] From the various discussions it emerged that it was Treasury that had been resisting paying the wage rise. Officials of Treasury had argued that the rise granted to the merchant marine engine room personnel had been in the nature of a special allowance that ought not to flow on to naval personnel. Their argument had deadlocked consideration of the issue in the Defence (Conditions of Service) Committee, which consisted of public servants from each of the three Service departments, the Department of Defence and the Treasury.

Spurred on by the events at Garden Island, the meeting of the relevant Ministers rapidly resolved the deadlock. They decided that the increase had to be paid, and backdated it to 7 July 1969. The Minister for Defence, Malcolm Fraser, announced the rise of

$8 per week which would affect about 6000 naval personnel and some RAAF and army personnel who worked in sea-going categories. The Government stated that 'the increases had been granted on the recommendations of the Defence (Conditions of Service) Committee after an examination of relevant navy pay rates in the light of the Maritime Industry Allowance awarded last year . . . to the civilian maritime industry'.[18] The announcement made no reference to the events at Garden Island. The fact that naval authorities decided not to take action against the men who refused duty and thereby mutinied indicated to some that they sympathised with the situation of their men. One newspaper remarked: 'Observers in Canberra say the Navy's decision not to take disciplinary action against the men indicates the degree of interdepartmental inaction over delays in granting Navy wage increases'. The mutiny at Garden Island in 1970 is one instance of naval authority tacitly admitting that the men were justified in their actions.

There was one other result of the events of that day. Defence Minister Fraser agreed to expedite an investigation into general terms and conditions of service in the armed forces, and to allow continuing review of those terms and conditions. There have been no mutinies in Australia's armed forces since that time, although concerns over conditions led to the eventual formation of the closest thing imaginable to an armed forces trade union.

15

Mutiny in the Australian Army and Air Force

It would be wrong to think that only the RAN suffered from mutiny or collective disobedience. This chapter contains a selection of incidents that amounted to mutiny in both the Australian military and air forces.

During World War I, around 330 000 Australians enlisted in the Australian Imperial Force (AIF). Considering the number who enlisted, it is perhaps surprising that so few were involved in incidents during the war years that may have fallen within the definition of 'mutiny'. The Australian Army was, however, in a different legal situation to the Navy when hostilities commenced in 1914. The 1910 *Naval Defence Act* had brought the Australian Fleet entirely under Admiralty control and made Australian sailors subject to British naval discipline. The Australian Army remained under the *Defence Act* 1903, which was developed from legislation inherited from the various colonial assemblies. This Act held, for example, that Australian soldiers were not subject to the death penalty except for crimes such as desertion to the enemy or mutiny. Perhaps for that reason, there were far fewer courts martial for mutiny in the Army than there were in the Navy, despite the vastly greater numbers who served in the AIF. This is not to say that there were fewer courts martial overall. During World War I, there were nearly nine men in prison per thousand Australian soldiers, compared with one per thousand for British units, and 1.6 for Canadian, New Zealand and South African units.[1] However, no Australian soldier was executed during that war compared with 346 British soldiers who suffered the death penalty.[2]

Yet there were some dramatic incidents, even if no men were charged for collective insubordination. In early 1916, hundreds of raw recruits who were mustered in a camp at Casula (on the outskirts of Sydney) protested against their living conditions. At a mass meeting, they elected spokesmen and marched in orderly ranks to a neighbouring camp at Liverpool where, in numbers now estimated at 2000, they confronted camp authorities and demanded that conditions be improved.[3] The authorities listened and responded. They agreed to see that conditions were reviewed and improved where possible. The mainly orderly protest was marred when some men later rioted and looted shops in Liverpool. A small number of men, mostly drunk from looted alcohol, then boarded a train bound for Sydney's Central Station, where they clashed violently with military police. One of the rioters was killed. Nine were injured.[4]

This incident is more properly considered a riot than a mutiny because there was no intent to subvert military authority and it is debatable whether the men actually disobeyed a direct order. In a subsequent incident (described later in this chapter), a new defence against mutiny was mounted which might have helped the Casula 'mutineers'. It was argued that to be charged with mutiny it was essential that a serviceman had actually refused to obey a direct order. Such insubordination was necessary for the specific offence of mutiny to be committed. Actions against men absent from duty or ignoring standing orders could not fall within the proper definition of mutiny. Were it to be otherwise, the crime of mutiny would be committed every time a group of men overstayed leave or paraded with unpolished boots.

For these very reasons, the riot of Australian and Scottish soldiers at the holding camp at Etaples in France in September 1917 should not be termed a 'mutiny'. Many Australians considered the conditions at the camp 'unduly severe'.[5] This incident was basically a violent reaction against strict, even brutal, training and discipline for troops returning to duty after being wounded. The fact that the trainers were military police who often had no active service themselves added to the bitter resentment that the troops felt against the camp authorities. At least one historian of the period agrees that the Etaples affair was 'not a politically aware mutiny against the war, its methods, or its aims, but a riot about camp conditions and treatment of the men'.[6] A riot, although a violent outburst against authority, is not normally considered a mutiny.

In September 1918, however, there were a number of incidents in France that possibly came within the bounds of mutiny. One group of incidents clearly fell within the meaning of the term mutiny. Australia's official military historian, Charles Bean, referred to them as 'the only serious mutiny before action that occurred in the AIF', although he did suggest by way of footnote that 'There had during this period been slighter incidents, of which only hints are given in the records'.[7]

PERONNE, FRANCE, SEPTEMBER 1918

The 1st Battalion at Peronne in France was to withdraw from the line of trenches in late September after fruitless efforts to break the German Hindenburg Line. However, instead of being relieved, the battalion was ordered to go forward to the attack again. It was an instance of men being asked to do too much. Three platoons refused to advance although they were twice ordered to do so. In Bean's words, 'after a week of repeated efforts and continuous strain [the unit] had no sooner reached its bivouac and settled to sleep than it was summoned to the line again to follow the enemy's retirement'. The men were supported in their actions by their officers, who gave them some moral support, a significant element in the unfolding mutiny. Another 80 men of the battalion attacked as ordered. Despite the mutiny, the advance was considered a success.[8]

One hundred and nineteen of the battalion's men were subsequently tried for mutiny; 118 of them were found guilty not of mutiny but desertion. The court martial ordered that all the offenders be imprisoned. General Monash made representations to the unit's senior officer, Major General the Honourable Sir Thomas Glasgow, to remit the sentences, but Glasgow refused. The men followed their division in a virtual state of limbo for the remaining weeks of hostilities. They were considered prisoners yet they still participated in battalion operations. Eventually, the commander of the Australian Corps, Lieutenant General Sir Joseph Hobbs, recommended remission, and a difficult situation was resolved. The men of the 1st Battalion returned to Australia without serving their sentences.

The whole issue behind this mutiny was, however, overshadowed by another series of incidents. Army authorities decided that to maintain the strength of each battalion in the eight Australian brigades then serving at the front, one battalion in each brigade should be disbanded to reinforce the others. This reorganisation was a reaction to recent heavy losses among the Australian forces. But those planning this apparently simple and straightforward change did not seem to recognise that the Australian soldier of World War I had an especially strong loyalty and attachment to his unit. This was due, in part, to the creation of units from particular areas in Australia. It was also a function of the men being so far from home, without leave for almost all of their service overseas. To dismantle a unit was a most serious action. As Bill Gammage points out: 'To every Australian soldier, his company, his battalion, was his home. Here lived our truest and most trusted companions, brothers who would share their last franc or crust with each other, bound together till victory or death'.[9]

The men of the eight battalions identified for redeployment refused to disband as ordered. At a parade on 22 September, the men agreed that they would obey every command but the last: the order to march to their new units. They considered the matter a strike rather than a mutiny and remained in their camps. They elected leaders when their officers left and maintained strict discipline. They received a great deal of sympathy from other units which sent them rations recorded as being 'lost' from their own supplies. One unit, the 60th Battalion, disbanded, but only after a personal appeal from a popular officer, Brigadier General 'Pompey' Elliott. The others survived until some weeks later, when the whole division was brought out of the line. The commanding officer of the first battalion to be notified of its disbandment, Colonel Story, lodged a protest over the head of his brigadier directly to General Monash. For this breach of discipline, Colonel Story was relieved of his command. He would be the only casualty of the incident.

As Bean has covered these events in Volume VI of his official history[10] they need not be repeated here, other than to mention these incidents as possible mutinies. No charges were laid against any of the men, nor was the matter treated as mutiny by any British or Australian authority. Whether it was large-scale mutiny or not is uncertain. The incidents could not be regarded legally as a 'strike' because the term 'strike' does not exist in military law. The key question is whether disobeying orders to report to a new unit constitutes mutiny or desertion? If the disobedience is collective the offence is probably mutiny. However, this affair was never tested in a legal forum. It remains an oddity and further proof that mutiny is a complex offence in both naval and military law. In any event, the end of the war was only weeks away. With demobilisation imminent, some units were less patient of military discipline. These were the final incidents of their kind in World War I.

MUTINY IN THE RAAF, SEPTEMBER 1941

A number of men gathered secretly in Hut 70 at the Benalla base of RAAF No.11 Elementary Flying Training School in the early evening of 8 September 1941. The group consisted of corporals and airmen who wanted to discuss a number of shared grievances. Someone started writing down a list of their complaints. After a short period, one man asked: 'How many's that?' Another said: 'Read them out'. Someone else shouted: 'You read them out, Wilkie'. The latter responded: 'Why me?' The answer was: 'You're a renegade from Laverton'. (Laverton was a RAAF training base near Melbourne.) Leading Aircraftman Wilkie stepped forward and picked up the list, then went over to the doors of the hut and locked them. This was to ensure that no-one else could enter the hut or hear what he was about to say. Then he stood up on a bed and said words to the effect: 'I was in a strike at Laverton. We got what we wanted there, and we'll go on strike in the morning—and if we don't get what we want, we'll go on strike again next week'.

Wilkie read the list of grievances. He then pronounced: 'We'll go on strike in the morning. All those in favour put up your hands'. Most of those present shot their hands up. There were a few reluctant to do so. Wilkie added: 'We've got to stick together'. He waved at the dissenters and said with a laugh: 'You're standing around as though you had a load of the pox'. There were few smiles at the joke. A group of the airmen then moved on to Hut 68, taking the list of grievances with them. Wilkie read out the list of complaints and again spoke about what he and others had purportedly done at Laverton.

Considering the seriousness of the action they took, the men's complaints were relatively minor. They wanted one day off per week in lieu of irregular duties. When leave was due, they wanted it granted in periods of more than four days at a time. This would give those who lived away from Melbourne an opportunity to travel home for a day or two of their leave. They demanded that technicians should not be rostered on guard duties. When guard duties were necessary, non-permanent guard members should be entitled to the same privileges as permanent guard duties in respect to time off. They wanted all 'bribery as regards, Best Dressed Guard, Neatest Hut, etc., to be eliminated'. In their view, aircraftsmen should have the same access to hot running water as aircrew. The men also wanted no marching or rifle drill after 5pm (the words 'before 8am' were added) and no mass-marching to the station when proceeding on leave. They did concede that 'personnel would be willing to march on Sunday through the town'. Finally, they demanded that there should be 'conveniences' (washing machines) for clothes.[11]

The following morning, Tuesday 9 September, the unit was roused by the customary bugle call at 7am calling men to parade. There was a second warning call at 7.10. A large number of men did not respond to either call to parade. Squadron Leader Thompson was obliged to look for his men. He found that 140 of them had assembled in the unit recreation hall and found that the doors of the hall had been locked. He summoned his adjutant, Flight Lieutenant Creighton, the orderly officer and two other officers, and instructed them to bring the airmen out of the hall. By the time the group of officers reached the building, one set of doors had been unlocked. The officers entered and found the airmen seated on forms. They were absolutely silent but as the officers entered, some immediately started to leave by whatever means of exit was available. Some of the airmen, although it was unclear exactly who they were, called out: 'Look on the table'. The adjutant, apparently just hearing a number of voices and not realising the import of what they were saying, snapped, 'That's enough of that!'

On the table next to the unlocked doors was the handwritten list of grievances. The adjutant picked up the list, read the grievances and left the hall. By this time most of the airmen had also left. Leaving the list on the table near the only set of unlocked doors meant the document could not be overlooked. This was a deliberate ploy, the airmen calculating that the grievances could be brought to the command's attention without any one of them being held responsible. They also hoped this arrangement would prevent someone being nominated as ringleader. The airmen returned to their usual routine, leaving the command with a conundrum. Clearly there had been a challenge to authority. The list of grievances could not be considered as anything other than a piece of evidence to support charges of mutiny. But who could be charged?

The facts did not support specific charges of mutiny. A large group of men had failed to parade and had gathered in the recreation hall instead. The officers had not witnessed any actions by the men and no-one had spoken up. Only one comment had been made in the recreation hall: 'Look on the table'. Several airmen had uttered the statement but no-one could be identified positively. An investigating officer from RAAF Headquarters in Melbourne, Flight Lieutenant E. Rosewarne, was called in. He began interrogating the men of Huts 68 and 70 the following day. As the interrogation progressed, the difficulty of sustaining mutiny charges quickly became evident. In essence, no-one had refused an order when the men failed to parade. It was, however, obvious that there had been a discussion beforehand concerning a strike. From a legal point of view, those wanting to secure a conviction had to concentrate on those prior discussions with a view to establishing a case of conspiracy to commit mutiny. This had more chance of success than prosecuting an uncertain case of actual mutiny.

As Flight Lieutenant Rosewarne focussed on what had transpired in the huts on the evening of 8 September, Wilkie's name was mentioned by a number of men. There was also evidence suggesting that Leading Aircraftman Geier had actually penned the offending list of grievances which, far from being the means to resolve the men's complaints, had become the principal piece of evidence against them. A further problem for the prosecutor was that all the men interrogated agreed that a 'large number' of men in both huts had voted for what they believed would be a strike. LAC Wilkie cooperated with the investigating officer and agreed that he had addressed the meetings in both huts. With that admission, it was decided that Wilkie would be charged with 'endeavouring to persuade others to join in a mutiny' and the prosecution would later ask the members of the court martial 'to infer that that was mutiny'.[12] The specific words from Wilkie that were quoted to support the charge were: 'We shall all stick together—you stand around as though you had a load of the pox'. This was evidence of Wilkie's attempt at persuasion and proof that he intended more than one person to be involved. This was tantamount to conspiracy.

As many witnesses were either unclear or contradictory concerning the role of other men in the huts, it was considered safer to charge the other principal participants—six in all—with '[Failing] to inform Commanding Officer of conspiracy to mutiny'. This charge could be proved simply by demonstrating first, that those men were in the huts, and second, that they understood the action proposed for the next morning. This charge, however, depended upon a determination that Wilkie's actions were mutinous or that he had conspired to commit mutiny.

The courts martial were held over 25–26 September 1941. The presiding member was Group Captain J. H. Summers, with Wing Commander W. Rae, and Squadron Leaders R. Francis, B. Eaton and A. Garrisson as members. Flight Lieutenant A. Smith was the prosecutor. Flying Officer C. Burgess-Lloyd was the defending officer. The prosecutor contended before the court that Wilkie's offence, and his breach of Section 7 of the *Air Force Act*, would be proved if the prosecution showed that he tried to persuade members of the RAAF to join a mutiny. The definition of a mutiny in the Act was 'collective insubordination' and 'organis[ing] defiance of authority'.[13] The other accused would accordingly be found guilty unless they could show that they had either taken steps to inform an officer or attempted to stop their fellow airmen from assembling in the recreation hut.

Wilkie's defending officer did not deny any of the facts put forward in evidence. Rather, he based the defence around the definition of mutiny contained in the *Air Force Act*. He argued that mutiny is 'a word of very grave significance . . . We all connect it . . . with instances in history which have to us all . . . a very grave significance . . . which is vastly different to the kind of thing we have been told about in the last day or so'.[14] The defence could point out that the understanding of mutiny in the armed forces legislation required the participation of two or more people deliberately combining to disregard an order given by an officer. Disregarding a routine order, such as that posted on a noticeboard to attend parade, was a lesser offence. It was similar to infringing regulations or standing orders. Burgess-Lloyd went on to argue that unless there was a direct and specific order, a personal command for the airmen to go on parade, the aircraftsmen could not be guilty of mutiny. If Flight Lieutenant Creighton had ordered the men to go on parade and they had disobeyed, they would have been guilt of mutiny. Instead, 'there was no intention at any time to do more than stay away from parade until someone of authority came along and found out that they had stayed away'.[15]

The court did not accept the argument. It judged that a combination of two or more persons resisting or inducing others to resist lawful Air Force authority was mutiny. Wilkie, although one individual, had tried to persuade his comrades to disobey orders. He was sentenced to two years gaol with hard labour to be followed by dishonourable discharge from the service. The sentence was later commuted to eighteen months' gaol by Air Vice-Marshal Wrigley, the Personnel Member on the Air Force Board. Four out of the five other defendants received six months' imprisonment, reduction in rank and subsequent discharge. So ended the only case where a court martial considered the constituent parts of a mutiny in the RAAF.

NO.3 DETENTION COMPOUND, NUSEIRAT, PALESTINE, 1942

The mutiny at Nuseirat in 1942 resulted in the largest number of soldiers being convicted of mutiny in Australian military history. Two courts martial were conducted, on 2–9 May and 6–12 May, under the presidency of Lieutenant Colonel T. M. Conroy, with Lieutenant Colonel Burton, Majors Lubke and McKechnie and Captain Miles sitting as members. Lieutenant Colonel W. T. Charles was Judge Advocate. At the first court martial, eight men faced the court; at the second, there were 13 men answering charges. All were privates and detainees of No.3 Compound at the Nuseirat Detention Camp.

The men at Nuseirat suffered under discipline that would have tested the strength and patience of ordinary men. The camp was a detention compound where soldiers served sentences for a variety of offences including absence without leave, habitual drunkenness and insolence. Most of the sentences were comparatively short, ranging from a few days to several weeks. The senior non-commissioned officers were apparently brutal men beyond the effective control of the camp commandant, who appears to have been unsuited for this position. Private Wardrop, at his court martial, made a number of accusations against the commandant:[16]

> I was deeply shocked at the criminal mal-administration of the Compound . . . On the second day that I was at the Compound, that is 22 April, the Commandant appeared on the parade ground under the influence of liquor. Later in the afternoon . . . the Commandant made some disgusting insinuations concerning my wife's fidelity . . . and he began asking me questions in a drunken and sneering tone of voice as to when the child was born and how long I had left Australia . . . he . . . selected me as a target for his venom and I was subjected to indecent language from him. On Sunday, 26 April, he was again drunk and I saw him embrace a young woman outside his tent . . . The woman in question was seated in a car just outside the main gate of the compound at about 0900 hrs the next morning . . . Next morning, I asked three members of the staff whether I could see the RSM, Staff [Sergeant] Bidewell, in order to be paraded before the Commandant. All . . . told me that the Commandant and the RSM had been away all night and were now 'sleeping it off' in their quarters—'sleeping off the effects of their drunken carousals'.

Private Wardrop's testimony was supported by other soldiers in the compound. Another soldier testified that the commandant was frequently 'under influence of liquor' and while drunk would come into the compound after 'lights out' and enter the men's tents and their beds. He was also seen putting rice and foodstuffs into a car driven by two Arabs. Some men were denied medical attention. The diet of rice in inadequate quantities led to either constipation or dysentery. Those with dysentery had to ask permission to use the latrines and the staff sergeant would refuse them permission for up to half an hour. The men were denied any rags or means to clean the latrines. Another strongly felt complaint was that the soldiers in the Compound were not allowed cigarettes. The intense heat was also a trial. Several men complained at being made to parade without hats. Others spoke of being 'doubled' to meals before being made to stand waiting in the sun without hats. On the day before disturbances broke out, a Private Heron stated that after parading without hats in the sun for 20 minutes the men were put through full drill including a stint of marching on the spot in pack drill. This lasted 37 minutes.

At their courts martial, some soldiers said that when they tried to make complaints, they were told by the staff sergeants that officers were not available to hear them. A Lieutenant Ward of the Provost Corps, Assistant Commandant of No.3 Detention Compound, testified that he fully informed soldiers under sentence of the complaint procedures on their arrival. While they had every opportunity to express grievances, this officer claimed there had been no complaints. Furthermore, no complaints had been made to the staff sergeants either. In the same page of testimony, the lieutenant admitted that he knew only one soldier in the camp by name.

The mutiny began with a mood of deep dissatisfaction which spread throughout the camp in the latter part of April after a rumour had circulated that the prisoners would have their sentences commuted to mark Anzac Day. This did not happen. Lieutenant Ward described events five days later—30 April:

> Something of an unusual nature happened at the Compound that day at approx. 1210 hrs. The first things I heard was the banging of tins which came from the compounds onto the parade ground. I saw those tins on the parade ground. They had no right to be there. As a result of that I sent for the Acting RSM, Staff Sergeant Bidewell, and gave him certain instructions. I saw Staff Sergeant Bidewell go the compounds, acting on my instructions, after the tins had been flung onto the parade ground ... he made a report to me. I later issued further instructions to Warrant Officer Morrison and Staff Sergeant Bidewell ... and

Warrant Officer Morrison called out the names of each man in the compounds and he gave instructions for the men he called to form up on Staff Sergeant Bidewell's right . . . I was approximately three yards from him when he gave the order.[17]

The men did not respond but remained in their tents. It was in the middle of the meal break and most men testified that they were eating their rations.

Private Hill explained that he was one of those halfway through eating when the Sergeant got 'very excited' and said: 'On your feet, No.3 Compound unless you wish to face a charge of mutiny'. The private said that he had no time to get onto the parade ground and 'there was hardly sufficient time to get on our feet' before the sergeant stated: 'Consider yourself on a report charged with mutiny'.[18] The staff sergeant reported to Lieutenant Ward who ordered him to go back to the Compound (a few yards away from the officer) and ask for a spokesman to come forward and explain the actions of the men. No spokesmen volunteered their services.

According to the soldiers, it was at this point that the sergeant informed them that they all were being charged with mutiny. Lieutenant Ward denied that he told the sergeant to do so but testified that he had told the Sergeant only to warn the men that they were engaged in 'mutinous conduct'. He found out only later that some of the men had been charged with mutiny. Under the admonishments of the warrant officer and the staff sergeant, the men were formed up on parade, but this was considered too late to avoid the charge of mutiny. A roll was called. There were 58 men in the Compound and all were held in detention pending charges for mutiny. In the event, only 21 of the men were formally charged that they 'joined in a mutiny by combining amongst themselves to resist the authority of Warrant Officer Class II Morrison, their superior officer in the execution of his duty'. The men whose names had been called by Morrison were court-martialled in Jerusalem one week later. The others were not charged because they were not identified as having been ordered to fall-in. The defence offered by most of the men was that there was no agreement to resist lawful authority and that each man had reacted as an individual in failing to obey the order.

The legal question to resolve was whether there had to be a specific agreement between the men to refuse duty before they carried out that refusal. The charged soldiers all denied having grievances. Although this was unlikely the matter was not pressed. They also claimed to have acted on the spur of the moment without prior discussion. The Judge Advocate was allowed to put forward the proposition, without challenge from the defence, that the definition of the act of mutiny required only that men act together. 'It is not necessary, however, for men to agree expressly to act in disobedience of orders to constitute mutiny'.[19] However, a close reading of the statutes and the normal use of language would seem to require that a 'conspiracy' or a 'concerted action' required some element of planning and prior agreement. Without prior agreement, simultaneous action by a group of men would be more in the nature of riot than mutiny. The definition used by the Judge Advocate in the Nuseirat courts martial appears to be inconsistent with both statute and practice.

The defence of no agreement to resist authority was dismissed. Several of the men then raised grievances about conditions in the camp, despite Lieutenant Ward having denied that any soldier had any grievances or cause for dissatisfaction in the Compound. His confident assertion was met with sarcasm from the defending officer: 'Well, do you think they would be happy and then suddenly mutiny?'[20] On the dismissal of their defence, the soldiers were found guilty. The defence then put forward as a mitigating circumstance that most of the men had only days left to serve of their original sentences of detention and would not have jeopardised their release if they had realised the seriousness of their actions. This argument also was set aside and the men received sentences ranging from sixteen months to five years and two months with hard labour, to be followed by 'discharge with ignominy'. One private had offered as a defence that he was too sick to comply with the order. This was not accepted and he was sentenced to five years and two months. Another soldier had argued that he did not hear the order. This argument too was rejected and he too was found guilty. The men later made representations to higher military authority in Australia and in October 1942 their sentences were suspended. The majority of those charged served a total of six months imprisonment for their part in the 'mutiny'.

NO.14 DETENTION BARRACKS, TAMWORTH, NEW SOUTH WALES, JUNE 1945

At Tamworth in New South Wales from 25–27 June 1945, Brigadier B. Klein presided over a court martial of seven of thirteen men (all privates or gunners) charged with joining in a mutiny of His Majesty's Military Forces, in that 'at or about 1120 hours on 29 May 1945, [they] joined in a mutiny by combining with other confinees of 14 Australian Detention Barracks in an attempt to break out of the said barracks by force and violence'.[21]

The other members of the court were Lieutenant Colonel J. Moyes, Majors C. Howie and J. Maroney and Captain D. Black. Major F. Myers was the Judge Advocate. The men were to be tried under Section 7 of the *Army Act* which, although not strictly defining the act of mutiny, made it an offence for a 'member of the Defence Forces' to 'cause or conspire with any other persons to cause any mutiny or sedition in any of His Majesty's military, naval or air forces'; or to 'seduce any person . . . from allegiance to His Majesty'.

The facts of the matter were not disputed. The thirteen men had planned to escape from the barracks at mid morning, outnumbering and overcoming the guards on duty at the gatehouse with their bare hands, and then making good an escape cross-country into the town of Tamworth. Six of the charged men were represented by Mr W. Bradley KC of Sydney, a high level of representation necessitated by law. The relevant legislation stated: 'As the offence under Section 7(3) of *Imperial Army Act* of joining in a mutiny is punishable by death each accused is entitled . . . to be defended by Counsel assigned by and at the expense of the Crown'.[22]

The first man on the list of those charged with mutiny was 23-year-old Private Bruce Smith. Smith had enlisted in the AMF on 23 June 1943. Over a year later, he went absent without leave for a long period. In effect, he deserted. On being apprehended, Smith was sentenced to be discharged from the Army and jailed for twelve months from 19 October 1944. The sentence was confirmed and Smith was transported to the military detention barracks at Tamworth. When Bradley was asked how Private Smith responded to the charge of mutiny, he made a response that startled the officers of the court.

> When it is alleged that he joined in a mutiny in His Majesty's Military Forces, the answer is that the other persons who were involved in this disturbance were not members of His Majesty's Military Forces. So that neither Smith nor those associated with him were legally capable of committing the offence of mutiny, as required by Section 7, or at all.[23]

One can sense the perplexity of the court members in the *verbatim* transcript of proceedings:

Justice Starke: How do you meet section 158(2) of the *Army Act?*
Mr Bradley: We say that it does not apply at all to a discharged soldier in Australia.
Justice Starke: You say he is not subject to Military Law at all?
Mr Bradley: That is so.
Justice Starke: Those are the main points?
Mr Bradley: Yes, and . . . the reason we say that is that the *Army Act* only becomes applicable to Australian soldiers during a time of war . . . and the *Defence Act* makes it applicable only to members of the Military Forces . . . So that Smith was neither a member of the Military Forces nor on war service.[24]

The court martial was suspended and the issue was referred to the High Court. That court agreed with Bradley and, in its summing up, confirmed that: 'the accused is not subject to military law on the general ground that he is a citizen of the Commonwealth and . . . no citizen can commit the offence of mutiny and . . . an ordinary citizen of the Commonwealth is not amenable to be tried by a military tribunal'.[25]

Thus, the court agreed that the charge was not a valid one, being *ultra vires* and moreover, was 'bad law'. Smith was returned to the detention barracks with the other charged men to serve out his original sentence and was released in due course.

The previous discussion makes two points clear. First, mutiny has been more of a problem for the Navy than the other two services. Although large numbers of Army and Air Force personnel have been charged with mutiny, there have been far fewer mutinies in those services. The second point is that no obvious pattern emerges from either Army or Air Force mutinies. Other than the common theme of sub-standard living conditions causing tensions not alleviated by a proper grievance-handling process, each of the mutinies had its own peculiar characteristics. In accounting for the higher incidence of mutiny in the Navy, the most probable reasons arise from the sheer physical hardships of sea-going service, the isolation of sailors from higher authorities to which they can address a grievance, and the absence of satisfactory complaint resolution procedures. For the greatest part, governments have avoided intervention in the management of naval discipline. However, the spirit of social and democratic liberalism that marked the Whitlam Government's tumultuous three years in office in 1972–75 unintentionally eroded a principal pillar of naval discipline and created a precedent that may have served as an encouragement to mutiny. This government's handling of protest action against French atomic testing in the South Pacific is the focus of the next chapter.

16

Volunteers and mutiny

When the Whitlam Labor Government took office after the federal election of 2 December 1972, one of the foreign policy problems it inherited was French atmospheric nuclear testing at Mururoa.[1] France had decided in 1963 to move its nuclear testing centre to the Pacific to Mururoa Atoll, an island group of the Tuamotu Archipelago 1200 kilometres south-east of Tahiti in French Polynesia. The traditional name for the atoll, Moruroa ('Island of Secrets'), was changed to Mururoa in the 1960s by the French military. There France would atmospherically test atomic and hydrogen bombs.

The change of test site was prompted by two developments. The first was the adoption by the United Nations of the partial Nuclear Test Ban Treaty of 1963 which prohibited nuclear tests in the atmosphere, outer space and underwater, but not underground. The concession on underground testing enabled the United States and the Soviet Union to continue their testing programs in that environment. The second reason for shifting the test site was the successful agitation by African states to end French atmospheric and underground tests in the Algerian Sahara after Algeria achieved independence in 1962. The French felt that Australia and the Pacific Island states would be less resistant to testing at Mururoa, which was some distance from public opposition centres, because Australia and a number of Pacific island states had been the actual site of atomic testing in the past two decades. There were two subsidiary reasons for the move. By having a major defence facility in the Pacific, France could show that she was still a world power with interests in the Pacific, and had grounds for regular deployments to the region of warships. The French Navy would re-supply the sites at Mururoa and Fangataufa (while the latter was in use) in addition to patrolling restricted zones during the tests. These patrols, it was asserted, were to ensure the safety of any craft near the test site.

Australia sent a number of communications to France expressing opposition to atmospheric nuclear testing in 1963. The Minister for External Affairs, Sir Garfield Barwick, pointed out that 'scientific knowledge of the effects of radio-active fallout was incomplete', and the impact of even a small increase in the general level of radioactivity was unpredictable. If the tests were as safe as the French asserted, Australia protested, they should be conducted on a French island closer to France, such as Corsica, Guadeloupe or Martinique. Sir Garfield told the French that Australia's concern 'was not merely with hazards to health, but at the danger of further testing and the proliferation of nuclear weapons'. There was also a fear that French testing would provide a pretext for other countries not to sign the test ban treaty or for extant signatories to find an escape clause. With France continuing to claim the tests were safe, Australia moved to monitor French safeguards with France initially expressing its willingness to accept Australian observers.

The first test was conducted at Mururoa in 1966 and, in a highly symbolic gesture, was witnessed by President De Gaulle from a French cruiser. Further tests were conducted in 1967, 1968, 1971 and 1972 without any evident biological hazard. The South Pacific Forum at its first meeting in 1971 expressed concern over 'the potential hazards to health and to marine life which is a vital element in island subsistence and economy', and urged France to make the tests of 1971 the last. The 1972 tests were met with heightened opposition. In September 1972, the Foreign Ministers of Australia and New Zealand called a meeting of those regional states affected by the French nuclear testing and urged concerted action at the United Nations General Assembly. The result was a draft resolution sponsored by Australia, New Zealand and eleven Pacific island and littoral states calling for an immediate halt on French atmospheric testing in the Pacific and anywhere else in the world, the suspension of all nuclear testing disregarding the environment and the prompt negotiation of a complete test ban treaty.

Within Australia the trade union movement had organised its own action against France with black bans and boycotts. As the Coalition Government of Prime Minister William McMahon made little comment on these activities they were perceived abroad as a component of official policy. On gaining office in December 1972, Prime Minister Gough Whitlam decided immediately to increase Australian pressure on France. He ratified the Nuclear Non-Proliferation Treaty that his predecessors had signed but not ratified. In January 1973, a note was sent to France conveying Australia's view that the tests were unlawful and warning that Australia would take international legal action unless France gave assurances that no further tests would be carried out. The French Government replied for the first time to Australian protestations, asserting the legality of their actions but indicating that discussions could be held to examine the differences of opinion. At a meeting in Paris in April 1973, it was made clear that France would not agree to cease atmospheric testing and was intending to conduct another series of tests in the near future. Whitlam decided to arraign France before the International Court of Justice at The Hague and to criticise France publicly and with great virulence for its 'illegal' testing program. So strong was his attack on this aspect of French policy that trade and economic relations between the two countries suffered as a consequence.

There was no question that Whitlam had the weight of Australian popular opinion behind him. In earlier years, support for British atomic testing at Maralinga in South Australia had fallen from 58 per cent in 1952 to 38 per cent in 1956. By 1965, opinion was divided on the question of France's right to test 'on one of their islands in the Pacific': 47 per cent thought they should be allowed, 43 per cent were opposed. Just seven years later, after the French had conducted several series of tests, opposition had risen to 72 per cent while only 20 per cent were in favour. Later that year with the survey question slightly altered from France's right to test on their own territory to general approval of the test program, one poll recorded a 90 per cent disapproval of French testing. In New Zealand opposition ran just as high. In 1971, nearly 81 per cent of respondents to one survey believed the New Zealand government should oppose French testing. By 1976, nearly two-thirds of all New Zealanders would be in favour of sending private boats into the test zone as a protest. In fact, the idea of sending a warship to protest directly against French atomic testing at Mururoa originated in New Zealand at this time, principally with the Labour Prime Minister, Norman Kirk.

It was Kirk's idea to deploy an RNZN frigate to Mururoa in an effort to attract international attention to the suffering endured by the Pacific Island nations as a result of the testing. This was part of the Kirk Government's concerted effort to improve and strengthen New Zealand's relationship with its South Pacific neighbours by promoting New Zealand's image as a Pacific Island state. Kirk said that 'New Zealand has a special concern, and acknowledges a special responsibility, to assist and co-operate with its neighbours in the South Pacific'.

The relationship between Australia and New Zealand was as close as it had ever been at that time with left-wing governments in power in both nations. At a meeting between the two Prime Ministers, at a time when cooperation in foreign policy reached a new and dramatic intensity, Whitlam decided that Australia should support New Zealand's action by deploying an Australian frigate. Certainly, Whitlam considered, Australia should not do less than New Zealand to halt the French testing, while the Federal Opposition accepted 'the necessity for all reasonable steps to be taken to try to prevent future nuclear explosions in the atmosphere, whether by the People's Republic of China or France', although not convinced that dispatching a ship to the test site would achieve anything of tangible value. The majority public opinion was in favour of the deployment. In an opinion poll conducted at that time, respondents were asked whether they were in favour or opposed to the suggestion of stationing a ship near the test site 'to stop the French exploding a nuclear device'. Of the 2259 people polled, 55 per cent were in favour while only 25 per cent were opposed.

It seems neither government was aware that the frigates then in service in both navies were incapable of reaching the test site without refuelling or that a continuous supply of fuel was required if they were to remain in the test area for an extended period. Given that the dispute was with France, refuelling at French Tahiti was obviously out of the question. After Whitlam was informed of this constraint, the Navy was asked whether the Tide Class fleet tanker HMAS *Supply* could be deployed to Mururoa to both represent Australia in the protest and refuel the RNZN frigate. The Fleet Commander advised that *Supply* was then undergoing a refit and could not be sent. The only other alternative was to send the converted aircraft carrier-cum-troopship HMAS *Sydney*, which had given such valuable service in supplying the Australian military effort in South Vietnam. *Sydney* had a refuelling capability and the capacity to remain on station for a prolonged period. The RNZN was faced with the same question about ship availability. The *Rothesay* Class Type 12 frigate, HMNZS *Otago*, was chosen. *Otago* was neither a new ship nor very well equipped but it was entirely capable of making the trip and remaining on station. Launched in 1958, *Otago* was equipped with a quadruple Seacat short range missile system, two 4.5-inch guns in a twin turret and two limbo 3-barrelled DC mortars. The only weapon that would have been used if the French retaliated in any way would have been the 4.5-inch guns.

The requirement for a support ship conveniently allowed Australia to take a back seat to New Zealand. As Defence Minister (and Deputy Prime Minister) Lance Barnard told Federal Parliament, Australia's main protest action was its claim before the International Court of Justice: 'It is the Government's view that emphasis should be placed on this protest in this way'. Barnard went on to say:

> I made it perfectly clear to the Prime Minister of New Zealand that the Australian participation would be to the extent that the vessel would be outside the fallout area [and] that the exercise would be regarded as a naval exercise ... We as a Government believe that we have a responsibility not only to fulfil our obligations in co-operating with New Zealand but also to ensure that we make whatever protests are available and within the capacity of this Government.

It is noteworthy that Barnard here makes the point that Australia would conduct the deployment as an 'exercise'; a signal to the French that they had apparently nothing to fear by the deployment. It also meant that any escalation of tension would see the New Zealand ship the first target for reprisal. As *Sydney* would be stationed 240 kilometres to the west, any trouble at the test site would give *Sydney* time to beat a hasty retreat.

The nomination of *Sydney* caused some concern for the Navy as the vessel was in the process of being modified for possible future use in an amphibious warfare role. Nonetheless, the firm decision was made that *Sydney* was to be deployed and, in preparation for a long 'exercise' off Mururoa, was given a docking and hull scraping. A request by *Sydney*'s commanding officer for utility helicopters to be embarked in the former aircraft carrier was denied. *Sydney* would proceed to Auckland and refuel before undertaking the 3600-kilometre passage to rendezvous with the New Zealand ship off the test site. While *Sydney*'s ship's company were preparing for the deployment, Labor Party frontbencher Jim Cairns made a number of emotive statements about the public health dangers of French atomic testing so close to Australia. Senator Frank McManus (Democratic Labor Party) asked the Minister assisting the Prime Minister, Senator Don Willesee, how the Government could assert that sailors in *Sydney* would be safe when 'we who are thousands of miles further away from the explosions are in danger?' Willesee replied:

> it is not envisaged that it [HMAS *Sydney*] will go directly into the area of the explosions. I understand that there will be an immediate fallout and that there will then be thrown into the atmosphere the dangers that will go on in varying quantities over many years. All I can say is that we certainly will not willingly be putting anybody into more danger than the normal French tests will bring about.

It was a feeble and unconvincing response that did nothing to allay what were legitimate fears. Not surprisingly, it prompted an immediate outcry from the wives of sailors posted to *Sydney*. Many were concerned for their husbands' safety such a short distance from the actual test site. After the women's protestations received widespread media attention, Whitlam announced in Parliament that no sailor would be forced to take part in the deployment.

The significance of this well-meaning but dangerous gesture should not be overlooked. This was the first time in the history of the RAN as a disciplined and entirely volunteer service that an operation was made optional. Barnard tried to deny that it was without precedent:

> It ought to be, and I am sure it is, understood by honourable members that in these circumstances applications will be made, as they have been made on other occasions by servicemen to opt out of an exercise, and these crew members are exercising their normal rights. I have sufficient faith in those who serve in the RAN to know that in these circumstances and because the question that is involved is one of very great significance to this country, there will be adequate numbers of naval men to man . . . whichever ship is used on this exercise.

That participation by anyone under the *Naval Defence Act* in any naval exercise was optional was plainly untrue, and there was no precedent within the RAN of any sailor being given an opportunity to withhold his service.

The Navy had always argued that once an individual had volunteered to join the service they were legally liable for service wherever and whenever the Naval Board directed them to serve, that they recognised they were forgoing certain rights and prerogatives when they volunteered for service. While conscripts had never been obliged to serve in the RAN, both conscripts and National Service trainees had the opportunity of electing to serve in the Navy. Whitlam's attempts at placating the objections of some naval families to the Mururoa protest undermined the culture of obligation which the Naval Board had adamantly maintained during the 1950s and 1960s. The Naval Board, in common with both the Army and Air Force Boards, believed the Government and the public had the right to expect service personnel to serve wherever they were ordered to serve. If the Services were being maintained in peacetime to prepare for war, the nation could fairly assume that they would be available to serve the national interest in wartime without condition or qualification. To expect otherwise would be to erode public confidence in the operational capacity of the Services. Worse, it would politicise the Services and allow individual discretion where absolute loyalty and obedience could properly be demanded. It is for this reason that the conscientious objection provisions in the *Defence Act* and *National Service Act* do not apply to volunteer personnel. The same thinking underlies Australia's resistance to recognising any form of selective objection among both volunteers and conscripts. The danger in allowing individual personnel to decide whether or not they would offer or withhold their service lay in the probability of one individual influencing another in the decision they would make. Ensuring that this influence was not mutinous was almost impossible. Furthermore, where and how would a line be drawn between those aspects of service which would be optional or mandatory?

Had the Australian Government made naval service in waters off Vietnam optional some eighteen months earlier, the Navy's ability to man and deploy its ships would have rested on an unstable basis.[2] Given the level of public opposition to Australian participation in the war, the attitude of naval officers and sailors to Vietnam was unpredictable. And the question could rightly be asked, 'What makes the war in Vietnam different from the Mururoa deployment?' No-one could argue that Australia's national interests were more or less at stake in South Vietnam. The problem for the Australian Labor Party was that it had not advocated making naval service in Vietnam optional while in Opposition. Had it done so, there might have been more consistency in its decision to offer an opt-out opportunity to *Sydney*'s ship's company. It was not surprising, then, that the decision to make the deployment optional led the Government into all kinds of difficulties—which it attempted to resolve by semantic obfuscation. In the Senate, the Minister representing the Minister for Defence, Senator Reg Bishop, said that:

although the deployment would be treated as a normal naval operation and the ship will be manned by its normal ship's company, any member of the ship's company who had special reasons for not proceeding with the ship could submit a request for re-posting and would get it. It is intended that the ship will operate clear of the nuclear fallout area, and questions of danger and contamination do not arise.

What the objections to participating in the operation might be exactly were not made clear, but the Government implied that no request would be denied, however spurious or specious its foundation. Barnard suggested possible objections would be 'political reasons or conscience'. While it was unclear whether such objections ever existed in the minds of sailors, that the Government suggested they might exist probably fostered their creation. 'Political reasons' could only have been an opinion that the French were entitled to conduct the tests and that this right should not be challenged, to which the Government was entitled to respond that political objections had no standing in a disciplined force and that any opposition to the deployment should be expressed at the ballot box. Furthermore, majority public opinion in Australia firmly opposed the testing. As to the grounds of 'conscience', only in the fear that the ships might be involved in a violent confrontation could grounds for conscientious objection have arisen. But as the Navy was a volunteer force, it is unlikely that those with such an objection would have joined the Navy in the first place. Given that political pressure had not been applied to the Government in relation to this matter, it was a curious step to take and one the Labor Party would come to regret.

Sydney's commanding officer, Captain Andrew Robertson DSC RAN, mustered the ship's company and informed them of the Prime Minister's announcement on the optional status of the deployment and its consequences for them, at the same time reminding the sailors that the ship needed every one of them if *Sydney* were to go to sea. He disagreed with the Government's decision and attempted to minimise its effects on *Sydney*'s preparedness for sea. From a ship's company of over 600, there were 18 compassionate cases in which sailors requested not to undertake the deployment. Fourteen of these had nothing to do with the protest or an exercise of political or conscientious rights, being related to the effects an extended deployment would have on family and domestic situations, and on the courses some sailors were programmed to attend for promotion and career advancement. Just four sailors requested re-posting on political and health grounds. The Navy was entitled to be pleased with the commitment and the dedication of its personnel.

In spite of the enthusiasm that accompanied the decision to join New Zealand in the protest deployment, the Australian Government took a long time to finalise details. The delay was intentional, the Government having resolved that the RAN ship would not be deployed 'until all other means of protest have been exhausted'.[3] In fact, the delay was so long that the Navy's first choice for the task, *Supply*, completed her refit and was then made available to undertake the operation. As *Supply* was a purpose-built underway replenishment ship with a vastly superior refuelling capability, a greater storage capacity and required less than 200 personnel, the nomination was changed, *Supply* was equipped with two double 40/60mm Bofors guns and two single Bofors guns.

When a signal from the Fleet Commander was sent advising that *Supply* would undertake the deployment in lieu of *Sydney*, the commanding officer, Captain Geoff Loosli RAN, cleared the lower deck and explained to the ship's company that the optional nature of the deployment applied to them just as it had applied to *Sydney*'s ship's company. He stated that there would be no recrimination against anyone who honestly and conscientiously believed he should not participate in the operation because of its nature. Anyone with such an objection was to request a new posting elsewhere in the Fleet. To ensure objections were not partly motivated by a desire to avoid sea service, those requesting to be drafted elsewhere would be sent to another sea-going ship rather than a shore establishment and would return to *Supply* on its arrival back in Australia. Twelve requests for draft were received, partly prompted by the indefinite nature of the deployment. As *Supply* was scheduled to take part in RIMPAC (Rim of the Pacific) exercises commencing in late August off Hawaii, it was possible that the ship would sail from Mururoa to Hawaii and that the deployment might be well over six months in duration. As a consequence of the uncertainty, sixteen drafts planned for late June, July and August were brought forward and reliefs were sent early.

The nine cases classified as compassionate would have been approved whatever the operation because of the uncertainty of the time away from Sydney. It was also essential that the need for compassionate leave be reduced to a minimum after the ship departed as it would be difficult to return any sailor to Sydney once under way. Three sailors asked not to go on the grounds of 'political' objection. The nature of their objections were neither stated nor questioned and remain unknown. That there were only three conscientious objectors taking advantage of the Government's unique concession again reflected a strong commitment to duty. This did not mean, however, that the ship's company or the Navy supported the protest in general, or that they shared the Government's opposition to French nuclear testing. Quite the converse seems to have been true. The RAN has always been known for its political conservatism and most officers of the time supported the right of France to conduct nuclear testing on French sovereign territory. They did not share the community's fear of the dangers of the testing to Australian public health and felt that Australia should support France's efforts to develop a nuclear capability which would further deter the Soviet Union. As for community protest, the feeling among officers was that protest action was for 'radicals and university students', recalling that the previous eight years were the years of protest against Australian involvement in the Vietnam conflict. One suspects that the Navy felt it was above 'mere protest action' and the political sentiment that was embodied in the deployment.

Supply sailed from Sydney on 25 June 1973 for the eight-day passage to Mururoa. The ship was not completely squared away and entirely ready for sea, as the refit had not been completed until 22 June and near-Herculean effort was expended in readying the ship's machinery for the trip. Adequate naval stores for 180 days were embarked while there were sufficient dry and frozen provisions, canteen stores and beer to last 90 days. The departure of the Navy's largest ship on what was described as an 'historic' deployment was covered by a very large media group including television crews from the United States and Japan. As the ship sailed past Bradley's Head, supporters waved while others had painted 'Good Luck *Supply*' on one of the old colonial harbour defences. The Navy had declined to give the ship's destination, its ports of call on the way to Mururoa, or what the ship would be doing when it arrived, and the sailors' wives were still concerned. Margaret Maksimovic, wife of Leading Seaman Thomas Maksimovic, told the press she was concerned about her husband: 'My husband is happy about it, but I'm worried. I don't trust the French any more'.

In New Zealand, the departure of *Otago* was an event of national importance. Prime Minister Kirk indicated that all 20 members of Cabinet, including himself, had volunteered to sail with *Otago* to the test zone and that a ballot had been held to decide the matter. The Minister for Immigration and Mines, Fraser

Colman, was the eventual 'lucky' winner. Colman, who was married with three daughters, was asked how his wife felt about his success in the ballot: 'Naturally, she has reservations, but she will be no different from all the wives and families of the crew of *Otago*'. Kirk was prepared to be more open than the RAN about the nature of the deployment: he said it would be of four to six weeks' duration and would not enter French territorial waters. To coincide with the ship's departure, Kirk sent a 750-word message to the heads of government of all member and observer states of the United Nations and all countries in the Pacific which were not members of the UN, calling for their support and their solidarity with Australia and New Zealand in persuading France to abandon the tests.

Supply passed the northern tip of New Zealand's North Island on 29 June 1973 and rendezvoused with *Otago*, under the command of Commander Alan Tirrel RNZN, 400 kilometres east of North Cape. A non-delaying exercise program was arranged while the pre-wetting system in *Supply*, which was not working to a satisfactory standard, received the attention of the ship's engineering staff. The highlight of the passage for fourteen of the Australian sailors was a jack-stay transfer to *Otago* and the chance to experience a rum issue, no longer part of RAN custom. *Supply* arrived off Avarua Harbour on Rarotonga in the Cook Islands on 5 July. The next day Captain Loosli met the Premier of the Cook Islands, Albert Henry, and the New Zealand High Commissioner, George Brocklehurst. Later in the day, some of the personnel from *Supply* traveled to Nikao Airfield to meet the RAAF C130 Hercules transport aircraft which had brought mail and stores from Australia. This was the first and last port of call for the Australian ship before joining the New Zealand frigate in the designated 'support area' to the west of the test site.

With the imminent arrival of the two 'Anzac ships', the French notified their intention on 8 July of establishing a security zone extending 115 kilometres out from Mururoa. There was a swift Australian response. *Supply* was to increase speed from 14.5 knots to 17 knots in an effort to replenish *Otago* earlier than planned to enable the frigate to be inside the declared zone by noon on 10 July. The transfer of 2500 kilograms of stores and 227 tonnes of fuel was carried out between 10pm and 11:30pm in rough seas. By late on 10 July, *Supply* had arrived in the support area in which she steamed for the next two days. During that period the tanker was over-flown by French aircraft on three occasions. Radiac instruments were manned continuously and air samples were taken every two hours. Air-sampling at two-hour intervals was maintained whenever the ship was within 800 kilometres of the atoll; beyond that distance sampling was done every 24 hours. No readings of significance were recorded throughout the month. During this initial period in the support area NBC (Nuclear-Biological-Chemical) exercises were carried out each forenoon and all procedures for dealing with contamination tested so that the ship could confidently have steamed into an area of nuclear fallout.

After replenishing *Otago* again on 12 July, *Supply* returned to Rarotonga. Less than two hours after the arrival of the C130 aircraft from Australia, all of the provisions had been transferred to *Supply*, which was then ready to return to the Support Area. Shortly after 8am on 15 July, France detonated the first device in the latest series of tests. At the time of the detonation *Supply* was 560 kilometres from Mururoa Atoll and no hint of the explosion was observed. The yield of the device was estimated by *Otago* to be about five kilotons. After the explosion, *Supply* replenished *Otago* with fuel and stores before the frigate returned to the 'observation' area. HMNZS *Canterbury*, which was to relieve *Otago*, had arrived in the support area but was unable to effect the changeover because of problems with a contaminated engine-room boiler. When the problem was rectified, the relief was effected on 25 July. *Canterbury* was a much newer ship which had arrived in New Zealand in August of the previous year. Capable of a comparable top speed but with better endurance than *Otago*, *Canterbury* was armed with one quadruple Seacat missile system, two 4.5-inch guns in a twin turret, two 20-millimetre anti-aircraft guns and two Mark 32 torpedo tubes. She also carried a Wasp helicopter. *Supply* replenished both ships and returned to Rarotonga. After a two-day stay in Avarua, *Supply* again departed for the support area, refuelling *Otago* 560 kilometres to the east of Rarotonga to enable the frigate to make the return passage to Auckland. During this replenishment the second French detonation took place. On returning to the support area, *Supply* was met by *Canterbury* which was refuelled and reprovisioned. It was now the end of July. The future requirement for both ships to remain in the area was unclear, as the next air-supply flight to Rarotonga had not been arranged and news reports indicated that all French naval vessels had left Mururoa Atoll and arrived at Papeete for a stand-down period. At 8pm on 29 July, *Canterbury* unexpectedly detached from *Supply* and returned to the observation area. The Australians were not advised of the reason. *Supply* remained in the support area.

Although intelligence and news reports indicated that the French had entered a stand-down period, *Canterbury* made its presence felt by remaining in close proximity to Mururoa Atoll. This clearly annoyed the French, who could do nothing to move the vessel. It was not until 3 August that the uncertainty ended, when the New Zealand Defence Minister, A. Faulkner, announced that *Supply* and *Canterbury* would be leaving the Mururoa area at 2pm on 5 August. After refuelling *Canterbury* on 4 August, *Supply* departed for Rarotonga to collect stores and mail, but not before the two ships were over-flown by a French Neptune aircraft sent to ascertain whether the ships were really intending to leave. *Canterbury* returned to the observation area for another 29 hours before departing for Auckland.

Supply arrived off Sydney Heads at 9am on 17 August after 53 days continuously at sea, having steamed 24 625 kilometres. There was extensive press and television coverage of the ship's return and a flood of signals from both Australian and New Zealand authorities expressing appreciation for the role *Supply* had played during the deployment. In the period that the ship had been off Mururoa, the French had defied the 22 June decision of the International Court and detonated five nuclear devices. Prime Minister Whitlam kept the issue alive by raising it at the Commonwealth Heads of Government meeting in Ottawa later in the month but received no support from the British Conservative Government of Edward Heath which was unwilling to jeopardise its relationship with the European Economic Community.

The action brought by Australia did not come before the International Court again until July 1974. By then the French Government had made a number of statements making it clear that atmospheric tests would not be conducted after 1974. On 8 June 1974, the French president issued a statement that 'in view of the stage reached in carrying out the French nuclear defence program France will be in a position to pass on to the stage of underground explosions as soon as the series of tests planned for this summer is completed'.

To coincide with the conclusion of this test program, the French Minister for Foreign Affairs told the United Nations General Assembly, 'We have now reached a stage in our nuclear technology that makes it possible for us to continue our program by underground testing, and we have taken steps to do so as early as next year'. Three weeks later, the French Minister for Defence announced that there would be no atmospheric testing in 1975 as France was ready to proceed underground.

In fact, the 1974 tests were the last. On 20 December 1974, the Court decided by a majority of nine to six that there was no dispute between the two nations and that the claim by Australia no longer had any object. The Court then declined to rule on its jurisdiction or the admissibility of the application. By then Whitlam had lost most of his vigour for the fight. After the Australian Council of Trade Unions joined forces with the New Zealand Federation of Labour to impose bans on French shipping, Whitlam was disinclined to further antagonise the French or the Americans over nuclear testing issues. He even refused to support a New Zealand proposal to declare the Pacific a nuclear-free testing zone.

Was the protest a success, given that the French very soon after moved the testing underground, a less efficient and more costly option? Although it is difficult to ascribe a particular result, the enormous international awareness of the testing and the pressure exerted on France generated by the protest played a large part in forcing France to alter its policy. A protest action featuring warships from two countries attracted enormous attention and helped to internationalise the dispute. The warships made the protest much more compelling and forceful and, combined with the flotilla of private protest craft in the area, created a powerful image that France could do little to counter.

The Navy had varying views as to the effectiveness and wisdom of the deployment. Mururoa was an unconventional use of one of the Navy's ships and many naval people were clearly uncomfortable with it. There had been occasional veiled use of the Navy in conjunction with national protest action but none as formal or as obvious as this, which demonstrated very little subtlety and not much discretion. Concerning the testing, naval officers had no particular views although the French government was thought to be potentially volatile and unpredictable. The deployment was described by some as a clear case of 'a boy being sent to do a man's work'. Sending a fleet tanker and an obsolete and poorly armed frigate to Mururoa could have resulted in an embarrassing diplomatic backdown for Australia and New Zealand had the French attempted to order the ships out of the area with their warships as escort. There could be little control of the way the deployment was perceived internationally but fortunately it was favourable. That the French actually detonated devices with the ships in the area was widely condemned as arrogant, defiant and uncaring. The world seemed to be on the side of Australia and New Zealand and nothing would change that.

It was considered within the Navy that despatching a warship had meant that Australia was serious about halting French atomic testing and was, in the final event, prepared to use that ship in a military role. Instead of the carrier, the sentiment was expressed that Australia should have sent a detachment of ships led by the Flagship, the aircraft carrier HMAS *Melbourne*. This, however, would most likely have been interpreted by the French as a hostile act, while the despatch of an ageing tanker which was very lightly armed could only be interpreted as a symbolic act designed principally to attract worldwide attention. While it could be argued that France had just as great an opportunity to make its point by turning the ships away, something it tried to do with the proclamation of an illegal exclusion zone around Mururoa, the weight of international opinion was clearly against the French, who were forced to weather the storm of protest and widespread condemnation.

The consequences on naval discipline of the Government's decision to allow an option to serve would not be apparent for another two decades, when the precedent created by the Mururoa deployment would be used to incite mutiny among Australian naval personnel bound for the Persian Gulf following the Iraqi invasion of Kuwait in August 1990.

17

Conscience and mutiny

The relationship between mutiny and conscientious objection has rarely been explored. In some countries, mutinies within the armed forces have been justified on the basis of service personnel being ordered to commit acts contrary to their conscience. Citing these objections, those personnel have individually and collectively withheld their service and, effectively, mutinied. To avoid such instances, many governments recognise in law a right to object to compulsory service in the armed forces on the grounds of conscience. In these instances, the objection must be declared and recognised before the individual is conscripted. But the legal recognition of such a right is not a straightforward matter in either its theory or application. In this chapter, attention will be turned to the possibility of legislation recognising a right of conscientious objection working to increase the likelihood of mutiny in the armed forces.

Objection to military service always implies some degree of conflict of values between the authorities and the person who objects. Pacifists, including Christian pacifists, normally represent a dissenting opinion held only by a relatively small number in society. This may explain why Australian governments have traditionally agreed to a compromise with those who genuinely hold *absolute* pacifist convictions. But when the objector is not a pacifist, but selectively objects to participation in military service because of the alleged immorality of the purpose or the illegality of the means and methods used in combat, the conflict of values becomes much more acute and resolution becomes much less satisfactory. Consequently, governments have consistently refused to recognise objection other than that based on absolute pacifism.

Recognising a right of *selective* objection has two major consequences for conscript and volunteer military service. First, it establishes the principle that wars and conflicts waged by a government can be judged by the electorate to be just or unjust. The second consequence follows from the first: military service needs, therefore, to be conditional, with provision for exemption for those who exercise their right and possibly judge a war, otherwise requiring their participation, to be unjust. During the Vietnam War, a number of individuals supported by various community organisations appealed to the Commonwealth Government and the courts for recognition of selective conscientious objection. Those seeking the legislative recognition of such a right claimed they would take up arms to defend Australia but that Australian security was not at stake in South Vietnam. Noting the conclusions of an American Presidential Commission which inquired into all forms of conscientious objection during 1969, the Government steadfastly refused to acknowledge any right to selective objection in Australian law.

With Australian involvement in the Vietnam War ended in late 1972, there was little discussion of conscription and conscientious objection for more than a decade. The debate prompted by the Vietnam War lay moribund. Shortly after the Labor Party gained office in the federal election of March 1983, Michael Tate, a Labor senator from Tasmania, a member of the Catholic Commission for Justice and Peace and a pacifist by personal conviction, introduced a Private Member's Bill into the Senate proposing changes to the *National Service Act* (1951).[1] The draft bill, which sought to amend the grounds for recognising conscientious objection, was referred for inquiry to the Senate Standing Committee on Legal and Constitutional Affairs on 31 May 1983.[2] The most controversial aspect of the draft bill was the proposal to recognise selective objection.

In its submission to the Standing Committee inquiry, the Defence Department was totally opposed to altering any legislation relating to conscription. Its concerns were not prompted by fears of civil disobedience or the difficulty of determining the validity of selective objection, but on the effect such legislation would have on the volunteer force and the conduct of operations. A Defence internal minute noted:

> If the proposed changes to eligibility for exemption on conscientious grounds are adopted *they should logically be available during service, whether compulsory or voluntary.* In this context, should regular [volunteer] members of the Defence Force gain exemption and thus not be available to perform the duties for which they have been trained, any national investment which

has been made in their training will have been wasted. Further, operational capabilities which are essential components of an effective national defence force could be rendered inoperative if specially trained personnel manning critical functions were granted exemption.[3] [emphasis added]

The Australian Defence Force (ADF) was in no doubt that such a provision would influence the whole nature of operational planning. In future, military planning staff would need to ensure that particular operations were palatable to the prevailing moral climate within the ADF. The alternative would be to withhold information about future operations until after the necessary forces were committed. For the sake of contingency planning, the ADF believed it would thus be justified in maintaining a register of the particular objections of its members in advance of any conflict. Such a policy would no doubt injure the morale of those who confessed no objection and who would be forced to remain in an area of operations. It would also adversely affect the professional posting and promotion prospects of those who did register an objection.

But how broadly could the exemption be understood if the grounds for objection included 'particular types of warfare'? The Australian Army had a somewhat glib outlook:

> If objection is to be allowed on these grounds there can be no certainty that members already serving will be available to continue to serve as a conflict progresses. It is possible that a member could object to rendering further service based on his objection to tactical decisions, or the employment of certain weapons with which he does not agree.[4]

The RAAF had a similar perspective:

> The processing of such cases [of selective objection] in a combat situation would be extremely difficult, to say nothing of the likely deleterious effect on morale and operations generally. It is unlikely that a conclusive consensus could be achieved before embarking on an operation, and the prosecution of defence objectives by the commander, which depends on the discipline and obedience of the men under his command, would be seriously impaired.[5]

After receiving a very diverse body of evidence during its inquiry, the report of the Standing Committee was tabled in the Senate on 28 May 1985. It defined conscientious belief as that which:

> ... involves a seriously based conviction which is part of the core fundamental values of a person and which is expressed as an imperative having primacy in the life of the person concerned. To be coerced by law into acting in a way contrary to this imperative would be to experience a violation of one's integrity as a person.[6]

In effect, an individual may have a belief about something but it may not be so strongly held as to amount to a conscientious belief. However, the Standing Committee believed it was worthy of recognition and exemption from military service.

In so broadening the basis for conscientious belief, including the admission of political convictions, which one submission argued could be held by people who 'may be speaking in political terms and expressing themselves in a political way but their relationship to politics is a conscientious one',[7] the Committee concluded that 'the formation of a specific conscientious belief will commonly involve an interaction between the fundamental values of a person and his assessment of current history and politics'.[8] This was extended to provide for the right of selective objection for conscripts.[9] Curiously, as it appeared to the ADF to be a logical extension of the same principle, the Committee did not recommend its extension to volunteers, although some of the things to which conscripts might object could in theory also be offensive to volunteers.

The Committee concluded that given the small number of people likely to exercise the right of selective objection, its provision in law would apparently not impede in any appreciable way a government's efforts to recruit the necessary number of combatants to defend Australia in time of war. This assertion went completely without substantiation. Furthermore, 'the more popular the war the more volunteers would be attracted to military service and the more conscripts could be expected willingly to participate'.[10] The Committee thought that if selective objection were ever to pose a recruiting problem, the Government would be required either to improve the case it had presented to justify Australian involvement or reconsider the need for any involvement. The Government's chances of success would be minimal. The Standing Committee also challenged the notion that selective objection was based on political, rather than religious, belief: 'Dissent from the government's decision or programs is not always to be described as "mere political dissidence". Recognition that some dissent can be conscientiously based is a mark of a democratic society'.[11] However, the Committee seemed unaware of, or perhaps was ignorant or unconcerned by, the difficulties identified and faced by the American Commission in this area some fifteen years earlier.

There was never any dispute that moral convictions and politics shared common ground. Establishing any means, any test, any criteria of assessment, of distinguishing between them, and the implicit rejection of political opposition to particular wars as a legitimate basis for objection, were not covered by the Committee's report. In this sense, it was negligent in failing to consider the key issues associated with recognising selective objection—the exercise of such a right for the consequences of granting such a right on the political community as a whole. It would appear that the Committee, led by Senator Tate, was predisposed to establishing the recognition of such a right but gave virtually no thought to its application in time of war. In effect, the Committee undermined the authority of the political order and the force and effect of laws passed by the Parliament.

For the next four years, the draft legislation proceeded very slowly through the necessary stages of development and consultation. One academic commentator, Dr Hugh Smith, doubted in 1989 that the Government would proceed with the legislation.

> [No] further action has so far been taken and the government may well have had second thoughts about allowing citizens to seek exemption from service in a particular war—all the more so, when such provisions are opposed . . . by the Department of Defence and the Australian Defence Force. Clearly this would be a bold move by any government and Australia would again find itself at the forefront in legislating for the protection of conscience.[12]

The Bill was still in draft form when Iraq invaded Kuwait on 2 August 1990. Prompted by the possibility of hostilities with Iraq, and the unlawful abstention of Leading Seaman Terence Jones from HMAS *Adelaide* which was bound for the Gulf of Oman to enforce UN sanctions against Iraq,[13] Independent Senator for Western Australian, Jo Vallentine, introduced a private bill into the Senate for *An Act relating to conscientious objection to certain Defence service*. Recalling the Labor Government's 'opt-out' concession during the Mururoa Protest in 1973, Vallentine claimed there was a precedent which ought to apply to the Gulf War. She praised Leading Seaman Jones for being 'aware, informed and intelligent'. This prompted a hastily convened group calling itself the Bring the Frigates Home Coalition to picket the RAN ships as they prepared to leave for the Gulf war. The group also placed posters and placards around Garden Island Dockyard which claimed that every sailor had the right to request exclusion from the deployment. A copy of one handbill held by the authors was headed: 'An Appeal to RAN Personnel on [sic] HMAS Sydney and HMAS Brisbane'. It proclaimed:

> Do not go to the Gulf on 12 November. The Terry Jones case proved that you can make a formal approach to your captain, state your objections to service in the Gulf, and he has to let you off. The Defence Minister has said that there is no compulsion for RAN personnel to go to the Gulf. Decide Now! Do not go!

This was a serious misrepresentation of the truth which bordered on incitement to mutiny. First, commanding officers of RAN ships were not at liberty to recognise any claim to conscientious objection. Second, the Defence Minister stated that as RAN personnel were not under any compulsion to join the Navy, they were, by extension, not compelled to go to the Gulf. In the wake of the confusion created by the Bring the Frigates Home Coalition, the Chief of Naval Staff, Vice-Admiral Michael Hudson, sent a detailed signal to all ships and shore establishments clarifying their obligation to serve.

> Many of you will be aware of the publicity given recently to the notion that volunteer servicemen and women are entitled to choose which operations or duties they are willing to take part in or to perform. This notion is sometimes referred to in terms of an alleged right to 'conscientious objection on the grounds of political belief'. Such views are of concern not only because they are wrong but because they may be causing unnecessary confusion or doubt among some of our younger members and among families.
> ... unless the government should choose otherwise, voluntary service in the Navy and indeed the ADF generally, does not carry with it any right by which individuals for reasons of political or other beliefs, whether conscientiously held or not, may selectively choose to avoid discharging duties lawfully imposed on them.[14]

Consequently, there were no defensible grounds on which Leading Seaman Jones could absent himself from HMAS *Adelaide*.

At his court martial, which began on 24 September 1991,[15] Jones was found guilty of being absent without leave and was sentenced to 21 days detention, reduction in rank to able seaman, the forfeiture of four days' pay and dismissal from the Navy. Despite the severity of the punishment, which was intended to make an example and to highlight the seriousness of Jones's untimely abstention, a paper prepared within the Naval Support Command shortly after the court martial noted that:

> In practice a considerable degree of flexibility has been shown in attempting to accommodate personnel who have genuine difficulties in participating in particular operations. This flexibility was exercised in the Gulf deployment where commanding officers agreed to allow a number of people to post off the ships for a variety of reasons, some less compelling than conscientious objection. The ability for commanders to do this is obviously useful and should be retained provided it is not seen as a *de facto* right of conscientious objection on the part of the individuals concerned.[16]

The initiation of proceedings against Jones prompted an inquiry from the Human Rights and Equal Opportunity Commissioner, Brian Burdekin, who was concerned that the absence of any right of selective conscientious objection offended against the spirit of the *Human Rights and Equal Opportunity Commission (HREOC) Act* (1986) and was contrary to the *International Covenant on Civil and Political Rights* (ICCPR) which was incorporated into Australian law by the *HREOC Act*. The subsequent lack of follow-up action from Burdekin regarding this matter was probably a consequence of the demonstrable weakness of his objection. No specific article of the ICCPR recognises a right of conscientious objection. Conversely, article 8 provides an exemption to the prohibition of forced or compulsory labour in the case of 'any service of a military character and, in countries where conscientious objection is recognised, any national service required by law of conscientious objectors'. However, the contention that the non-recognition of conscientious objection is discriminatory is usually based on the view that this situation results, or is likely to result, in a person holding a particular political or religious belief being treated in a worse manner than persons not holding such a belief. This worse treatment could arise in two ways. First, where a person holding a conscientious objection is automatically disqualified from service in the ADF. Secondly, in a failure to recognise conscientious objection in the terms of employment which are offered by the ADF.

The prevailing view within the Defence Force is that the obligation to participate in combat or in particular operations is defensible as 'an inherent requirement of the job' under section 3(7) of the *HREOC Act*. Furthermore, the ADF has asserted its right to punish those who seek to avoid this obligation.

> An expectation that all *lawful* orders will be obeyed is fundamental to the maintenance of discipline within the RAN and the ADF. Concomitant with this expectation there must exist a right . . . to take disciplinary action where breaches of this fundamental obligation occur. In other words the right to enforce the obligation to serve is reasonable and not discriminatory. Accordingly, so far as volunteers are concerned, there is no scope for allowing for conscientious objection with respect to specified operations, or indeed combat generally, unless the matter is raised as a ground for discharge at own request. As a matter of practice, the RAN would restrict its capabilities to an unmanageable extent if every male volunteer had the right to choose not to make himself available for duty in particular operations or in combat.[17]

It is noteworthy that all Defence agencies avoided using the word mutiny throughout the debate and dealt with the matter as though selective objection could be restricted to isolated individuals deciding to object alone. In a letter to fellow Member of Parliament, Harry Woods, the Minister for Defence Science and Personnel, Gordon Bilney, stated:

> The ADF has consistently taken the view that members join voluntarily and take an oath or affirmation to serve in the defence of the nation. Such volunteer service does not carry with it any right by which individuals for reasons of political or other beliefs, whether conscientiously or not, may selectively choose to avoid discharging the duties lawfully imposed on them. Specific conscientious objection by serving members would imply that the oath or affirmation was not binding, raising issues of principle well beyond that of conscientious objection itself. Furthermore, in practical terms, it would be detrimental to Australia's security if the obligation to adhere to a lawful direction of Government to defend Australia, or Australia's interests, were to be put in doubt at the time the Armed Forces were needed.[18]

Despite the brief resurgence of interest in conscientious objection during the Gulf War, the progress of Senator Tate's bill through Parliament was not hastened. The *Defence Legislation Amendment Bill*, as it was by then known, was introduced into the House of Representatives on 26 February 1992. It was considered one week later by the Senate Standing Committee for the Scrutiny of Bills, which offered no comment.

In his speech at the second reading of the Bill, Minister Bilney stated that the Government had been persuaded by the conclusions of the Senate Standing Committee and agreed that 'in some cases, an individual's sense of personal integrity could be violated by compulsion to participate in a particular military conflict but not in other conflicts'.[19] Greg Pemberton, writing in the *Sydney Morning Herald*, regarded the introduction of the Bill as a continuation 'of this country's little-known 90-year-old record as a world leader in terms of liberal laws covering the obligation of citizens to fight'.[20] He commented that the new Bill upheld a strong tradition in 'British liberal political theory dating from Thomas Hobbes which suggests that the issue of war is so destructive . . . the State does not have the right to commit a person to war against his or her will'.[21] Community groups such as the RSL, which supported the ADF in its opposition to the amendments, were not so sure.[22]

Despite the unanimous support for the Report's recommendations within the Standing Committee, the Federal Opposition opposed the inclusion of a right of selective objection in the new Bill. In response, the Minister for Defence, Senator Robert Ray, stated that selective objection would not include military service required in the event of invasion of the Australian mainland. The Australian Democrats moved an amendment to the Bill in the Senate which would give volunteer ADF members the right to object to service in specific conflicts. This was rejected outright by the Government.[23] The Bill was finally passed by the Senate on 23 June 1992 and generated very little publicity, in contrast to the turbulent reception that had greeted any change to conscription legislation during the Vietnam War.[24]

The new provisions were seriously flawed. On the one hand, the recognition of a right of selective objection ought to have extended beyond an objection to a Government's decision to go to war to include objection to the manner in which the war was being fought. This would have reflected both aspects of the just war theory: the need for the war to be just and the means by which it was fought to be fair. On the other hand, the new objection provisions made no mention of the ways in which individuals would or could determine that a conflict or the conduct of an operation was ethically acceptable. Given that ethical decision-making usually occurs in dialogue with others, would discussion of the ethical quality of a war or an operation, with a view to either accepting or refusing participation, amount to mutiny and incitement to mutiny? And if an individual refused duty on the basis of an ethical judgment that was later shown to have been made on inadequate information or deeply flawed logic, could the individual be charged with insubordination or mutiny?

Of course, the practical difficulties of implementing the selective objection provisions in the Act were legion. For example, how would the Government determine whether an objection was ethical or political? Given the absence of a state religion and the enshrinement of religious plurality in the Australian Constitution, on what basis would judgments be made about the ethical quality of one set of religious propositions and beliefs over and above another? And what would happen when a conscript, inducted into the armed forces at a time when a certain strategic environment which was not conscientiously unacceptable prevailed, later found that an unforeseen scenario developed to which a conscientious objection did arise? Would it be legal to quarantine that individual and isolate his view to avoid others developing a similar objection?

Although effected without fanfare, these amendments to the *Defence Act* have essentially transformed the manner in which Australians regard military service. The objection provisions in the Act allow, and even promote, individual judgment to be made on the moral standing of any war against a more diverse and more demanding range of criteria. In acknowledging the possibility of an unjust war, the Government has tacitly accepted that the population will in future be much more critical of the reasons which are given in support of Australian involvement in any war. Being mindful of the manner in which modern warfare is conducted, one is justified in doubting that any future conflict in which Australia might be involved could be free from objection on the grounds that it failed to comply with even the basic tenets of just war theory. In other words, will it be possible not to have a selective objection?

The ADF expects that a volunteer member will probably try to claim exemption from service on the grounds of selective objection when Australian forces are next committed to an overseas conflict or major operation. Although a test case of this kind is unlikely to succeed, the amendments being very specific in that only conscripts can claim selective objection, its abiding significance will lie in its inevitable legal defeat prompting demands for further amendment to the *Defence Act* granting volunteers a similar right of selective objection. It will take a strong government to resist such demands, not to mention the added strain such political controversy would bring to bear on ADF recruitment.

The primary role of the ADF is the defence of Australia and its sovereign interests. In our opinion, the protection of conscience and the recognition of certain human rights, essentially individual matters, cannot be accorded such precedence that they intrude in a deleterious manner on the national interest. Most serious of all, the effect of the selective objection provisions in the Act will be to undermine the confidence of any commander in the willingness of those under his authority to comply with a legitimate order. There will always be the fear that some ethical objection to the conduct of a particular operation might emerge and that a 'mutiny' might ensue. This is an anxiety that the ADF does not need.

18

Looking back and moving on

Popular opinion may envisage mutiny as involving eye-patched desperadoes, swords in teeth, swarming across open decks to seize their officers before hanging them from the yard-arm. The reality is that most mutinies in warships, as opposed to merchant vessels, have been free of personal violence while none has occurred in the face of imminent enemy action.

Of the 400 000 sailors who served in the RN during World War I, 56 were charged with mutiny. By way of comparison, the RAN consisted of only 4000 sailors among whom seventeen (only two being RN-trained) were tried for mutiny. During World War II, 61 RAN sailors faced courts martial; 49 of these were tried for offences relating to resisting or defying authority. There were many other instances in which ships were sabotaged either as part of an attempt to have them remain alongside or as a means of drawing attention to some unacknowledged grievance. In the period 1915–45, charges of mutiny were laid formally against men serving in the RAN five times. On other occasions, events were described by those in authority as 'mutinies' but were dealt with summarily as lesser offences under another name. There were still more incidents, probably as many as eleven, that technically conformed to the legal definition of mutiny but which were resolved by negotiation and compromise. Of those events described officially as 'mutinies', the participants were charged with offences under the *Naval Discipline Act* (NDA). Four led to courts martial and convictions for mutiny.

In terms of the number of sailors involved and subsequently punished, the 1947 New Zealand mutiny was the largest after World War II. There were also more units involved in the New Zealand mutiny (six—*Black Prince, Bellona, Arbutus, Hautapu* and the shore establishments *Philomel* and *Tasman*) than in any other comparable incident. The 1947 mutiny stands out not just for being one of the largest (around 20 per cent of lower deck personnel then serving in the Navy were discharged or punished for mutiny) but because the punishments inflicted upon the personnel who took part were severe and indiscriminate.

What, then, can be said about the causes and course of mutiny in Australia and New Zealand? First, men do not mutiny without a cause. The principal causes of unrest are poor living conditions, destructive leadership and excessive or inconsistently applied discipline. Nelson's contemporary, Admiral Collingwood, considered that an act of mutiny reflected more upon deficiencies in the leadership capabilities of officers than upon the character of sailors who resisted naval authority. It is difficult to escape the conclusion that in almost every instance since 1915, the mutineers were provoked into taking drastic action by defective leadership, management or administration. Sailors do not refuse duty lightly.

Second, most of those charged with mutiny were young men who mistakenly believed that a simple refusal of duty would bring attention to their grievances with the probability of an acceptable resolution. In most instances, the first reaction of their officers was to take strong action to protect authority rather than to consider the grievances prompting the action. Just as often their officers were either unaware or unconcerned about the unhappiness of their men or the grounds for any grievance. The mutinies that did least damage to the overall wellbeing of the Navy were those where officers took firm but considerate action, as at Garden Island in 1970.

Third, although a number of mutinies have involved large numbers of men, usually only a small number are selected for court martial, either as suspected ringleaders or scapegoats. Many courts martial spent much of their time considering the technical definition of mutiny and determining whether the offence had been committed. None of the courts martial considered the grievances that lead to the mutinies as a justification for the action taken.

Fourth, mutiny has always been considered a very serious offence. Consequently, punishments were usually gaol sentences followed by dismissal. These punishments were often the subject of political debate. On several occasions the sentences were commuted through political intervention, to the bewilderment and chagrin of service authorities.

Fifth, the initial response to mutiny is often an official denial, with naval administrators, especially, playing down the importance of what had occurred. Navies appear to be particularly sensitive to the deleterious effects of mutiny on corporate morale and self-esteem, and on recruiting. Mutinies are not normally followed by renewed public interest in naval careers.

Sixth, in five cases, the protagonists were not Australian or New Zealand officers, but Royal Navy commanding officers who insisted upon the strict application of traditional naval discipline with no variation for local conditions. This attitude made compromise impossible.

Seventh, in six of the incidents, unrest among naval personnel coincided with industrial unrest on the waterfront or among merchant seamen. Young sailors (most mutineers described in this book were men aged in their early twenties) observed civilians taking direct action over perceived injustices and reasoned: 'Why don't we do that as well?'

Eighth, in many cases, those charged and convicted of mutiny claimed they did not realise the gravity of their actions nor did they comprehend that their complaints or disobedience of routine orders could be construed as mutiny. The naivety, even idealism, of young Australians and New Zealanders clashed with traditional discipline where disobedience was not tolerated. The past loyalty and service of a sailor accused of mutiny does not seem to have altered the gravity of the offence as far as most commanding officers were concerned.

Ninth, none of the mutinies took place while the units involved were under threat of enemy action. Australian and New Zealand servicemen proved that they were prepared to accept any hardship when it was demanded in the face of the enemy. It was only in peacetime or reserve areas that they were not prepared to accept what they considered to be unfair pay and deplorable living conditions.

Tenth, none of the mutinies described in this book involved violence on the part of the mutineers, although in some cases press reports sensationalised the events and even implied the sailors had violent intent.

Eleventh, very few instances of unrest and mutiny have been well recorded. Indeed, official histories make almost no reference to what were key events in the development of the armed forces. In possible collusion with politicians and naval administrators, historians have tended not to use the word 'mutiny', loaded as it is with connotations of violence and bloodshed, and have preferred euphemisms such as 'strike' although there was no provision in naval life or law to distinguish a mutiny from a strike.

It is ironic that in many cases when servicemen claimed to be on 'strike' the authorities immediately condemned them as 'mutineers' and punished them as such. Yet after the fact, the same actions were referred to in informal records as 'strikes'.

Given the patent need and the obvious desire of sailors for more vigorous representation of their interests, especially the frequency of instances where grievances were not taken seriously, it was not surprising that moves were eventually made to create an external advocacy service for Australian service personnel. Curiously, the impetus came from the other two services rather than the Navy. In the early 1980s, when Australia was feeling the effects of recession and government was trying to reduce expenditure wherever possible, the Defence Forces were subjected to a wage freeze, wastage of personnel was at an all-time high, and morale was low. A small group of serving members in Canberra was considering the need to form a lobby group to express the needs of service personnel. These people realised the extreme difficulties they faced. An attempt in the late 1970s to form a Services Union had not surprisingly, been unsuccessful. Service personnel were politically conservative while the notion of forming a union had appeared to many as a threat to command and discipline. The Federal Government had also made clear its opposition to the formation of a new union. The organisers, who had sought clearance from the Defence hierarchy before forming their union, were promptly identified and posted far away from each other.

The key players in the 1980s formation of the Armed Services Federation, notably Wing Commanders Mike Alves and Clive Huggan, had learned from the previous attempt at forming a union and kept their plans discreet. After canvassing personnel from each Service, a group of all ranks was invited to an informal meeting at the Carillon in Canberra during September 1984 to discuss forming a professional association to represent Service personnel. About twenty personnel attended this meeting. A 'Committee for the Time Being' was formed to progress the Federation's cause. The Police Federation was contacted for advice on framing the ground rules and drafting a constitution. Key office bearers for the Federation were identified, and work began on preparing its foundation.

A public meeting to establish the Armed Forces Federation of Australia was held at the Ainslie Football Club on 28 November 1984 following a leaflet drop to every car at Campbell Park and Russell Hill advising Service personnel of the meeting.

Approximately 200 serving personnel (and the media) attended, a turn-out which encouraged the organisers. A constitution was proposed and ratified, office bearers were elected, and the Defence Headquarters Branch was established. Following the success of the public meeting, recruitment of other members proceeded in earnest. Lieutenant Colonel Bob Copley, who was elected to the inaugural Federal Executive Committee, was assigned the task of forming and coordinating branches in each major concentration of military personnel. As the Federation was intended to represent all personnel, an attempt was made to gain representation at every major base. Forty-five branches were formed nationally.

Very soon there were approximately 3000 financial members, which lent credibility to the Federation's claim that it genuinely represented all Service personnel. The Federal Executive Committee also obtained the support of the Labor Government whose policy platform pledged support to worker organisations. This eased political pressure on Federation members and prevented any government or Defence agency trying to abolish or disband it. As in any broad-based organisation, the first few years of the Federation's life were turbulent. There was considerable disagreement about the Federation's public profile. Those who joined because they were dissatisfied with pay and conditions of service wanted the Federation to be an adversarial organisation. Others suggested a more moderate and measured approach.

There was an eventual consensus that the Federation would foster, protect and promote the welfare and conditions of service of members of the Federation in their capacity as members of the Australian Defence Force. The Federation would act on behalf of its members and under their guidance (through the Federal Council) to protect and improve wages and conditions of service. It would also provide legal, financial and social benefits to its members. Its specific objectives were to ensure:

- current conditions of service are not taken for granted and are protected;
- possible changes to conditions of service are discussed openly;
- an alternative, independent and unbiased view is presented to the DFRT;
- pressure is maintained to keep conditions of service under review;
- Defence recognises community standards and the changing expectations of today's military personnel;
- that ADF members have an independent voice.

But what of complaints and grievances? How would the Federation assist in their expression and resolution? The Federation advised its members that it would

> assist with the resolution of genuine grievances for members. These grievances could include Equal Employment Opportunity, Occupational Health & Safety, Compensation, or other conditions of service matters. It is important to note that the Federation is not about undermining the Chain of Command. Members should seek assistance only after established procedures within the ADF, such as a Redress of Grievance or representation to the Defence Ombudsman, have failed to satisfy the complaint.

In other words, the Federation would involve itself only when all of the established official procedures had been exhausted. This was a wise limitation of its role.

Had an organisation like the Armed Forces Federation existed during the 1920s and 1930s, many of the hardships endured by sailors would have been the subject of greater discussion and more likely alleviation. Far too many officers, from the rank of lieutenant to admiral, lacked genuine concern for the wellbeing of those for whom they had a burden of care. It is most unlikely that either the RAN or the RNZN will ever again witness the extent of unrest and dissatisfaction which plagued both navies before 1950. The sailor's lot has improved considerably, with quality control mechanisms in place to monitor living conditions and external advocacy groups ensuring the willingness of young people to serve in the naval forces is not taken for granted by politicians.

These remarks apply, however, only to peacetime service. During active service, the readiness of sailors to respect authority and obey orders will be tempered by the operational competence of officers and the quality of the leadership they exert. It is for this reason that navies must continue to reflect on the development and expression of leadership at sea in naval ships. While warships continue to be instruments of foreign policy and national interest, conflict at sea will continue. The possibility of mutiny will, therefore, never end.

Endnotes

1 THE EVOLUTION OF MUTINY

1 Hugh Edwards, *Islands of Angry Ghosts*, soft cover edition, Angus & Roberston, Sydney, 1973, p. 12.
2 John Noel and Edward Beach, *Naval Terms Dictionary*, 5th edition, US Naval Institute Press, Annapolis, 1988, p. 191.
3 L.F. Guttridge, *Mutiny—A History of Naval Insurrection*, Ian Allan Publishing, Maryland, 1992, pp. 235–6.
4 ibid., p. 235.
5 ibid., pp. 281–2.
6 *Commonwealth Record Series* (hereafter CRS), A7111/1, Australian Archives (hereafter AA).
7 ibid.

2 MUTINY AND THE ROYAL NAVY

1 Sir Geoffrey Callender, *The Naval Side of British History*, Christophers, London, 1952, p. 93.
2 M. Oppenheim, *Administration of the Royal Navy*, (Lane, London, 1937) p. 240.
3 Michael Lewis, *The Navy of Britain: An Illustrated Portrait*, Allen & Unwin, London, 1948, p. 302.
4 Admiralty minutes dated 10 March 1746, Naval Records Society (hereafter NRS), *Naval Administration, 1715–1750*, Spottiswoode Ballantyne Press, London, 1977.
5 Admiralty minutes dated 11 March 1746, p. 74.
6 Admiralty minutes dated 6 February 1746, p. 139.
7 Admiral James Steuart to Admiralty Secretary, Spithead, 29 May 1746, pp. 142–3.
8 ibid., p. 143.
9 Admiral John Byng (Vice-Admiral of the Blue) to Admiralty Secretary, *Boyne*, Vado Bay, 3 October 1747, p. 157.

10 Daniel A. Baugh (ed.), *Naval Administration, 1715–1750*, Navy Records Society, London, 1977, pp. 157–8.
11 William Bligh, *A Narrative of the Mutiny on board HMS Bounty . . .* facsimile edition, Libraries Board of South Australia, Adelaide, 1969.
12 Edward Christian, *A Short Reply to Captain Bligh's Answers*, London, 1795.
13 Rolf du Reitz, *The Causes of the Bounty Mutiny*, Almqvist & Wiksell, Uppsala, 1965.
14 Gavin Kennedy, *Captain Bligh: The Man and his Mutinies*, Duckworth, London, 1989, p. 72.
15 Richard Hough, *Captain Bligh and Mr Christian: The Men and the Mutiny*, Cresset, London, 1972.
16 Madge Darby, *Who Caused the Mutiny on the Bounty?*, Angus & Robertson, Sydney, 1965.
17 Greg Denning, *Mr Bligh's Bad Language: Passion, Power and Theatre on the* Bounty, Cambridge University Press, Melbourne, 1992.
18 NRS, *Nelson's Letters to His Wife*, Spottiswoode, Ballantyne and Co., London, 1958, p. 187.
19 ibid., p. 265
20 Rear-Admiral H. G. Thursfield (ed.), *Five Naval Journals: 1789–1817*, NRS, 1951, p. 354.
21 Lewis, op. cit., pp. 302–3.
22 *Nelson's Letters to his Wife*, p. 328.
23 Quoted in 'Peter Cullen's Journal' in *Five Naval Journals*, p. 88–89.
24 'Letters from the Lower Deck, 1794–1811' in H. G. Thursfield (ed.), *Five Naval Journals, 1789–1817*, Navy Records Society, London, 1951, p. 357.
25 *Nelson's Letters to his Wife*, p. 330.

3 THE NEW SOUTH WALES CORPS

1 For an account of the political and economic power of the Corps see A. G. L. Shaw, 'Rum Corps and Rum Rebellion', *Melbourne Historical Journal*, 1971, Vol. 10.
2 These events are assessed in further detail in F. M. Bladen, 'The Deposition of Governor Bligh', *Journal of the RAHS*, Vol. 1, 1905.
3 Details of the charges are quoted in Owen Rutter 'The Rum Rebellion' in *Fifty Mutinies, Rebellions and Revolutions*, Odhams, London, 1938, p. 334.
4 *A Charge of Mutiny: The Court Martial of Lieutenant Colonel George Johnston for Deposing Governor William Bligh in the Rebellion of 26 January 1808*, introduced by John Ritchie, National Library of Australia, Canberra, 1988, pp. 408–9.
5 Paul Brunton, 'Arresting Bligh', pp. 80–97 in *Mutiny on the Bounty*, State Library of NSW, Sydney, 1991.

4 MUTINY IN THE AUSTRALIAN COLONIAL FORCES

1. See T. R. Frame, *The Garden Island*, Kangaroo Press, Sydney, 1990, p. 114.
2. Remarks in the Queensland Legislative Assembly, reported in the *Brisbane Courier*, 26 October 1888.
3. ibid.
4. ibid.
5. Correspondence, Captain Townley Wright to RA Commanding the Australian Squadron, Admiralty Folio (AF) 12224, AA (ACT).
6. Correspondence respecting the Dismissal of Captain Wright, presented to the Queensland Houses of Parliament, 1888, p. 301.
7. ibid.
8. ibid.
9. ibid.
10. *Brisbane Courier*, 25 October 1888.
11. ibid.
12. Correspondence, AF 12224, AA (ACT).
13. ibid.
14. Correspondence, AF 12224, AA (ACT).
15. ibid.
16. *Brisbane Courier*, 27 October 1888.
17. ibid.
18. Memorandum to the Secretary of the Admiralty, AF 12224, AA (ACT).
19. *Brisbane Courier*, 26 October 1888.

5 A DEMOCRATIC NAVY

1. For a description of Creswell's contribution to Australian naval defence see Stephen D. Webster, 'Vice Admiral Sir William Creswell' in David Horner (ed.), *The Commanders*, Allen & Unwin, Sydney, 1984, pp. 44–59.
2. See *Naval and Military Forces of the Commonwealth*, Senate Printed Paper, 24 July 1903 in Printed Papers Naval, Vol. 1, Defence Department Library. Also Stephen D. Webster, 'Creswell: The Australian Navalist', unpublished PhD dissertation, Monash University, 1976, p. 43 ff.
3. Memorandum by Lord Selborne submitted to the 1902 Colonial Conference, reproduced in George Macandie, *The Genesis of the Royal Australian Navy*, Government Printer, Melbourne, 1949, p. 105.
4. A. T. Mahan, 'Considerations Governing the Disposition of Navies', *National Review*, January 1902, p. 709.
5. Memorandum to the Minister for Defence by Captain W. R. Creswell, Naval Director, *Commonwealth Parliamentary Papers* (hereafter CPP), Vol. II, 1908, p. 370.

6   See Tom Frame, *Pacific Partners: A History of Australian–American Naval Relations*, Hodder & Stoughton, Sydney, 1992, p. 20.
7   Quoted in Macandie, p. 240.
8   Quoted in Macandie, pp. 244–5.
9   CRS A5954, Item 1001/1, AA (ACT), CID Memorandum dated 1910, enclosure to Hyde to Minister for Defence.
10 *Sydney Morning Herald*, 18 July 1914.
11 *Report of the Royal Australian Naval College, 1916*, CPP, 1916.
12 Brian Beddie, 'The Australian Navy and Imperial Legislation', in *War & Society*, pp. 73–88, Vol. 5, No. 2, September 1987, p. 73 quoted.
13 Admiralty memorandum of August 1910.
14 Memo. from the Naval Director to the Minister for Defence, 8 February 1911.
15 Naval Board Minutes, 3/24 June 1910, CRS, A2585, AA (ACT).
16 CRS, CP 78/22/1, 136/1912, AA (NSW).
17 *Commonwealth Parliamentary Debates* (hereafter CPD), Vol. LXXI, 13 September 1913, p. 369.
18 CPD, Vol. LX, 13 October 1911, p. 1402.
19 CPD, Vol. LX, 13 September 1911, p. 369.
20 Robert Hyslop, *Australian Naval Administration, 1900–1939*, Hawthorn Press, Melbourne, 1973, p. 105.
21 CPD, Vol. LXIX, 12 December 1912, p. 6956
22 CPD, Vol. LXIX, 17 December 1912, p. 7267
23 CPD, Vol. LXIV, 20 June 1912, p. 61
24 CPD, Vol. LXXI, 24 October 1913, p. 2520.
25 ibid., p. 2521.
26 CPD, Vol. LXIX, 17 December 1912, p. 7267.
27 Hyslop, op. cit., p. 41
28 Beddie, op. cit., p. 74.
29 A contemporary news cable quoted by Arthur Jose, *Official History of Australia in the War of 1914–18*, Vol. IX, *The Royal Australian Navy*, A&R, Sydney, 1928, p. 2.
30 A. W. Jose in his *Official History of Australia*, states on page 78 that the firemen's 'essential grievance' was 'refusing to take the vessel outside Australian waters'. The Inquiry into the incident (CRS 1914/0486 AA) makes no reference to this.
31 Captain John Glossop in *Sydney* reported that the message was: 'Want assistance. Mutiny.' The Defence Signals log records the former wording, AWM 35, 24/48.
32 John Glossop, HMAS *Sydney* Letter of Proceedings dated 9 September 1914, CRS MP 1049/1, 1918/0185 AA (Vic).
33 ibid.
34 ibid.

6 WORLD WAR I

1   Unit records AWM 37/63.
2   Unit records AWM 37/59.

3 A. W. Jose, *Official History of Australia in the War of 1914–1918*, Vol. IX, *Royal Australian Navy*, Angus & Robertson, Sydney, 1939, p. 398.
4 Unit records, AWM 37/59.
5 ibid.
6 ibid., p. 399.
7 Tom Frame and Greg Swinden, *First In, Last Out! The Navy at Gallipoli*, Kangaroo Press, Sydney, 1990, p. 141.
8 Unit records AWM 37/62.
9 Message of 25 January 1916.
10 CRS, AIF 251/2/231, 22/11/1916, AA (ACT).
11 CRS, AIF 251/2/231, 18/2/1917, AA (ACT). One officer and ninety-seven men transferred to the Army; nine officers and 194 men were discharged.
12 ibid., 4/7/1917.
13 AWM Collection, Captain Bracegirdle, A1247 and A1272
14 CRS, AIF 251/2/231, 6/8/1917
15 C. E. W. Bean, *Anzac to Amiens—A Shorter History of the Australian Fighting Services in the First World War*, Australian War Memorial, Canberra, 1946, p. 310.
16 ibid., p. 311.
17 CRS, MP 1049/1, 1920/04444, AA (Vic), Report of Court of Inquiry, December 1920.
18 Jose, op. cit., p. 231.
19 ibid., p. 218.
20 ibid., p. 219.
21 ibid.
22 CRS, A7111/1, AA (ACT).
23 ibid.
24 ibid.
25 CRS, MP 472/1, 5/21/11552, AA (Vic).
26 CRS, MP 472/1, 5/21/11318, AA (Vic), Captain's Report to Fleet Commander, 29 July 1917, included in minutes of proceedings of courts martial.
27 ibid.
28 CRS, 17/6899, AA (Vic), Admiralty note of 28 November 1917.
29 CRS, MP 1049/1; 1920/0444, Cablegram No. 49 to Admiralty.

7 MUTINY IN WHOSE FLAGSHIP?

1 2DRL/0032 (AWM) George Williams' 'Diary', quoted in Kathryn Spurling, 'Life in the Lower Deck of the RAN, 1911–1952', unpublished doctoral dissertation, UNSW (ADFA), 1999, p. 127.
2 *Argus*, 12 June 1919, p. 4.
3 ibid.
4 ibid.
5 There is no reference to the Fremantle mutiny in the official naval history which states simply that *Australia* returned to its home

country after the war and reached Fremantle 'after an uneventful voyage'. A. W. Jose, *Official History of Australia in the War of 1914–1918*, Vol. IX, *Royal Australian Navy*, Angus & Robertson, Sydney, 1939, p. 346.
6 Patsy Adam-Smith, *The Anzacs*, large format edition, Nelson, Melbourne, 1985, p. 247.
7 CRS, MP 1049/1, 1919/0120, AA (Vic), Minutes of courts martial proceedings.
8 ibid.
9 ibid.
10 Robert Hyslop, 'Mutiny in HMAS *Australia*', *Public Administration*, Vol. XXIX, No. 3, September 1970, pp. 284–96.
11 CPD, Vols. LXXXVIII–XC ff.
12 ibid.
13 ibid.
14 CPP 78/23/1, 19/89/679, AA (NSW).
15 CRS A2585, AA (ACT), Naval Board Minutes No. 747.
16 Hyslop, op. cit., p. 108.
17 CRS A2585, AA (ACT), Memo to Naval Board dated 25 June 1919.
18 Hyslop, op. cit., p. 293.
19 B. N. Primrose, 'Australian Naval Policy 1919–1942', unpublished doctoral dissertation, ANU, 1974, p. 61.
20 CRS, MP 1049/1, 1920/0444, AA (Vic).
21 CRS, MP 1587/1, File No. 23U 1923–1929, AA (Vic), extracts from a letter received by Admiral Allan Everett from the Acting First Naval Member, 11 October 1923.
22 Quoted in the *Times*, 23 December 1918.

8 THE TURBULENT TWENTIES

1 Guttridge, pp. 172–3.
2 ibid., p. 182.
3 B. N. Primrose, 'Australian Naval Policy 1919–1942', unpublished doctoral dissertation, ANU, 1974, p. 59.
4 ibid., p. 60.
5 Greg Swinden, 'Charting the Northern Coastline: HMAS *Geranium* 1919–1927', unpublished paper.
6 *Jane's Fighting Ships of World War I*, Studio Editions, London 1990, reproduction of 1919 edition, p. 87.
7 ibid.
8 *The Open Sea: Journal of the Tingira Old Boys Association*, quoted in Swinden, op. cit.
9 *Brisbane Courier*, 18 August 1923.
10 *The Guardian*, August 1923.
11 'Recollections of Able Seaman Alec Fowler', quoted in Swinden, op. cit.
12 CRS A2585, AA (ACT), Naval Board Minutes 603/201/53.
13 CRS A2585, AA (ACT), Naval Board Minutes 332/5/14.

9 DEPRESSION DISPUTES

1. Kathryn Spurling, 'Life and Unrest in the Lower Deck of the RAN in the 1930s', *Journal of the Australian Naval Institute*, No. 1, 1997, p. 3.
2. ibid., p. 5.
3. Admiral Sir Michael Hodges had been hospitalised in Portsmouth with pleurisy. Tomkinson was the next senior officer in the Atlantic Fleet.
4. Paul Hasluck, *Official History of Australia in the War of 1939–45, The Government and People 1919–41*, AWM, Canberra, 1952, Chapter 2.
5. Robert Hyslop, 'Mutiny in HMAS *Australia*', *Public Administration*, Vol. XXIX, No. 3, September 1970, pp. 284–96.
6. Quoted in Tom Frame, *Where Fate Calls: The HMAS* Voyager *Tragedy*, Hodder & Stoughton, Sydney, 1992, p. 2.
7. Tyler Dennet, 'Australia's Defence Problem', *Foreign Affairs*, Vol. 18, No. 1, October 1939, p. 118.
8. ibid.
9. ibid., p. 126.
10. Quoted in Tom Frame, *Pacific Partners: A History of Australian–American Naval Relations*, Hodder & Stoughton, Sydney, 1992, p. 34.
11. Cordell Hull, *The Memoirs of Cordell Hull*, Vol. I, Macmillan, London, 1948, p. 630.
12. CRS A2585, AA (ACT), Naval Board Minutes 603/251/3157.
13. Spurling, op. cit., p. 2.
14. ibid., p. 3.
15. ibid., p. 6.
16. ibid., p. 8.
17. CRS A5954/1 AA (ACT), Report of the Chief of Naval Staff, *Discipline in the RAN*, December 1934.
18. ibid.
19. Report of the Chief of Naval Staff, op. cit., p. 3.
20. CRS A2585, AA (ACT), Naval Board Minutes 452/201/499.
21. ibid.
22. ibid.
23. *Age*, 7–11 November 1932.
24. ibid.
25. ibid.
26. ibid.
27. *Age*, 9 November 1932.
28. CPD (Senate), 9 November 1932.
29. *Age*, 10 November 1932.
30. ibid.
31. Spurling, op. cit., p. 7.
32. *Age*, 11 November 1932.
33. ibid.

34 CRS A2585, AA (ACT), Naval Board Minutes, No.14, 16 January 1932.
35 Hyslop, op. cit., p. 127.
36 CRS A7111, AA (ACT), HMAS *Canberra*, Punishment Returns, April 1933.
37 ibid., March 1933.
38 ibid., August 1933.

10 THE TUMULTUOUS THIRTIES

1 *Jane's Fighting Ships of World War I*, Studio Editions, London 1990, reproduction of 1919 edition, p. 86.
2 CRS A2585 AA (ACT), Naval Board Minutes 556/201/561.
3 R.J. Hardstaff, *The Hydrographic Service, Royal Australian Navy 1920–1995*, Sydney 1995, Part 1.
4 CRS A2585, AA (ACT), Naval Board Minutes, 407/210/25.
5 CRS A2585, AA (ACT), Naval Board Minutes, 407/222/216.
6 CRS A7111, AA (ACT), HMAS *Moresby* Punishment Records, 1934.
7 CRS A5954, Item No. 1003/13, AA (ACT), Report of Chief of Naval Staff, 17/1/35.
8 ibid., Appendix C, p. 1.
9 The facts and quotes are taken from the report of Lieutenant Commander Martin to the Court of Inquiry, CRS A2585, AA (ACT), AF 836/411/17.
10 Report of the Chief of Naval Staff, 17/1/35.
11 ibid.
12 CRS AF 836/411/17, AA (ACT), Report of Court of Inquiry 7 September 1934.
13 Kathryn Spurling, 'Life and Unrest in the Lower Deck of the RAN in the 1930s', *Journal of the Australian Naval Institute*, No. 1, 1997, p. 9.
14 The papers of Stoker Norm King, AWM MSS 1502, p. 51.
15 ibid.
16 ibid.
17 AWM 78, HMAS *Perth* Letter of Proceedings, August 1939.
18 AWM 78, HMAS *Perth* Letter of Proceedings, June 1940.
19 Norm King papers, p. 58.
20 ibid., p. 56.
21 Much of the information about Farncomb's career has been obtained from A. W. Grazebrook, 'First to a Flag: The Life of Admiral H. B. Farncomb' in T. R. Frame, J. V. P. Goldrick and P. D. Jones (eds), *Reflections on the RAN*, Kangaroo Press, Sydney, 1991, pp. 189–205.
22 Two histories of the RAN College have been written: Frank Eldridge, *A History of the RAN College*, Georgian House, Melbourne, 1949; and Ian Cunningham, *Work Hard Play Hard*, AGPS, Canberra, 1988.
23 'Chephren', 'The RAN College—Its history and development', *Journal of the Royal United Services Institute*, Vol. 38, No. 3, January–March 1930.

24 The site originally proposed for a naval college was in Sydney. Admiral Sir Reginald Henderson, in his report to the Commonwealth Government of March 1911 (generally known as 'Recommendations') assessing Australian naval defence needs, stated that the College should be located at Middle Head in Sydney, near the present site of HMAS *Penguin*. However, it was soon decided to site the College at Jervis Bay with existing buildings at Geelong to be utilised until the permanent site was ready for habitation in 1916. Papers Relating to the Henderson Report, mimeographed minute, AWM 124, 'RAN Historical'.
25 CRS A5954, Item 1004/4, AA (ACT), 'Naval Defence Report of Admiral of the Fleet Viscount Jellicoe, 1919', p. 7.
26 Promotion to the rank of lieutenant commander was, in the normal course of events, automatic after eight years in the rank of lieutenant.

11 WORLD WAR II

1 R. Dymond, *The History of HMAS* Voyager I, Southern Holdings, Hobart, pp. 76–7.
2 One is recorded in the diary of Petty Officer Cooper; the other was related to R. Symonds by a member of *Voyager*'s ship's company.
3 AWM record PR00908, Diary of AB Bob Skinner, 3/3/45.
4 ibid., 11/1/44.
5 AWM record PR 91/106, Diary of W. Fitzgerald.
6 See *Corvette*, Newsletter of the RAN Corvettes Association (NSW) January 1992, No. 44.
7 AWM record PR00904 File No. 97/0338 J. W. Evans.
8 Accounts of incidents involving N Class destroyers and corvettes are also included in *Corvette*.
9 AWM record PR00904 File No. 97/0338 J.W. Evans.
10 AWM record MSS 1454; 93/0074 F. C. Tregurtha, p. 102.
11 AWM record PR00908, Diary of AB Bob Skinner.
12 AWM record PR 91/106, Diary of W. Fitzgerald.
13 ibid.
14 AWM record PR00464, J. C. Searle, p. 7.
15 ibid.
16 ibid., p. 9.
17 ibid.
18 CRS MP 1049/5, AA (Vic), HMAS *Westralia* Letter of Proceedings, 3 November 1941 to 10 January 1942.
19 AWM record PR00464, J. C. Searle.
20 CRS MP 1049/5, AA (Vic), HMAS *Westralia* Letter of Proceedings, 3 November 1941 to 10 January 1942.
21 AWM record PR00449, R. Penglase.
22 ibid.
23 See L. Audette, 'The Lower Deck and the Mainguy Report of 1949', in James Boutillier (ed.), *The RCN In Retrospect: 1910–1968*, University of British Columbia Press, 1982, p. 236.

24 An extended account of the mutiny is contained in B. Glenton, *Mutiny in Force X*, Hodder & Stoughton, London, 1986.

12 VANITY AND MUTINY

1 This chapter has drawn extensively on personal recollections from former members of the ship's company of HMAS *Pirie* printed in various editions of the *Journal of the HMAS* Pirie *Association*, and Robert Gillam's account of the mutiny published in that journal.
2 W. S. Robinson, 'Corvettes—Their Limited Speed, Firepower and Endurance', *Corvette*, January 1992, No. 44, p. 9.
3 Les Lawler, a former member of *Pirie*'s engine room staff described the experience of working in a corvette's engineroom in *Corvette*, July 1993, No. 50, p. 11.
4 H. Campbell, *Notable Service to the Empire—Australian Corvettes in the British Pacific Fleet 1944–45*, Naval Historical Society of Australia, Sydney 1995, p. 70.
5 Nicholas Monsarrat, *The Cruel Sea*, Penguin Books, 1951, p. 18.
6 Related by a former sailor in the RNZN corvette *Arbutus* to the authors.
7 Campbell, op. cit., p. 45.
8 ibid., p. 44.
9 The report of the action is in *Pirie*'s Report of Proceedings, April 1943, AWM 78.
10 ibid.
11 SBA Harvey wrote to friends after the action. His letter is quoted in Vic Cassells, *For Those in Peril*, Kangaroo Press, Sydney, 1995, p. 199.
12 ibid.
13 CRS, A7111/1, AA (ACT), HMAS *Pirie*, Punishment Returns.
14 *Pirie*'s story is outlined in Iris Neasdale, *The Corvettes—Forgotten Ships of the Royal Australian Navy*, self-published, 1982.

13 MUTINY IN NEW ZEALAND

1 Author not noted, *Naval Historical Review*, Sydney, October 1982, pp. 21–2.
2 A. Tonson, 'The Royal New Zealand Navy', *Naval Historical Review*, Sydney, August–September 1981 pp. 3–7.
3 Author not noted, Dido *Class Cruisers*, Ensign Publications, London.
4 G. Howard, *The Navy in New Zealand*, A. H. & A. W. Reed, Sydney, 1981, p. 97.
5 ibid.
6 *New Zealand Herald* [hereafter *NZH*], 2 April 1947.
7 Howard, op. cit., p. 97.
8 *NZH*, 3 April 1947.
9 ibid.
10 *NZH*, 4 April 1947.
11 Howard, op. cit., p. 97.

12 *NZH*, 8 April 1947.
13 *NZH*, 11 April 1947.
14 *NZH*, 10 April 1947.
15 ibid.
16 *NZH*, 26 April 1947.
17 *NZH*, 30 April 1947.

14 POSTWAR DISAPPOINTMENT

1 M. K. Roy, *War in the Indian Ocean*, Cancer Publications, Delhi, 1995, pp. 43–50.
2 B. C. Dutt, *Mutiny of the Innocents*, Sandhu Publications, Bombay, 1971, p. 76.
3 *Report on Certain 'Incidents' Which Occurred on Board HMC Ships* Athabascan, Crescent *and* Magnificent *and on Other Matters Concerning the Royal Canadian Navy*, Department of National Defence, Ottawa, 1949.
4 See L. Audette, 'The Lower Deck and the Mainguy Report of 1949', in James Boutillier (ed.), *The RCN In Retrospect: 1910–1968*, University of British Columbia Press, 1982, p. 239.
5 ibid., p. 244.
6 Unattributed article, 'The Thai Navy', *Warship International*, 1986, p. 244.
7 HMAS *Moresby* Report on Proceedings 1943, AWM 78, 225/1.
8 ibid.
9 Outlined in John Betty, 'The RAN Hydrographic Branch, 1942–45' in David Stevens (ed.) *The Royal Australian Navy in World War II*, Allen & Unwin, Sydney, 1996, p. 156.
10 AWM 78, 35/D/505.
11 Betty describes the typical day's duty in a survey ship in Stevens, op. cit., pp. 161–62.
12 J. O'Connell, 'HMAS *Moresby*, 1925–1946', Naval Historical Society of Australia, 1994, No. 38, p. 11.
13 ibid.
14 R. J. Hardstaff, *The Hydrographic Service Royal Australian Navy, 1920–1995*, Sydney, 1995.
15 O'Connell, op. cit., p. 11.
16 A history of Garden Island from 1788 is contained in Tom Frame, *The Garden Island*, op.cit.
17 Subsequent events were reported in the *Age* and the *Sydney Morning Herald* on 18 August 1970.
18 *Canberra Times*, 18 August 1970.

15 MUTINY IN THE AUSTRALIAN ARMY AND AIR FORCE

1 Outlined in Bill Gammage, *The Broken Years—Australian Soldiers in the Great War*, Australian National University Press, Canberra 1974, p. 28.

2 ibid.
3 Eric Andrews, *The Anzac Illusion—Anglo-Australian Relations During World War I*, Cambridge University Press, Melbourne, 1993, pp. 105ff.
4 ibid., p. 105.
5 ibid.
6 C. M. Wrench, *Campaigning with the Fighting Ninth 1914–1919*, Boolarong Publications, Brisbane, 1985, p. 495.
7 C. E. W. Bean, *Anzac to Amiens: A Shorter History of the Australian Fighting Services in the First World War*, Australian War Memorial, Canberra, 1946, p. 487. The footnote reference is Volume VI, p. 875.
8 Patsy Adam-Smith, op. cit., pp. 319ff.
9 Gammage, op. cit., p. 229.
10 Bean, op. cit., Vol. VI, pp. 935–40.
11 CRS, A471/1, item no. 780066, AA (ACT), Court martial records.
12 ibid., Appendix C, p. 3.
13 ibid.
14 ibid., Appendix D, Section a.
15 ibid., Appendix D, Section f.
16 CRS MP 742/1, W/1/32, AA (Vic), A. H. Wardrop, Report of Conditions at Jerusalem Detention Barracks.
17 CRS A471, item no. 36806, AA (ACT), Court martial records.
18 ibid., Transcript of court proceedings, p. 9.
19 ibid.
20 ibid., Summary papers, pp. 45ff.
21 CRS, A471, item no. 36806, sheet 15, AA (ACT).
22 ibid., sheet 6.
23 ibid., sheet 13.
24 ibid., sheet 37A.
25 ibid., sheet 7.

16 VOLUNTEERS AND MUTINY

1 For other treatments of Australia's protests against French atomic testing at Mururoa see Tom Frame: 'Island of Secrets', *Canberra Times*, 4 August 1990, p. B1; 'An RAN Triumph of Diplomacy', *Canberra Times*, 5 August 1990; and 'Gunboat Diplomacy?: The RAN and RNZN at Mururoa', *Journal of the New Zealand Institute of International Affairs*, 1992, pp. 20–25.
2 Conscription could also take place under section 60 of the *Defence Act* (1903) which allows the Governor-General, by means of a proclamation, to call upon certain male persons to serve in the Defence Force at a time when there is a real or apprehended attack on or invasion of Australia. This Act does not recognise any right of conscientious objection. The proclamation of the *National Service Termination Act* in 1973 ended all obligations under the *National*

Service Act. Provisions relating to national servicemen were removed from the *Defence Act* in 1975.
3 Hansard, Senate Question Time, 17 May 1973, p. 1683.

17 CONSCIENCE AND MUTINY

1 Senator Michael Tate, 'Conscientious Objection—Australia', *National Outlook*, August 1983.
2 *Commonwealth Parliamentary Papers* (hereafter CPP), Senate Standing Committee on Constitutional and Legal Affairs, Transcript of Evidence: *National Service Amendment Bill* (1983), AGPS, Canberra, 1983.
3 ibid.
4 Chief of Personnel—Army minute 399/83, 7 July 1983.
5 AF 68/1/271, 15 July 1983
6 *Conscientious Objection to Conscripted Military Service* [hereafter *Tate Report*], Report by the Standing Committee on Constitutional and Legal Affairs, AGPS, Canberra, 1985; p. 10, para. 2.16. See also Tate's tabling address, *CPD* (Senate), 28 May 1985.
7 Submission by Denis O'Donnell, Evidence, p. 81.
8 ibid., p. 13.
9 *Tate Report*, op. cit., para. 2.34.
10 ibid., p. 26
11 *Tate Report*, op. cit., para. 4.21.
12 Hugh Smith, 'Conscience, Law and the State: Australia's Approach to Conscientious Objection Since 1901', *Australian Journal of Politics and History*, Vol. 35, No. 1, 1989, p. 25.
13 Tom Frame, 'Navy deserter faces music in band hall', *Canberra Times*, 25 September 1990, p. 2.
14 HMAS *Harman* Temporary Memorandum 216/90 dated 9 November 1990.
15 Frame, *Canberra Times*, 25 September 1990.
16 Naval Support Command (NSC) letter, Annex C, 'Human Rights Aspects of Conscientious Objection', to Assistant Chief of Defence Force (Personnel), October 1990, NSC file N90/32170, folio 56.
17 NSC letter.
18 Bilney to Woods, 5 March 1991. Copy held by author.
19 Defence file A91/9883, Director of Army Legal Services letter 1491/92 dated 30 April 1992.
20 *SMH*, 27 March 1992.
21 ibid.
22 *Reveille*, January–February 1991, p. 4.
23 *CPD* (Senate), 23 June 1992.
24 *Canberra Times*, 24 June 1992, p. 19.

Index

Aboriginals, 139, 143
Achilles, 187–9
Ackell, Able Seaman, 93
Adelaide, 254
Admiralty influence, 123–4
advocacy service, 263
Albatross, 125
Albion, 47
Alceste, 47–8
Allied Navies, 161–3
Almirante Latorre, 121–2, 134
Alves, Mike, 263
Anzac, 216
Anzac Cove, 79
Arabis, 189
Arbutus, 189–92, 201, 260–1
Armed Forces Federation of Australia, 263–5
Army, 219–22, 227–33, 251
Athabascan, 208–9
Atkins, Richard, 33–43
Australasia Naval Defence Act, 49
Australasia Naval Defence Act, 49
Australia, 67–8, 97–110, 113–14, 127, 149, 160–1, 179, 187, 217
Australian Council of Trade Unions, 247
Australian Naval & Military Expedition Force, 75–6

Banks, Joseph, 33–4
bans, boycotts, 235–6
Barnacle, Henry, 10
Barnard, Lance, 238–9

Barr, Stoker, 92
Barwick, Garfield, 235
Batavia, 1–3
beer issue, 46–9
Bell, Able Seaman, 141–2
Bellona, 188–90, 190, 203, 205–6, 260–1
Bennett, Harry, 117–18
Berrima, 76
Bidewell, Staff Sergeant, 227–9
Bilney, Gordon, 256–7
Bishop, Reg, 240–1
Black Prince, 188–90, 192, 202–3, 260–1
Blake, Robert, 21–2
Bligh, William, 15–20, 33–44
Bombay, 207
Bond, Lieutenant, 82–5
Bounty, 15–20
Bracegirdle, Leighton Seymour, 78–9, 84–6, 181
Bradley, W., 231
Brass, Driver, 84
Brazil, 112
Brett, John, 13
Brisbane, 216, 254
Burdekin, Brian, 255–6
Burnett, Joseph, 149
Bushell, Charles, 90–1
Byng, John, 14–15

Cabena, W., 97–8
Cadzow, Able Seaman, 141–2
Cairns, Jim, 238
Calliope, 186
Canada, 161, 207

279

Canberra, 127, 135–7
Canterbury, 245–6
Captain, 13–14
career service, 48
Carr, Able Seaman, 141–2
Casula, 219–20
causes and course of mutiny, 261–2
Chile, 121–2, 134
Christian, Arthur, 83
Christian, Fletcher, 16
civilians and incitement to mutiny, 8, 128
Collins, John, 149
Colman, Fraser, 243–4
colonial forces, 45–57
Colonial Naval Defence Act, 49–50
Commonwealth Defence Act, 57
Communists, 128, 214
conditions of service, 67–8, 98
Conroy, T. M., 227
conscientious objection, 249–59
Constellation, 8
Cook, James, 19, 71
Cook, Joseph, 62, 106
Copley, Bob, 264
Cornelisz, Jeronimus, 1–2
Creighton, Flight Lieutenant, 224, 226
Crescent, 208
Creswell, William Rooke, 58–61, 71
Crookshanks, Captain, 13
Crutchley, Victor, 179–80
Culloden, 23
Cumberlege, Claude, 94, 100–2, 109
Cussen, Leo, 130–1
Cutler, Steward, 140

Davies, Acting Engineer's Mate, 92
de Wardt, Stoker, 66
De Zeven Provincien, 132–5
Deakin, Alfred, 59–62
Dean, Dixie, 172–3
Defence Ombudsman, 265
Delhi, 111
Depression, the Great, 121
Dhanush, 207

Dhonburi, 209–10
Dili, 210
discipline, 65–7
Dixon, J. P., 117–18
Downes, Jim, 168
Dumaresq, John Saumarez, 100–2, 104, 107–9

Edwards, Edward, 17
Elliott, 'Pompey', 222
Emu War, 128
English Civil War, 11–12
Etaples, 220
Evans, J.W., 155–6

Fairfax, Henry, 56
Fantome, 87–94, 109, 114, 138, 210
Farncomb, Harold, 145–9, 160–1, 179
Faulkner, A., 246
Ferguson, Ronald Munro, 64–5
Finlay, Dr, 199–201
Fletcher, Able Seaman, 140, 141–2
food, 46, 121
France, 111, 234–48
Fraser, Peter, 193–202
Fremantle incident, 98–110, 113–14
Fryar, John, 16–17

Gambia, 188
Garden Island, 213–18, 261
Gayundah, 50–6
Geier, Leading Aircraftman, 225
General O'Higgins, 121–2
Geraldton, 161
Geranium, 114–20, 138
Germany, 75–7, 94–6
Gillam, Bob, 167
Gilmour, Stoker, 92
Glasgow, 207
Glasgow, Thomas, 221
Glossop, John, 88, 104
Gorman, Eugene, 130–1
Gorman, Ronald, 131–2
Grand Fleet, 95, 98, 99
Grant, Percy, 107–8
Greaves, Able Seaman, 140
Gulf War, 253–7

INDEX

Hautapu, 190, 202–3, 260–1
Hermione, 20–1
Heron, Private, 228
High Seas Fleet, 94–6
Hill, Private, 229
Hipper, Franz Von, 95
Hobart, 144
Hobbs, Joseph, 221
Hodsoll, Captain, 14–15
Hoffman, F. G., 177
Holman, Bruce, 80
Holmes, Colonel, 73, 75–6
Hudson, Michael, 254
Huggan, Clive, 263
Human Rights and Equal Opportunity Commission, 255–6
Humphrey, Able Seaman, 141–2
Hunter, John, 31–2
Hyde, George Francis, 126–30, 140–1

Imperial Conference, 61–2
India, 207
Invergordon, 122–3
Iraq, 253–7
Iroquois, 161, 208

Jacobsz, Ariaen, 1–3
Jellicoe, John, 113–14, 148, 187
Johnston, George, 33–44
Jones, Lewis Tobias, 89–93
Jones, Terence, 253–5
Jumna, 207

Kanowna, 72–4
Kiel, 94–6
King, Norm, 145–6
King, Philip Gidley, 32
Kirk, Norman, 236–8, 243–4
Kitty Hawk, 8
Klein, Brigadier, 230–2
Kronstadt, 112–13
Kuwait, 253–7

Laing, Captain, 205
Langdale, Driver, 82, 84
Langridge, Petty Officer, 140
Lawless, Able Seaman, 93
Leander, 187–9
Lewis, Vaughan, 119

liability for service, 239
Lingard, Harold, 80
Lithgow, 161
Loosli, Geoff, 242, 244
Lorains, Robert A., 167, 176, 181
Loring, William, 48
Lothian, 162–3

Macarthur, John, 33–44
McDougall, Allan, 66
McDougall, Leading Seaman, 141–3
MacIntosh, William, 103–6
McKenzie, K., 119–20
Magnificent, 208, 209
Mahan, Alfred Thayer, 59
Mainguy, E. R., 208
Manhattan mutiny, 209–10
Martin, W., 143
Mayfield, John, 28
Melbourne, 10, 216–17
Mills, Charles Ferry, 165–84
Moir, Able Seaman, 93
Monash, General John, 221–2
Monin, Maurice Henry, 87–8, 92
Morehead, Boyd, 51–6
Moresby, 138–43, 210–14
Morris, Stoker, 92
Morrison, Warrant Officer, 228–9
Mururoa, 234–48
mutinous influence, 240
mutiny, causes, definitions, 3–10, 25, 261–2

Napier, 153–4, 156–7
Naval Discipline Act, 6
Neave, Able Seaman, 140, 143
Nehru, Jawaharlal, 207
Nelson, 122–3
Nelson, Horatio, 8, 23, 26–8
Nestor, 155–6
Netherlands East Indies, 132–5
New South Wales Corps, 30–44
New Zealand, 185–206, 235–7, 242–8, 260–2
New Zealand, 187
Nizam, 154–5
Nore, The, 25–9
Norfolk, 122–3
nuclear testing, 234–48
Nuseirat, 227–30

obligation, culture of, 240
O'Donnell, Stoker, 92
Ontario, 208
Orchard, Richard, 104–5
Ordinance for the Great Crusade, King Richard's, 5
Otago, 237–45

Paluma, 50–1
Pandora, 17
Papua-New Guinea, 75–6
Parker, Richard, 26–7
Patterson, Kenneth, 103–6
pay and allowances, 81–2, 193, 215–18
Payne, William, 130
Pearce, George Foster, 127, 130–1
Pelsaert, Francisco, 1–3
Pemberton, Greg, 257
Penguin, 125–7, 137
Peronne, 221–2
Perth, 144–7, 178, 179, 216
Philomel, 185–201, 203, 260–1
Phipps, Peter, 194–200
Pigot, Hugh, 20–1
Pirie, 163–84
Port Macquarie, 78–9
Port Moresby, 74
Powerful, 63
Prince Frederick, 14
Prince's Pier, 127–32
prize money, 47
Putland, Mary, 38–41

RAAF, 223–6, 232–3, 251
RAN Brigade, Bridging Train, 75–86, 181
RAN College, 64–5, 148
Ranier, Able Seaman, 141–2
Raphael, Able Seaman, 142
Ray, Robert, 257
Reed, Petty Officer, 141–2
Reeves, Alan, 174
Reid, Stoker, 10
Repulse, 122–3
Reuter, Ludwig Von, 95–6
Rice, Lieutenant Commander, 93–4
Richardson, Stoker, 66
Robertson, Andrew, 241

Rosewarne, Flight Lieutenant, 224–5
Royal Navy, 11–29
Royal Oak, 14–15
Royal Thai Navy, 207, 209–10
Rudd, Dalmorton, 103–6
Rudd, Leonard, 103–6
Russell, Sub-Lieutenant, 52–5
Russia, 112–13

sabotage, 250
Sandwich, 25–7
Sao Paulo, 112
Sardam, 2–3
Scott, Commander, 93–4
Searle, J., 158
Selborne, Lord, 59
selective objection, 240, 249–59
Ship Money, 11
Shipp, Bob, 174
Silvio, 138
Skinner, Bob, 156
Skinner, Clarence Farthington, 204
Smith, Bruce, 231
Smith, Hugh, 253
Smith's Weekly, newspaper, 129
Spithead, 24–5, 28
Sri Ayuthia, 209–10
Steuart, James, 13–14
Stevenson, H. David, 216–17
strike, 9, 222
Summers, J. H., 225–6
Supply, 237–48
Surabaya, 132–5
surveying, 114–20
Sutherland, 13
Swan, 216–17
Sydney, 67–8, 144, 216, 237–41, 254

Tahiti, 15–17, 192
Talwar Signal Station, 207
Tamworth Detention Barracks, 230–2
Tasman, 202, 260–1
Tate, Michael, 250, 256–7
Taylor, E. P., 52–6
Temeraire, 28
Thailand, 207, 209–10

INDEX 283

Thompson, R., 82
Thompson, Squadron Leader, 224
Thompson, Wilfred, 103–6
Thomson, D. L., 183
Tirrel, Alan, 244
Tomkinson, Wilfred, 122–3
Toowoomba, 161
Tregurtha, Lieutenant, 155–6
Truth, newspaper, 129–31, 141
Tryon, George, 49
Tui, 195
Turner, H. E., 139–40

United States Navy, 7–8

Valiant, 122–3
Vallentine, Josephine, 253–4
Velox, 111
Versatile, 111
Vietnam War, 250
Vindictive, 111

volunteers, 45
Voyager, 151–3, 178

Ward, Lieutenant, 228–30
Wardrop, Private, 227
welfare committees, 128, 195, 199, 208–9
Wemyss, Rosslyn, 84–5, 181
Weston, Able Seaman, 141–2, 142
Westralia, 157–60
Whitlam, E. G., 233, 236–40, 246–7
Wilhelmshaven, 94–6
Wilkie, Leading Aircraftman, 223, 225–6
Willesee, Don, 238–9
Windsor Castle, 23
World War I, 70–96
Wright, Henry Townley, 51–6
Wryneck, 111
Wylie, Able Seaman, 93